WELCOME *to*
the JUNGLE

A Business Officer's
Guide to Independent
School Finance and
Operations

Edited by Mari Brown & Marc Levinson

NB⬤A

National Business Officers Association

Find solutions. Exchange ideas.

www.nboa.net

Published by National Business Officers Association (NBOA)
P.O. Box 4576, Boulder, CO 80306, www.nboa.net

First edition

ISBN 978-0-9820107-0-9

Printed in Denver, Colorado, by NSO Press, Inc.

Printed on paper that is 100% recycled content, 100% post-consumer waste, processed chlorine-free, certified by the Forest Stewardship Council, and which uses inventory items manufactured with electricity that is offset with Green-E®-certified renewable wind energy certificates. For more information, see back inside cover.

About NBOA: The National Business Officers Association (NBOA) is the definitive professional resource and leading advocate for Independent School Business Officers. Through programs, online tools, and research on emerging issues, NBOA helps to develop solutions for effective and sustainable operations in independent schools. To find out more, visit www.nboa.net.

Book designer: Laura Ross

Book editors: Mari Brown, Marc Levinson

National Business Officers Association

DEDICATION

We are always struck by the fact that in this industry, people freely give of their expertise. Whether it's business officers helping other business officers or companies that serve independent schools sharing their knowledge, people in this community go out of their way to be generous with their time and expertise. This book is a testament to that generosity.

We would also like to acknowledge Will Hancock, one of the original co-founders of NBOA, for his vision of what this book might be.

National Business Officers Association

National Business Officers Association

Find solutions. Exchange ideas.

Our Mission

The National Business Officers Association (NBOA) is the definitive professional resource and leading advocate for Independent School Business Officers. Through programs, online tools, and research on emerging issues, NBOA helps to develop solutions for effective and sustainable operations in independent schools.

Our History

Founded in 1998, NBOA was, and remains, the only national professional association for the business officer in the country. Since its inception, NBOA has enjoyed continued success and expansion, with a membership that currently includes over 700 schools, representing every region in the country and several sites outside the United States. NBOA represents schools with enrollments from 26 to 5,412, with budgets from $400,000 to $112 million, and which have one year to 230 years of history.

Our Community

NBOA knows that it is all too common for the business officer to feel alone. As a member of the vibrant NBOA community, online and in person, the business officer suddenly feels surrounded by people who "get it." The community provides answers—person to person, business officer to business officer—to the myriad questions that challenge our schools every day.

Our Programs

From exciting national conferences to cutting-edge webinars, from our online discussion forum to our dynamic consulting service, NBOA gives its members the tools they need to stay at the forefront of industry knowledge.

Get Involved

www.nboa.net
National Business Officers Association
P.O. Box 4576   Boulder, CO 80306   Tel: 720-564-0475   Fax: 720-564-4951

Table of Contents

FOREWORD BY JAMES P. HONAN .... *page vi-vii*

1. GETTING YOUR BEARINGS .... *page 1*

2. FINANCIAL MANAGEMENT & REPORTING .... *page 11*

3. FACILITIES .... *page 35*
   part one: Planning .... *page 37*
   part two: Operations .... *page 47*

4. ETHICS .... *page 55*

5. HUMAN RESOURCES & EMPLOYMENT LAW .... *page 67*

6. REGULATORY COMPLIANCE .... *page 89*

7. RISK MANAGEMENT .... *page 107*

8. ADMISSION & ADVANCEMENT .... *page 121*
   part one: The Admission Office .... *page 123*
   part two: The Advancement Office .... *page 131*

9. TECHNOLOGY .... *page 137*

10. ENDOWMENT MANAGEMENT .... *page 151*

11. FOOD SERVICE .... *page 163*

12. SUMMER & AFTER-SCHOOL PROGRAMS .... *page 181*

13. AUXILIARY SERVICES .... *page 195*
    part one: School Stores .... *page 197*
    part two: Facility Rental .... *page 201*
    part three: Transportation .... *page 207*

14. ENVIRONMENTAL SUSTAINABILITY .... *page 213*

Foreword by James P. Honan

Over the past 15 or so years, I have had the good fortune to work with a wide range of independent school leaders—as a consultant, as a conference speaker, and as a teacher or faculty member in various professional development and executive education programs. My numerous interactions and conversations with independent school heads, administrators, teachers, trustees, and parents on issues of financial management, planning, and strategy development have provided me with a number of insights and lessons regarding the leadership, management, and governance of these unique and complex institutions. Right near the top of my "lessons learned" list is this one: the independent school business officer plays a key strategic role in the overall leadership and operation of the school. The required knowledge base and skill set for a high-performing business officer has gotten more complex over the years and will continue to become even more so in the future. Independent school business officers need to know—and know how to do—many things to be effective stewards of financial resources and strategic contributors to their school's overall financial health and sustainability.

In 14 chapters, all written by individuals who bring extensive knowledge of and experience in independent school financial management and leadership, Welcome to the Jungle: A Business Officer's Guide to Independent School Finance and Operations, offers both new and experienced independent school business officers pertinent and practical information and detailed examples of effective practices for addressing the key challenges one faces in this important leadership role.

This volume can serve as a comprehensive reference source for guidance and insight on many of the pressing financial challenges independent schools now face and will continue to face in the years ahead. Keep this book on or near your desk. You never know when you or a colleague at your school might need an insight, solution, or example of best practice on a new or emerging financial problem or dilemma. Good luck as you make your way through the jungle of independent school financial management and leadership—travel well!

James P. Honan
Senior Lecturer on Education
Harvard Graduate School of Education
Cambridge, Massachusetts
December 2008

James P. Honan
Senior Lecturer, Graduate School of Education,
Harvard University

James Honan has served on the faculty at the Harvard Graduate School of Education since 1991. He is also a faculty member at the John F. Kennedy School of Government and a principal of the Hauser Center for Nonprofit Organizations at Harvard University. He has served as a consultant on strategic planning, resource allocation, and performance measurement and management to numerous colleges, universities, schools, and nonprofit organizations both nationally and internationally. He is a member of the Board of Trustees of Marist College and the Dana Hall School. He served previously as a trustee of Fitchburg State College and the Plan for Social Excellence, a private foundation. He holds a BA from Marist College, an MA and EdS in Higher Education from George Washington University, and an EdM and EdD in Administration, Planning, and Social Policy from Harvard University.

Chapter One

GETTING YOUR BEARINGS

The Business Officer Meets the 21st Century

IN THIS CHAPTER:

- Who is today's business officer?

- Financial sustainability: the big picture

- Leadership vs. management

- Tips of the trade

- What can NBOA do for me?

by Sarah Daignault

Sarah Daignault

Executive Director, National Business Officers Association

Sarah Daignault is a founder and current Executive Director of the National Business Officers Association (NBOA), the definitive professional resource and leading advocate for independent school business officers. Through programs, online tools, and research on emerging issues, NBOA helps to develop solutions for effective and sustainable operations in independent schools. Since its inception, NBOA has enjoyed continued success and expansion, with a membership that currently includes over 700 schools, representing every region in the country and several sites outside the United States. Prior to founding NBOA, Sarah served as the Business Officer at Friends School of Baltimore and as the Business Manager at Bryn Mawr School for Girls. For eight years, Sarah was the President of the Board of Trustees of the Madeira School, where she chaired the school's capital campaign. She has also served on the boards of the National Association of Independent Schools (NAIS) and the National Coalition of Girls' Schools.

GETTING YOUR BEARINGS

The Business Officer Meets the 21st Century

As the new century unfolds, independent schools find themselves facing a variety of challenges: financial sustainability, government intrusion, and maintaining relevance in a rapidly changing world, to name just a few. It has become clear that the issues facing schools today are too complicated to address in a "silo" fashion. They demand the coordinated collaboration of traditional leadership (heads and trustees), the senior leadership team (admission, development, principals), and the person who stands at the nexus of all of them: YOU, the business officer. It is time for all business officers to recognize themselves as managers *and* as leaders, and understand what it takes to manage, as well as what it takes to lead. Yes, it's a jungle out there, but we're going to give you the map (and the machete) to help you find your way.

FINANCIAL SUSTAINABILITY: WE'RE AT A CROSSROADS

The 21st century is placing demands on the independent school industry, and at the top of any "current issues" list is financial sustainability. Independent schools are being forced to examine their financial structure, and ask hard questions about how it relates to delivery of services, demand in the marketplace, and relevance of mission. Independent schools offer a luxury product, which is priced accordingly. We want our student body to be diverse—in all ways, including economically diverse—so we offer financial aid for those families who need help paying tuition. Most schools rely on tuition as the major, if not only, source of revenue. And yet we do not even charge what it costs to deliver the education. We are at a crossroads. Do we increase our price to cover the cost? The very wealthy families can pay any amount. Then we may have more room to offer financial aid or tuition discounts to those in the middle class, supplementing the financial aid we already offer. Or do we change the mission/product we offer to be more cost-effective (like putting more kids in a classroom) and risk losing our identity and the very reason people will pay to send their children to our schools? These are very real questions for all of us.

The complexity of the answers is forcing us to do business internally in a new way, and this is where the new role of the business officer comes in: a team player who is both a manager and a leader. We can no longer afford to operate in isolation. At this moment in time, the sustainable future of independent schools is in question, and we need complex thinking to develop the solutions that will allow independent schools to go forward.

You, the business officer, are a key player in this discussion because of the information to which you have access. In this chapter, I want to transform your thinking about your "ownership" of that information, and give you a real sense of the strategic player you are. I want to give you tips on how to operate effectively as both a leader and a manager in the 21st century. And finally, I want to prove that your annual masterpiece, The Budget, is as much a statement of your school's mission as the mission statement itself.

WHO IS TODAY'S BUSINESS OFFICER?

"Business officer" is a generic title that is used to capture a set of responsibilities that are held by one person in an independent school. In reality, you see titles that span the gamut from "Business Manager" (the old way of thinking about this position) to "Chief Financial Officer" (and let's not even mention "Director of Finance and Operations," "Associate Head for Business and Finance," and "Assistant Head for Financial Operations"). No one title perfectly fits your job. Why? First, the position differs from school to school, depending on the unique mission and makeup of the school. Second, the responsibilities themselves are incredibly varied, and no single title seems to capture them all. "Jack/Jill of All Trades" might come closest. Another way to describe your work is:

If it is not academic and it is not fundraising, it is the business officer's job.

The average business officer today is 50 years old, and is just as likely to be female as male. This job is not their first—they have worked hard prior to coming to our schools, usually for a minimum of 10 years, in a wide variety of backgrounds. Business officers are former accountants, bankers, businesspersons, teachers, heads of school, human resource professionals, and military personnel. What traits do successful candidates have in common? They can juggle an amazing number of priorities at once. They are energized by the diversity of their work. They love to learn new things…all the time. They are committed to the missions of their schools in particular, and the work of independent schools in general. They work long hours because it is not possible to do this job in a regular 9-5 day. They understand that the knowledge base for the job is more than any one person can possess. They are therefore willing to ask for help—from colleagues at their schools, and from other business officers in town, around the state, and across the nation.

LEADERSHIP VS. MANAGEMENT

Your job title, in reality, is "Director of Resources." You manage the financial and physical resources of your school, which dictate the human resources. You manage risk to protect the institution (its physical entity and the integrity of its mission), as well as its students and staff. As the business of education has become more complicated, a debate has emerged about the business officer's role in managing the

school. To participate in this debate, it's important to understand the difference between leadership and management as these terms relate to the contemporary business officer.

Warren G. Bennis articulates it well in his book <u>Managing the Dream: Reflections on Leadership and Change</u>: leadership is quite different from management. The distinction is an important one. Leaders conquer the context—the volatile, ambiguous surroundings that will surely suffocate us if we let them—while managers surrender to them.

The problem for many independent school business officers, particularly those who have a limited number of staff members in the business office, is that they have to be both leaders and managers. Let's take some examples that Bennis cites and adapt them to independent school business officers:

> *The manager is a classic good soldier; the leader is his own person.*

In independent schools, the business officer answers to and works with the head of school. When this partnership is passably adequate, one can classify the business officer as a good soldier doing the work of the leader, the head. But when the partnership is truly effective, both are leaders, and they work as a team. The head defines the business officer's responsibilities and scope of work, but the rapport between these two leaders should be such that they constructively debate the pros and cons of school operations.

You can challenge your head's goals for the school, question ideas, and help refine the vision. You then take that vision and translate it into actual numbers that can become the basis for the strategic direction of the school. Remember: the spreadsheet—the bottom line—is as much a reflection of your school's mission as the mission statement itself.

It is not always easy to forge this partnership. You and your head likely have different professional backgrounds and opposite Myers-Briggs personality types. Yet it is precisely this difference that can make the partnership powerful: it creates synergy. You complement each other by viewing the same problem from different angles. When you are able to effectively share your viewpoints to develop solutions for the school, together you create an unstoppable combination.

Generational issues can also interfere with the development of this partnership. Older business officers, who dominate the profession, were trained to "be the best" as individuals, and not necessarily taught to move a team forward. A truly effective business officer has an awareness of collaborative learning and team approach, and recognizes that the senior team of a school comes to the table with a variety of learning styles. The business officer who excels in meetings is able to respond to these different learning styles by bringing in data and demographics (i.e., numbers), but also backing them up with articles (words), as well as graphs, charts, and web resources (images).

Other issues can prevent the business officer from being perceived as a strategic partner. If the person has come up through the ranks—started as a bookkeeper and taken on more and more responsibility—he or she may not have training in strategic thinking. Additionally, there's an outdated institutional view of business officers that needs to change: they're seen as the ones who just write the checks and pay the bills. Yet now that the business officer is responsible for such a wide spectrum of holistic issues, from keeping the school in compliance with regulations to dealing with environmental issues, no one can pretend the business officer simply takes orders.

> *The manager accepts the status quo; the leader challenges it.*

In today's average independent school, where tuition is rising with inflation plus 2-3% every year, the business officer must work with the head and board to think about the school's financial model in new ways. Accepting the status quo could deny the school a future. Because you are the one who knows the most about your school's financial systems, as well as the details and assumptions on which they are founded, you are in the best position to challenge the model and come up with new ways to deliver the mission. You can also take the ideas of the head and board and translate them into financial projections that can sustain the mission—or show how they can't. You have the power to prove, in numbers, what can make for a successful school over a long period of time, yet you also depend on the vision of your head and board to define what success is.

> *The manager has a short-range view; the leader has a long-range perspective. The manager has his eye on the bottom line; the leader has his eye on the horizon.*

The business officer in the 21st century school has to work with the head and board to strategically plan for the next 20+ years. But s/he also has to be involved in the day-to-day and year-to-year, like sending out the monthly budget reports to everyone on campus reminding them of where they stand. The business officer is ultimately responsible for bringing in the current-year financial operations on budget. This is a great example of the dichotomy of the job: short-range view on the current year and long-range perspective to help shape the future of the school. Large schools and those with greater resources can afford enough staff in the business office to have a controller. The controller can focus on the short-range financial information, allowing the business officer to look at the big picture and the long-range issues. But many of our schools do not have the luxury of having two people of this caliber to share these tasks. So one person has to wear both hats. This presents a challenge because these two jobs often require different skill sets. A person who is good at big-picture thinking may struggle to sustain focus on the details of the moment. A person who loves the exactness and minutiae of accounting may be hard-pressed to do the "what-if" work of strategic financial thinking. The business officer who looks to the horizon and forgets the bottom line will have a very serious problem, and vice versa.

> *The manager administers; the leader innovates. The manager maintains; the leader develops.*

Remembering that today's business officer is both leader and manager, let's evaluate this statement with some examples:

Example 1:
You work with outside resource people to develop an innovative health insurance plan for your school's employees, saving the school money while providing a quality benefit for your staff. You then have to actually administer the plan, making sure that forms are completed and timely payments are made.

Example 2:
You develop new approaches to the physical resource issues facing the school. You oversee construction of new facilities and the financing to make this construction possible. But you must still maintain the rest of the campus during this time, worrying about the effectiveness of the cleaning crew, allocating sparse resources to repair deferred maintenance, and constantly working the construction and repair around the school's program calendar (and summer camp).

> *The manager focuses on systems and structure; the leader focuses on people.*

The business officer who *only* looks at "systems and structure" is guaranteed to be unsuccessful in the job. People—staff, teachers, parents, and students—are what the job is all about. If you lose sight of that fact, you may make decisions for the wrong reasons. However, the school *relies* on you to develop and maintain good systems to manage the school's resources. Because schools are organizations whose focus is all about people, not widgets, the systems you create or improve must take into account the needs of the people. The effective business office is centered on customer service, whether it is helping parents afford the school by offering payment plans or helping faculty with good benefit plans. The truly great business officer does not just say "no" when asked for more resources (money, space, time, etc.). The truly great business officer says, "Let's see how this delivers the mission," and then, "Let's find a way to make it happen." This attitude can help an under-resourced school effectively deliver its mission without breaking the budget, and can help a rich-in-resources school stay that way.

> *The manager relies on control; the leader inspires trust. The manager does things right; the leader does the right things.*

The most effective business officers are totally trusted on their campuses. But they, more than anyone, know that blind trust can lead to disappointment. They must hold themselves to the highest ethical standards. They must realize that the segregation of duties, as well as checks and balances, are designed to protect the institution from misuse, or worse, misappropriation, of funds. The fiduciary responsibility for the school comes down to systems of control: who can sign checks, authorize purchases, drive the buses, access the databases, etc.

As the business officer, you hold up the ethical mirror to the internal processes at the school for the board. So you must "do the right things," yet because you are responsible for so many areas at the school, you must "do those things right," or the school will suffer.

It is important to add one more point. The business officer has control over the financial information of the school. As "manager," you will send information to whomever asks for it, whenever they ask. But as "leader," you will think about the need itself, and send people what they need, in a format they can understand, when they need it, without waiting to be asked. By sharing information this way, the governance team of the school can make informed decisions at the right time, being proactive rather than reactive.

TIPS OF THE TRADE

Be as active as possible: Get out of your office at least once a day. Eat in the cafeteria with your colleagues. Talk to the students. Hang out in the maintenance shed and get to know the building and grounds staff. Go to a sports game. Be visible and approachable. Remember, "customer service" should be the mantra of you and your office.

Join associations: Off-campus, participate in your local, regional, and national associations. These connections will give you access to new information that can make you look like a genius when you come back and present it—and give you a whole new cadre of colleagues. You have come to this job from other jobs where you have had a lot of responsibility. But the breadth of responsibilities that you now have makes it virtually impossible to stay on top of all of the information alone. You need help. Whether it is walking around campus and learning from your colleagues or going to a professional meeting and learning from others in the field, you need all the help you can get. And here's where we come in:

Participate in NBOA: NBOA is the only national association that focuses on the financial and operational health of independent schools. We are a solution-oriented community that honors collective expertise. Our dynamic knowledge base constantly updates itself online (through our website discussion forum and web-based resources), at events (stellar conferences and programs with award-winning speakers and hands-on workshops), through our publications, and with our personal consulting services. And NBOA needs YOU—it needs your knowledge, your bright ideas, your questions, your concerns, and your unique take on the financial and operational challenges facing independent schools today. This book will get your feet wet: then log on to *www. nboa.net* to really get in the game.

I DON'T HAVE TIME!

I can imagine that at this moment you are saying to yourself that you are too busy to do all of this. You do not have time to get out of the office. You do not have time to go to conferences in other states. You don't have time to eat lunch, let alone eat lunch with your colleagues! Many in this job feel like they are drowning under a tidal wave of tasks and expectations. Even if you've taken a time management course and mastered all the tricks to managing a

challenging environment, *you do not have control of your priorities.* You can develop a task list, prioritize it, and set your goals for the coming day. But when you arrive at your desk at 8am, and the phone is ringing, and it's your head of school on the line, you know that your tidy little list is going to have to wait. And if it's not your head, it's a broken cable that disconnected all the power to the campus. Or maybe there was an ice storm during the night and you have to help figure out how to get school open by 8am. Or there's an administrative assistant whose marginal performance has suddenly spun out of control and you need to develop an immediate termination process. Or the bus won't start and you have to find alternative transportation for the fifth grade field trip at noon, etc., etc., etc.

BUT AT THE END OF THE DAY… YOU LOVE THIS JUNGLE

The nature of this job is nonstop problem-solving. That is why there is a cadre of people drawn to it. They live for the thrill of fixing yet another problem. They live in fear of being bored in their professional careers. The business office is one place where that will never happen. Most of the solutions to the problems in the preceding paragraph needed a team approach to implement. You need to have developed relationships of mutual respect with the facilities staff to address the broken cable; the vendors need to know you and the school so they will want to respond quickly when you call. The campus community needs to trust your ability to address problems. When you say, "Give me an hour and I'll come back with some ways to fix this," they back off because they know you will deliver to the best of your ability. Those relationships are forged by those trips venturing out of your office. And NBOA is where you can turn when those relationships don't provide the answers you need. Our members can point you to a new vendor or resource that gets you on the path to a solution to your current problem.

Why do we do this job? Because the satisfaction of watching those fifth graders go on their field trip to learn something entirely new that may change their lives, knowing that you were partially responsible for making it happen, is great. (Perhaps YOU were the alternative transportation.) Once again, you have played a part in the delivery of the school's mission. Inside the classroom, teachers are teaching and students are learning; outside the classroom, you are making sure it happens. You are ensuring the school's future, one day at a time.

Chapter Two

FINANCIAL MANAGEMENT AND REPORTING

Everything You Always Wanted to Know But Were Afraid to Ask

IN THIS CHAPTER:

- Assessing your own internal controls

- Ulcer-free audit preparation

- GAAP vs. internal financial management

- Mastering pledge accounting

- Setting your annual budget

by Linda Myers Dennison

Linda Myers Dennison, CPA

Associate Director, National Business Officers Association

Prior to assuming her present position as Associate Director for NBOA, where she heads the association's consulting services program, Linda held various senior positions in independent schools. She was the Director of Finance and Operations for St. Anne's School of Annapolis, The Woods Academy, Pingree School, and Chapel Hill-Chauncy Hall School, as well as the Major Gifts Officer for Tabor Academy. She spent seven years in public accounting working for Coopers & Lybrand and Newburg & Company, LLP. Linda has served on several nonprofit boards, including Tabor Academy & Summit Montessori School. She is a frequent presenter on various independent school topics, including leadership, financial sustainability, and strategic planning. Linda holds a Bachelor of Science degree in Accounting from the University of Southern Maine and a Graduate Certificate in Business Leadership for Independent Schools from Johns Hopkins University. She is a member of the American Institute of Certified Public Accountants.

FINANCIAL MANAGEMENT AND REPORTING

*Everything You Always Wanted to Know
But Were Afraid to Ask*

When beginning as a new business officer (either as someone who is new to the profession or as someone who has changed schools), it is important to assess the overall business structure of the school in order to plan how you should best move forward. The most important part of the transition is establishing and developing relationships with business office staff, direct reports, and key school administrators, as well as the greater school community. One way to initiate those relationships is to solicit observations of the school's current business practices: find out what works well, what could be improved, what may not be getting done, and how you can best support your colleagues.

- Where is the school's money? How is it invested?

- How is money collected by the school for tuition, fees, camps, meals, field trips, books, sports, etc.?

- How do we pay our bills and how often?

- Who signs school checks?

- How is payroll processed? Do we need to move money in order to fund a payroll account?

- How is the school's cash flow? At any time during the fiscal year, do we rely on a line of credit? If so, when is it typically needed? Is there an outstanding balance at this time?

- What is the budget for the current year?

- What are the school's financial trends?

- Is enrollment greater than or equal to budget? If not, are there cash flow implications that should be considered?

- Is the school contemplating or in the middle of a capital campaign?

- Is the school contemplating or in the middle of a substantial construction project? Does the school have deferred maintenance?

- What reports and regulatory filings does the school prepare and how often? What are the typical due dates?

- When was the school's most recent audit completed? Were there any issues communicated by the auditor to the audit committee or to the school's management?

DIFFERENCES BETWEEN GENERALLY ACCEPTED ACCOUNTING PRINCIPLES AND INTERNAL FINANCIAL MANAGEMENT

Since 1973, the Financial Accounting Standards Board (FASB) has been the designated organization for establishing standards for accounting and financial reporting for the private sector, which includes most independent schools, whether for-profit or not-for-profit. FASB issues the pronouncements and technical interpretations that comprise Generally Accepted Accounting Principles (GAAP). In May 2008, FASB issued *Statement 162, The Hierarchy of Generally Accepted Accounting Principles*, a summary of which is available at ***www.fasb.org***, to help schools understand some of the complexities found within GAAP. While most schools prepare their audited financial statements in accordance with GAAP, they also tend to rely on concepts common to independent schools (and cash management) that are not compliant with GAAP. Understanding the key differences is crucial to proper financial planning, budgeting, and reporting.

Financial Reporting

Statement of Financial Accounting Standards (SFAS) 117, Financial Statements of Not-for-Profit Organizations, issued in June 1993, standardized the way in which nonprofit organizations publicly report financial information. It formally introduced net asset accounting: unrestricted, temporarily restricted, and permanently restricted net assets, and moved away from fund accounting, which segregated financial resources activity into separate funds by function: operations, endowment, debt, plant, etc. While schools annually prepare financial statements according to GAAP, many prepare monthly/quarterly internal reports on a cash basis or modified cash basis. It is imperative for each school to develop a way that the business officer, head of school, and board of trustees can best manage the fiscal resources of the school. However, consideration should be given to including a brief reconciliation to GAAP, since many debt covenants require minimum income and service ratios that are based on GAAP. In the worst case, excluding GAAP income and expenses from periodic reports and the annual budget may result in an unexpected loss that is reported in the school's audited financial statements and IRS Form 990. Also, providing a GAAP reconciliation of internal statements to the audited financial statements at the end of each fiscal year gives trustees and other overseers a consistent instrument through which they can analyze the school's financial picture that is "verified" annually through the audit.

Pledges Receivable

The treatment of pledges receivable is a common difference between internal financial reports and GAAP-compliant financial statements. *SFAS 116, Accounting for Contributions Received and Contributions Made*, requires that bona fide pledges be recorded in a school's financial statements in the year in which the pledge is received by the school (not the years in which the pledge will be paid). Most accountants deem a bona fide pledge to be one that is in writing and is clear about both the donor's intent for the gift and the

pledge payment schedule. While GAAP allows a school to establish a reasonable reserve with pledges the school deems may be uncollectable, the pledge and any estimated reserve would have to be recorded in the year in which it is received, regardless of when the cash is actually received. This timing issue between recording of the revenue and payment of cash can be challenging, particularly when a school is also beginning a major construction project or other cash-intensive initiative. Care should be taken to understand the revenue and cash implications of each gift.

Example:
In Fiscal Year (FY) 1, NBOA Academy will be in the "quiet phase" of its first capital campaign. The school hopes to raise 90% of its stated campaign goal from major donors before announcing the campaign to the general public. Mrs. Smith is so excited about the school's projects that she signs a $1,000,000 pledge in FY 1 to be paid in five equal, annual installments beginning in FY 2 and ending in FY 6. Mrs. Smith has been a loyal supporter of the school and is known to have assets sufficient to pay such a generous pledge. According to GAAP, the entire $1,000,000 pledge (and corresponding campaign revenue) would have to be recorded in FY 1 even though the cash would not be received until FY 2 and beyond. Depending on the timing of the school's projects, care should be taken to analyze cash flow to ensure coverage of all expenses.

Note: This pledge will also have to be discounted to present value based on the pledge payment schedule. Pledge reserves and discounts are further explored in the "Development Contributions" section of this chapter.

PROVISION FOR PLANT REPLACEMENT, RENEWAL, AND SPECIAL MAINTENANCE (PPRRSM) AND DEPRECIATION

The Provision for Plant Replacement, Renewal, and Special Maintenance (PPRRSM) is one mechanism through which independent schools plan and save money for future repairs and restoration to their physical assets. A school can analyze the existing condition of its physical assets and estimate the remaining life and timing of replacement costs associated with maintaining an excellent physical plant. This analysis can then be used to set aside the resources necessary to accomplish maintenance and repair on a schedule established by the school that is least disruptive to the program, rather than when the asset breaks and repair is absolutely necessary. GAAP does not specifically recognize PPRRSM as an accounting concept. Rather, physical assets with an estimated useful life greater than one year are recorded and depreciated. Any cash that may be "budgeted" to meet these goals in future years is not considered an "expense" by GAAP, but rather a board designation of the school's unrestricted net assets. A school can only expense depreciation and those repair and maintenance items (which do not increase the estimated useful life of the asset) that were incurred in the current fiscal year.

Cash Reserves

It is considered best practice for independent schools to save cash in reserve for unexpected future events. Many schools impose this discipline by having a reserve "expense" in their annual budget. Like PPRRSM, GAAP does not consider this an expense, but rather a designation of unrestricted net assets.

FINANCIAL REPORTING

An independent school typically needs to report its financial and operational outcomes to several internal and external constituents, including its board of trustees, bondholders, and letter-of-credit holders. A nonprofit school's financial information is also made public through the IRS Form 990, which a nonprofit organization is required to make available to the public when asked and which is typically posted on third-party websites such as *www.guidestar.org*.

As discussed above, the Financial Accounting Standards Board (FASB) requires schools to account for financial transactions and prepare external reports in accordance with Generally Accepted Accounting Principles (GAAP). Audited financial statements are explored later in this chapter.

For internal users, the business office should be preparing all financial reports that are provided to department heads, program managers, the head of school, and the board of trustees. The guiding principle should be the informational needs of the users (within reason).

Financial reports need to be designed to provide the head of school and the board with the information they need for financial oversight in a format they *each* can understand—not just those with financial acumen. The internal reporting cycle for each school varies depending on its size, financial complexity, existence of bonds and related financial covenants, and strategic plan initiatives. However, the finance committee of the board of trustees should, at a minimum, receive quarterly financial reports that include year-to-date activity with comparisons to budget, year-end projections relative to budget, project summaries relative to planned initiatives, a cash requirements report, and a narrative summary that analyzes all of the information contained within these financial reports and identifies the most important information. These reports should be sent to the finance committee electronically at least one week in advance of the meeting to allow time for review, leaving the committee's meeting time to focus on discussing issues and questions rather than summarizing results.

One way to streamline reporting to the full board of trustees is to create a one-page, quarterly executive summary that includes key financial indicators and an abbreviated written financial report that highlights items of significance. Again, an important part of the report is the narrative description of the financial issues that are revealed in the report. At appropriate times throughout the fiscal year, this report should include revenue, expense, and cash flow projections for the remainder of the fiscal year, and show the impact of all strategic decisions.

When designing internal financial reports for your school, it is important to consider your users, the questions they may have, and their level of financial acumen. It is also important to give the context for the school's numbers and provide insight into what the data means for the school.

Questions That Should Be Answered In Your Reports

- How do the current period results compare to the prior period (whether monthly, quarterly, year-to-date, or annually)?

- How do the current period results compare to the annual budget approved by the board of trustees? What are the reasons for significant variances? Are the variances mission-consistent and in line with the school's strategic objectives?

- How do the current period results impact the school's year-end projections? Given the experience to date, what is the impact to the overall bottom line? Does that affect the school's ability to meet bond covenant or cash flow requirements or present other significant issues that should be discussed by the board of trustees before the end of the fiscal year? Are mid-year adjustments necessary?

- How do the current period results compare to what is happening with other schools? Are they experiencing similar trends?

- How do current period results impact the school's ability to achieve what it has defined as success for the year? Can unexpected, unfavorable trends be managed to produce a more desirable result or is the trend driven by circumstances out of the school's control? How should the school use these trends to plan for its future sustainability?

Key Indicators

Identifying meaningful program, financial, and operating indicators allows a school a mechanism through which it can evaluate outcomes and directives relative to the school's mission. When these indicators are tracked over a period of time, a school can determine whether the trends it is experiencing are in line with the school's intended strategic direction.

Key indicators can include:

FINANCIAL

- Cash flow and liquidity ratios

- Percentage of unrestricted net assets to total net assets

- Functional spending allocations

- Financial aid as a percentage of gross tuition

- Capital spending

- Debt service ratios: debt service coverage and minimum net asset and cash flow requirements

- Staffing ratios

- Investment performance

- Level of cash reserves relative to stated goals

PROGRAMMATIC AND DEVELOPMENT

- Number of admission inquiries, applications, acceptances, matriculants, and rejections

- Percentage of gift participation by each constituency (parents, alumni, etc.)

- Number of graduates who went on to first- or second-choice schools

- Number of students participating in various programs

- Number of volunteers and analysis of participation

In analyzing these key indicators, ask:

- How do these trends compare with expected results?

- How do these trends compare to other schools?

- Are these trends sustainable over time?

The data resulting from a school's chosen key indicators should be interpreted and conveyed in clear narrative language to the school's board of trustees.

Annual Budget

A school's annual budget should be the financial translation of the school's mission and strategic vision. It should clearly support the school's program and intended outcomes as well as manage the school's cash flow to ensure smooth operations throughout the fiscal year.

There are many methods schools use to manage their budgeting process. Some schools develop a future year's budget based solely on amount expended in previous years. Others choose to begin each budget process with "zero," asking all budget managers to submit expected costs for the coming year, with explanations for all unusual costs or dollar requests. In either scenario, it is important to understand each program manager's current and future visions so resources can be planned and the mission seamlessly supported.

A participatory budget process provides the school with a systematic method to administer its finances so that available resources are directed toward matters of highest priority and areas of greatest importance for fulfilling the mission. While the head of school and the business officer should model the appropriate leadership in setting financial objectives, other school leaders should be involved in setting the budget. Giving administrators and others in charge of programs responsibility for their budgets (current and long-term) and sending them monthly budget-to-actual reports will encourage them to become more involved and accountable.

Transparency within the school is critical to the successful functioning of a participatory budget process. When items are not approved within the current budget cycle, the rationale should be explained to the person making the initial request.

The budget needs to be structured so all constituents can see the depth of their programs. For example, all strategic programming should be grouped by initiative and shown in total so directors can monitor the revenues and expenses associated with each program, as well as the overall bottom line.

One way to educate various community members about the budget is to establish an internal budget committee. Generally this committee is composed of the business officer, division heads/ principals, and, if appropriate, other business office staff. In smaller schools, the head of school is also typically a member of the committee. In addition, this committee may have one to three guest members from other areas of the school (academic department heads, development

director, facilities manager, etc.) who join the committee for a one-year period. The committee meets several times to discuss budget requests for the next year. The committee's goal is to balance these requests against the school's long-term strategic plan and the available resources in the budget. The committee may choose to schedule meetings with those who have significantly large areas of budget responsibility (academic department heads, plant facilities manager, computer services director, etc.). If the head of school is not a member of the committee, once the budget is balanced it should be presented to the head, then to the finance committee, for review and approval.

This process can be successful because the prioritization of spending requests is done by those individuals who know the program. The process promotes open dialogue so that the internal budget committee can understand the needs of the programs and the program heads can understand the limitations of a particular budget year.

Finally, when working with the budget, it is important to understand that one cannot correctly estimate every number. Developing a contingency reserve (typically 1-2% of the annual operating budget) allows the school some flexibility in the face of uncertain circumstances.

ANNUAL BUDGET TIMELINE

The timeline for completing a school's annual budget varies by school. Since many schools are significantly tuition-dependent, the budget timeline may be driven by the date by which a school sets its tuition rate for the following year. Other schools choose to set key budget drivers such as tuition, financial aid, and salaries several months in advance and finalize the budget once school opens for the year and final enrollment is known. In either scenario, the more information you have at the time tuition is set, the more informed the board can be.

Suggested Timeline

This timeline presumes tuition is set in early January in time to prepare re-enrollment contracts.

SEPTEMBER AND OCTOBER:

- Meet with the head of school and chair of the finance committee to discuss desired budget process. Assess their sensitivity to increases/decreases to major budget drivers and their perception of the "bottom line."

- Complete data input to National Association of Independent Schools (NAIS) StatsOnline and/or regional data collection vehicles to ensure future access to necessary benchmarking data.

- Prepare budget template and instruction sheet to be distributed to all program managers and department heads. The template should include space for immediate year requests (must have, nice to have, wish list), future requests, and staffing levels by head count as opposed to salary dollars.

- Ensure immediate prior-year fiscal results are entered into budget worksheets to serve as a reminder to all budget-responsible personnel.

- Examine current year enrollment relative to expectations and seek any

relevant demographic or economic data that may impact budget assumptions.

- If data is available, begin benchmarking relevant budget drivers: tuition, financial aid, salaries, benefits, physical plant, etc.

NOVEMBER:

- Meet with all budget managers to understand their program vision and goals.

- If applicable, assemble budget committee as described above and establish meeting dates that are consistent with all finance committee and board of trustee meeting dates.

- Assemble all budget requests into a preliminary budget as written.

- Meet with the head of school and chair of the finance committee to discuss preliminary requests.

- Finalize benchmark data for tuition, financial aid, salaries, and other critical budget drivers.

- Meet with the finance committee to gain an understanding of their expectations of the budget (e.g., must have a balanced budget that allows for a $50,000 contribution to cash reserves).

DECEMBER:

- Bring results from the finance committee meeting to the budget committee, if applicable, and begin prioritizing requests to achieve the expectations outlined by the board of trustees.

- Meet with the head of school and/or the treasurer to finalize the budget and its presentation to the board of trustees.

- Send packet to the finance committee for consideration prior to its final meeting before the board meeting.

- Meet with the finance committee to prepare budget (or key drivers) that will be presented to the board of trustees.

JANUARY:

- Send the budget package to your board of trustees at least one week in advance of the board meeting, including a narrative of why this budget is programmatically appropriate; outline strategic objectives that will be achieved through this budget plan.

- Present the budget to the board of trustees for discussion and approval.

- Work with the head of school to inform members of the school community of budget approval and any budget changes. Provide specific details to budget managers. Discuss the method through which items not currently approved will be tracked for future consideration.

FEBRUARY THROUGH SEPTEMBER
(for schools not finalizing their budgets until after opening enrollment is known):

- Work with budget managers to establish appropriate summer spending policies that reflect the financial realities of the school. For example, if it is possible the school will not meet enrollment projections and spending may need to be cut, budget managers should be informed of the maximum amount that may be spent until the budget is finalized.

- Update assumptions as new information becomes available.

- Inform the head of school and board of trustees if any change in assumptions will result in unfavorable circumstances.

- Present revised budget to finance committee for approval.

- Present revised budget to board of trustees for final approval.

LONG-RANGE FINANCIAL PLANNING AND SUSTAINABILITY

Financial sustainability should be of paramount concern for all business officers. One way to plan for the future is to create a multi-year financial plan that reflects the strategic direction of the school and thoughtfully evaluates the impact of current decisions on future operations. Multi-year plans should include relevant, strategic details and project the potential impact of major decisions (or current budget drivers): bond issuance, construction, staff transitions, etc. Preparing and finalizing such a plan allows the decision-makers to model the resources necessary to meet the school's strategic initiatives, while understanding any possible impact to the operating budget several years into the future. It allows the board of trustees to analyze possible scenarios and make the most educated choice given the current information. Finally, the school must be able to assess the sustainability of its present operations relative to its current and future resources. This includes analyzing, assessing, and developing long-range plans for all major budget drivers, including enrollment, tuition, financial aid, staff compensation, facilities, debt service, and technology expenses.

PREPARING FOR THE ANNUAL AUDIT

As discussed above, the Financial Accounting Standards Board (FASB) issues Generally Accepted Accounting Principles (GAAP), the basis on which audited financial statements must be prepared. The Auditing Standards Board (ASB) issues Statements on Auditing Standards (SASs), which govern how auditors prepare for, conduct, complete, and report their audits. While SASs are intended to govern how auditors complete their work, the impact to schools can be substantial, since most of the auditors' schedules must first be prepared by the school.

In March and May 2006, the ASB issued *SASs 104-111* (referred to as the *Risk Assessment Standards*) and *SAS 112, Communicating Internal Control Related Matters Identified in an Audit. SASs 104-111* have significant repercussions for all independent schools because the new regulations change the way auditors evaluate a school's system of internal controls, as well as how schools process and report financial information. The *Risk Assessment Standards* require the auditors to gain a more in-depth understanding of a school's operations and internal control environment in order to assess the risk of material misstatements in the financial statements. It also requires testing of your school's internal control systems so the auditor may develop additional procedures surrounding any perceived risks. Internal controls are discussed later in this chapter.

SAS 112 outlines the requirements under which internal control deficiencies are communicated to the board of trustees of the school. The Standard describes circumstances under which schools must receive written communications. Understanding these new standards and your auditor's interpretation of them will be critical to assessing their impact on your school's future audits.

SFAS 117, Financial Statements of Not-for-Profit Organizations, provides the framework with which independent schools report financial information. When preparing for the audit, a school is required to prepare its financial statements in accordance with GAAP, including all statements, footnotes, and additional schedules (if desired). Prior to the *Risk Assessment Standards,* auditors could assist schools in assembling these statements during the audit, but are no longer allowed to do so, since the financial statements represent a critical element in the reporting segment of a school's internal control structure.

SUMMARY OF KEY CONCEPTS AND REQUIRED SCHEDULES:

The crux of audited financial statements is to break net assets into three categories: 1) unrestricted, 2) temporarily restricted, and 3) permanently restricted. Temporarily restricted net assets and permanently restricted net assets are defined as donor-imposed stipulations relative to the use of the gift. For example, a donor's gift to endowment is a permanently restricted net asset whereas a board of trustees' designation of funds from operating surpluses to function as endowment is considered an unrestricted net asset. The board's designation can be acknowledged in the presentation of unrestricted net assets but does not change the nature of the asset from unrestricted to permanently restricted.

AUDITED FINANCIAL STATEMENTS

Statement of Financial Position

(also known as the Balance Sheet): this is a summary of the school's assets, liabilities, and net assets as of a particular date, usually the school's fiscal year end. When assembling, remember:

ASSETS ≡
LIABILITIES ✛ NET ASSETS

Create two big columns. Put all of your assets on the left in order of liquidity (cash, accounts receivable, pledges receivable, property, equipment, and other assets). Put the liabilities on the right in the order in which they must be paid (accounts payable, accrued expenses, short-term notes payable, long-term notes payable), followed by net assets in the following order: unrestricted, temporarily restricted, and permanently restricted. Make sure the totals of the left column and the right column are the same number!

Statement of Activities

(also known as the Income Statement): this is the summary of the school's revenues and expenses for a period of time, usually the school's fiscal year. This is the statement that most resembles the school's financial reports except that it must be consolidated— i.e., include all funds and/or net asset categories and include all financial activity occurring under the school's tax identification number (including associations and other decentralized operations that may otherwise seem immaterial to the school).

Statement of Cash Flow

This statement summarizes activity by three activity categories: operating, investing, and financing. It is also prepared for a period of time, usually the school's fiscal year. Following common interpretation of operations, investment, and financing will help you include the school's activity in the correct section of this report.

Notes to the Financial Statements

The narrative section of the financial statements, which provides details about accounting assumptions and allows for greater explanation of substantial accounts and activities. GAAP has several required footnote disclosures, including a summary of major accounting policies, reserve policies, depreciation schedules, investment schedules, debt payment schedules, and listings of temporarily and permanently restricted net assets. Using a prior year's footnotes is a great start to preparation, but measures should be taken to ensure any new pronouncement requirements are also included.

Supplemental Schedules

Schools can choose to present supplemental schedules of financial information within their audited financial statements. The school and the auditor need to agree in advance as to whether these schedules will a) be audited, and receive an opinion from the auditors as to their accuracy relative to the audited numbers, or b) remain unaudited, and be labeled as such. Examples of supplemental schedules include functional expense allocations of accounts listed on the Statement of Activities, report formats required by donor foundations, or a summary of activity by fund. Since supplemental schedules are not typically required, the school should consider the users of the audited financial statements and whether the supplemental schedules will provide critical information before including them.

INTERNAL CONTROLS

Since the Auditing Standards Board issued its *Risk Assessment Standards* in March 2006, schools have had to gain a deeper understanding of their system of internal controls, document that understanding, and provide mechanisms through which the controls are tested and modified as appropriate. Below is a brief summary of the components of a school's internal control environment as directed by the Committee of Sponsoring Organizations of the Treadway Commission (COSO). In 1992, COSO developed a model that has been adopted as the generally accepted set of guidelines for internal controls. More information is available at *www.coso.org*.

The COSO model defines internal control as "a process, effected by an entity's board of directors, management and other personnel, designed to provide reasonable assurance of the achievement of objectives in the following categories:

- EFFECTIVENESS AND EFFICIENCY OF OPERATIONS
- RELIABILITY OF FINANCIAL REPORTING
- COMPLIANCE WITH APPLICABLE LAWS AND REGULATIONS"

COSO promulgates that an effective internal control system utilizes the following five components to support the school's mission, strategy, and related financial objectives:

1. Control Environment

2. Risk Assessment

3. Control Activities

4. Information and Communication

5. Monitoring

These five components work to establish the foundation for good internal controls within a school through leadership, shared values, and a culture that emphasizes accountability and integrity. The school identifies and routinely assesses risk in all areas of the organization. Control activities, including segregation of duties, are proactively designed to address and mitigate significant risks. The entire system of internal control is monitored continuously and issues are corrected in a timely manner.

Segregation of duties is another component of an effective internal control structure. When discussing segregation of duties, it is important to understand which tasks are deemed to be incompatible:

- AUTHORIZATION
(review and/or approval of transactions)
- CUSTODY
(access or control over the physical assets, e.g., checks)
- RECORDING
(creating and maintaining the information in the school's accounting software)

- RECONCILING
(verifying the processing of records, including authorization)

For example, the person responsible for student billing should not be collecting or depositing cash. The person responsible for accounts payable should not be an authorized check signer nor should s/he mail the checks once signed.

How do I achieve segregation of duties with a one- or two-person business office?

When limited personnel does not allow optimal segregation of duties, the school should consider implementing as many mitigating controls as possible. Mitigating controls are designed to catch human errors or possible intentional misstatements by incorporating additional review and/or reconciliation procedures. Mitigating controls that help smaller schools improve their system of internal controls include:

- Asking an administrative person outside of normal business office functions to open mail and endorse and deposit all checks using a remote deposit machine before distributing to the appropriate record-keeper.

- Directing all cash receipts to a lock box at a local bank. While the associated fees are higher than with a regular checking account, the control achieved is far less expensive than employing or utilizing another person.

- Asking the head of school or the school's treasurer to directly receive, open, and review all bank statements for unusual and irregular items.

- Asking the finance committee to regularly review the totals (not details) of accounts payable and accounts receivable aging reports. Train them to ask if anything outstanding in either area is greater than 60, 90, or 120 days old, and ask them to require explanation.

- Providing monthly detailed activity reports to all department heads and budget managers along with training on how to read the reports and identify errors. Asking department heads to alert the business office in writing (including email) of any errors noted.

- Creating and maintaining a good tuition collections process that is diligently followed. A family that receives a collection letter on tuition already paid will surely call to find out what happened.

- Creating appropriate review and approval structures that examine payroll, accounts payable, purchasing, accounts receivable, and cash receipts. The review should be completed by persons outside of the custody and recording functions.

- Hiring an accountant (independent of your school's audit firm) to prepare or review financial data on a periodic basis.

POLICIES AND PROCEDURES MANUALS

A well-defined system of internal controls requires schools to have policies and procedures manuals that document procedures and their related reviews and mitigating controls. Also, business operations procedures manuals that address each of the major functions of the business office and outline the school's standard operating procedures will provide information necessary for the school to continue operating in the event a staff member becomes ill or leaves suddenly. These manuals allow for the completion of vital tasks and ensure business continuity. Periodically, the procedures in these manuals should be tested internally to ensure accuracy and to accomplish the testing of the control environment that is suggested by COSO.

Accounting Procedures Manual

An accounting procedures manual and usable computer operating instructions should be made available to all accounting personnel. The purpose of this manual is to describe job functions and duties, to detail procedures used in accounting for transactions, and to provide information on existing internal controls designed to produce reliable financial information. Appropriate revisions to policies or procedures should be made on a regular basis.

Payroll Procedures Manual

The purpose of a payroll procedures manual is to ensure the school's compensation program is administered within appropriate guidelines. It addresses compliance with all federal and state regulations, adherence to the approved budget, and ensures that compensation is objective and non-discriminatory in theory, application, and practice. A payroll manual typically includes a discussion of employee classifications, payroll changes, payroll deductions, compensatory time, wage and salary payments, time records, workers compensation, etc.

Cross-Training

There should be at least two people who know how to perform each critical function within the business office: payroll, benefits administration, accounts payable, cash receipts, and student billing. This cross-training will prepare the office to function in the event an employee is unexpectedly absent on a crucial day. While schools may rely on a set of accounting process manuals, that may not be enough to prepare the school for an unanticipated absence.

General Ledger Reconciliation

School accounts receivable and accounts payable subsidiary ledgers should be consistently reconciled with the general ledger throughout the year. Professional best practice recommends that each person (accounts payable, student billing, and payroll) be responsible for reconciling his or her subsidiary ledger to the general ledger monthly. These reconciliations should be reviewed and approved by a supervisor who is knowledgeable about accounting and regulatory requirements. Any resulting journal entry from this analysis should also be approved and posted by persons other than the initial preparer, for proper segregation of duties.

CASH MANAGEMENT AND TRANSACTIONAL ACCOUNTING

Authorized Check Signatories

When a school designs its system of internal controls, it is important to consider the role an authorized check signer can play in ensuring the integrity of the accounts payable process. Check signers should include staff who do not have direct responsibility for authorizing purchases or entering invoices into the accounts payable system, and who do not have responsibility for reconciling bank accounts. The school should consider requiring two check signers for large checks. While the bank will not verify the two signatories, it provides an opportunity for the school to strengthen its internal controls.

Bank Accounts

Historically, many schools maintained separate bank accounts for operations, plant, capital campaign, parents association, alumni association, etc. Having multiple bank accounts, varying by function, can cause inefficiency of cash transfers and increase the school's risk for misappropriation of assets. Schools should consider using one checking account through which all receipt and disbursement transactions flow. Schools and their finance/investment committees should then consider the appropriate investment vehicles that will maximize investment return and manage their endowment, reserves, and excess cash.

In smaller schools, bank statements should be received, unopened, by the head of school, who should review the account for unusual activity and initial the bank statement to indicate completion of the review. The account should then be reconciled and reviewed by persons who are not responsible for check signing, posting deposits, or accounts payable.

Purchasing

A school should consider whether it is spending a disproportionate amount of time processing purchases relative to the amount of money being spent, the size of

its overall budget, staffing, and culture.

Many schools allow their budget-responsible leaders to approve purchase orders and expense reimbursements within reason, relative to the size of the budget being managed. Budget managers should be given monthly activity reports so they can monitor their progress relative to budget, and should likewise be held accountable for any budget overages. This allows faculty to purchase supplies within reason, with only the approval of their department head.

Having business office personnel complete purchasing is no longer considered professional best practice, as it does not properly segregate the asset acquisition from the recording of the transaction. It has become best practice for schools to distribute purchasing responsibilities across academic divisions and administrative departments with the understanding that purchases must be approved in advance by the budget-responsible manager. When orders are received, the person placing the order should verify that all items expected were received, indicate approval of the shipment by initialing the packing slip, then forward the approved purchase order and the approved packing slip to the business office for invoice payment.

School Credit vs. Personal Cards

Within many independent schools, several staff members are responsible for purchasing, attending conferences, or arranging to send staff to conferences. Employees should not be expected to make charges to their personal cards and then request reimbursement from the school. The school should apply for credit or purchasing cards in the name of the school rather than rely on employees' personal credit to conduct school business.

Accounts Payable

Accounts payable is a critical area in which schools must operate efficiently and effectively. A poorly run accounts payable function has the potential to damage the school's credit rating, interrupt the school's ability to work with certain vendors (as they will not tolerate late payments), increase expenses due to late fees, and cause unnecessary inconvenience to staff needing to place orders (if they are not permitted to order until a previous bill is paid).

Schools should consider designating a specific day and time each week when accounts payable checks will be processed, signed, and distributed. The school should also designate a day and time by which all payables and related support must be submitted to the business office in order to be processed that week. For example, if the school chooses for all accounts payable checks to be ready by Friday at noon, then it might process all payables received by 3pm Wednesday. Schools should make every effort to develop a system that will encourage all staff to submit paperwork for reimbursements on time, and ensure that all invoices and reimbursements are paid in a timely manner. At the end of each check run, the business officer should review the list of outstanding invoices to ensure that all vendors are paid in a timely manner.

Capital Assets

Inventorying historical depreciable assets and implementing effective procedures in accounting for additions and disposals to these capital assets can be time-consuming and daunting to any business officer.

As a standard operating procedure, a month-end report should be generated detailing capital purchases. This may require identifying capital expenditures initially recorded within operating expense accounts. These should then be transferred by journal entry to the school's capital asset accounts.

Utilizing this report and corresponding invoices from an "additions" file, staff can enter each purchase into an inventory subsidiary ledger (either produced within an asset software program or an Excel spreadsheet). This ledger identifies each asset by asset number, date purchased, vendor, description, and physical location of the asset. Individual asset identification plates should be attached to each capital item when received. On a periodic basis, staff should reconcile each asset category from the subsidiary ledger to the general ledger. Any discrepancies should be researched. Staff should also prepare a yearly list of items that have been sold, retired, or disposed. These items should then be removed from the general ledger to ensure that depreciable assets, as well as the annual depreciation expense, are accounted for properly.

Student Billing, Accounts Receivable, and Collections

Information about the financial

situation of enrolled families must be accurate and complete at all times. In order for a school to be successful in a competitive independent school market and to balance the fiscal importance of remaining fully enrolled, but not overenrolled (due to possible occupancy permit restrictions), it is vital that both the business office and the admission office have accurate and complete information on currently enrolled families. It is imperative that schools treat all families fairly and in a manner that emulates the school's mission, particularly when dealing with business and financial matters.

Schools should develop collections policies and procedures that are discussed and endorsed by the head of school and board of trustees, and which are followed in the event of delinquencies. It is imperative that everyone agrees on the policies and procedures so that there is consistent treatment of all families experiencing difficulty with payment of tuition and fees.

These collection procedures should require written and signed documentation of any special payment arrangements with any family requesting an arrangement outside of the stated tuition payment policies. These documents should remain in the family's file until the account is paid in full.

Cash Receipts

Cash coming into a school is often a challenge for business officers, as schools often have a decentralized, inconsistent approach to cash receipts. This can result in checks not being deposited in a timely manner or checks being lost within a

school's process. Having decentralized cash receipts increases the possibility for misappropriation of cash. Schools should consider having one person designated to receive all cash receipts including checks. That person should be someone who is centrally located within the school and who is not also responsible for the recording of activity within the financial accounting process (promoting proper segregation of duties). That person should have access to a remote deposit machine (which is secured and out of sight when not in use) that allows daily deposits to be made directly to the school's operating account from a secure desktop computer within the school. Once a check is deposited, it is canceled, and can then be forwarded to the appropriate department for recording without risk of loss. The departments receiving checks must agree to return the canceled checks to the business office within two weeks so the checks can be destroyed. This promotes optimal segregation of duties and allows staff to focus on their program rather than worrying about the timely processing of money or photocopying checks.

Finally, business officers and their schools should determine all the different ways and times parents are asked to pay money to the school and consider consolidating as many of these as possible, to reduce the volume of cash and checks entering the school.

Endowment

While endowments are discussed at length in Chapter 6, there are certain business office implications that are noteworthy for this chapter.

Endowments are created when a donor gives a gift that is to be kept in perpetuity for a specific purpose or when the school's board of trustees designates otherwise unrestricted money to function as endowment. To maximize earning strategies, most schools choose to commingle endowment funds into one or two investment accounts and then allocate fees, earnings, and other gains and losses by each fund's proportionate share of the whole. This approach, called "unitizing," means that each endowment gift, or named fund, is assigned a unit share of the total endowment based on the size of the gift or fund relative to the total investment endowment as of the inclusion date (usually the gift date or the last day of the month or quarter in which the gift is received). That unit value is used to allocate income, gains, losses, and fees across all funds managed in that investment account. Unitizing lets the school know the value of named funds, or funds designated by purpose on a given measurement date; enables good stewardship reports to donors; and allows business officers to properly plan and budget spending of restricted gifts.

Many independent schools have endowment spending policies that state the amount of annual spending that is permitted from the endowment. Endowment spending is often used to offset operational expenses. Showing the draw as operating revenue in each fiscal year provides an appropriate matching of revenue and expenses, but does not meet GAAP requirements. While the true presentation of total endowment returns is dictated by state statutes (as some states' attorney generals mandate temporary restrictions on endowment revenue), it is common to present the draw amount as unrestricted and other net income, gains, and losses as temporarily restricted, below the operating line, of a school's financial reports.

Tax-Exempt Financing

Tax-exempt financing has become a cost-effective debt strategy for independent schools. While this chapter does not allow for a complete discussion of such financing, the business officer needs to be aware that in addition to the debt instruments, these arrangements can include many components including credit enhancement through a bank letter of credit, independent credit ratings, and interest rate swap agreements. Each piece has its own accounting that must be recorded within the school's financial statements. Tax-exempt debt and all related agreements have required footnote disclosures. The lending institutions will often have covenants with which the school must comply and which require periodic reporting.

OTHER BUSINESS OFFICE AREAS

Parent and Alumni Associations and Other Decentralized Operations

Many schools have parent and alumni associations that support the mission of the school through events, programs, fundraising, and other activities. These associations may operate under the school's federal identification and exemption or be separately incorporated. These associations offer many benevolent opportunities on behalf of the school.

However, the financial side of such associations should be actively managed.

When a school-related association is separately incorporated, it is likely using the school's name, e.g., "NBOA Academy's Parents Association." The school's name is a large factor in societal reputation and its integrity is crucial to the school's brand. As such, the association's activities should be monitored to ensure that the association is current with all required federal, state, and local regulatory filings, and that it is taking appropriate precautions against unauthorized activity. Since these organizations are typically led and run by volunteers, a collaborative relationship with the school's leadership should be forged to ensure all activities of these decentralized associations are consistent with the school's mission and comply with all applicable laws and regulations. Managing the school's reputation is critical.

When a school association is operating under the school's federal exemption, all of the concerns outlined above remain. In addition, the school must consolidate the financial activity of the association(s) into its financial results. Often this is politically difficult, because these organizations are run by accomplished volunteers who want to run outside of the school's business structure and be responsible for their own record-keeping. It is considered professional best practice to have all organizations or associations operating within the school's federal identification and exemption follow the same business processes as the rest of the school. Failing to do so presents a material risk to the school, its operating license,

and its nonprofit status, particularly if the association engages in activities disallowed by the Internal Revenue Code.

Every independent school has a separate and distinct culture, and this includes associations. When it is not possible for all activity of an association to flow through the business office, at a minimum the school should reconcile the association's bank account monthly and ensure all activity is recorded in the school's general ledger in a timely manner. This reconciliation should be performed by someone who is not an authorized check signer on the account, and the reconciliation should be reviewed by the business officer.

Auctions and Raffles

Many schools utilize auctions and raffles as fundraising methods. The rules that govern auctions and raffles vary by state; often, permits, licensing, and regulatory reporting are required. NAIS provides its members with an excellent summary of caution areas that should be reviewed early in a school's planning for one of these events.

Development Contributions

As discussed earlier, the treatment of pledges receivable is a common difference between internal financial reports and GAAP-compliant financial statements. *SFAS 116, Accounting for Contributions Received and Contributions Made*, requires that bona fide pledges be recorded in a school's financial statements in the year in which the school receives the pledge (not the years in which the pledge will be paid). Most accountants deem a bona fide pledge to be one that is in writing and is clear about the donor's intent for the gift and the pledge payment schedule. While GAAP allows a school to establish a reasonable reserve with pledges the school deems may be uncollectable, the pledge and its estimated reserve must be recorded in the year in which it is received, regardless of when the cash is actually received.

Pledge Reserves

A school should assess the collectability of each pledge when the pledge is received and, at a minimum, at the end of each fiscal year. If the school believes a pledge may be ultimately uncollectable, then the business office should work with the development office to develop a reasonable reserve similar to that of the school's tuition accounts receivable.

Example 1:
Remember Mrs. Smith? She signed a $1,000,000 pledge in FY 1 to be paid in five equal, annual installments beginning in FY 2 through FY 6. Let's assume that Mrs. Smith paid her pledge payment in FY 2 and FY 3, but that before making her payment in FY 4, Mrs. Smith loses all of her investments in a bad business deal. Mrs. Smith is bankrupt. The development office should work with the business office to establish a pledge reserve for the remaining three pledge payments totaling $600,000.

Example 2:
Using Mrs. Smith's intent to pledge above, now assume Mrs. Smith is not known to the school and has never previously contributed to the school. The school should carefully consider

Mrs. Smith's intent and her financial circumstances to determine whether the pledge should be booked with a reserve in the year it is received.

Pledge Discounts

GAAP requires schools to discount multi-year pledges to their net present value as of the end of each fiscal year. While this may feel like a complicated accounting principle, it is simply a matter of retrieving a comparable discount rate given the expected pledge payouts (read: as an annual interest rate) and applying it to the net expected pledge payments by year (net of any reserves). The difference between the face value and the total net present value is the discount. The total discount is recorded as a contra-asset account, similar to a pledge reserve account.

Let's assume that the current rate for three-to-five year treasury bills is 3%. This is a reasonable discount rate given that the pledge payments are to be received within the next five years. The pledge payment in the immediate coming year is considered to be at full value. For each future year, the present value is "discounted" by 3% annually.

Example 3:
With Mrs. Smith's pledge payments, we are approaching 6/30/x1. Knowing that the school is to receive $200,000 annually, calculate the present value as of 6/30/x1. The present value of Year 2's payment is 100%, as it is expected to be collected within the immediate next fiscal year. The present value of Year 3's payment is 97% of its original value (100% minus 3%), or $194,000. The present value of Year 4's payment is 94%

of its original value (100% minus 3% per year away from the valuation date), or $188,000. Year 5 is 91% and Year 6 is 88%.

Gift Stewardship

The school's development office is responsible for understanding the school's major donors and for managing the relationships with those donors. Many donors expect to receive reports on how their money has been used to advance the mission of the school. This is particularly true when donors give large sums of money to the endowment. Donors want to see that the school is properly managing its investment as well as spending those funds as the donor intended. It is common for the business office to prepare information on spending and fund values for the development office to report to donors. Accordingly, it is important for the business office to work with the development office to understand what information needs to be collected and when it needs to be distributed. If the school prepares an annual report for its donors and constituents, the business office needs to understand and provide the necessary information for it.

CONCLUSION

The ultimate responsibility for the management of a school's financial and physical resources rests with you, the business officer. While you are aided by other staff, and guided by the head of school and board, it is you who must take the lead in setting standards that will keep the organization running like clockwork… or as close to clockwork as possible. Sometimes, when you're at your desk at 9pm on a Friday night preparing for the audit, it's difficult to see the forest for the trees. Yet there is a great reward for all of this attention to detail: it is knowing that your work has truly ensured the future of the school.

NBOA

Chapter Three

FACILITIES

How to Get Your Campus Running Like Clockwork

part one:
Planning

part two:
Operations

IN THIS CHAPTER:

- The real cost of planning

- Why not to hire an architect

- "Surprise-free" scenarios

- Structuring your staffing plan

- The 411 on CMMS

part one by **Dr. C. Kenneth Tanner**

and part two by **Al Allen**

Dr. Charles Kenneth Tanner

Professor, REFP, Faculty of Engineering, University of Georgia

Dr. C. Kenneth Tanner focuses on research, service, and teaching regarding the impact of physical environments on student outcomes. He founded the School Design and Planning Laboratory at the University of Georgia in 1997 with the assistance of a Georgia Board of Regents grant. The Laboratory offers comprehensive guidance in school design and planning for public and independent schools. A member of the graduate faculty at the University of Georgia since 1982, Kenneth has written over 100 articles for educational journals, presented numerous research papers, and authored four books on planning. He is the lead author of a 2006 publication entitled "Educational Facilities Planning: Leadership, Architecture, and Management," published by Allyn & Bacon. He works as a consultant to public and independent schools in the areas of student population forecasting, pre-planning activities, and planning and development of concept design for educational facilities. He is currently developing materials to assess "green" schools.

FACILITIES: PLANNING

Charting Your Course

We all know the truism "if you fail to plan, then you plan to fail." Did you know that planning without a budget, goal, mission, and the authority to plan are equally irrational? When I am invited to participate in a school planning project, I ask three questions to ascertain whether people are truly ready to get started:

- HAVE YOU SET ASIDE A BUDGET FOR PLANNING?

- DO YOU HAVE A TIMELINE FOR THE PLANNING AND CONSTRUCTION OF AN EDUCATIONAL LEARNING ENVIRONMENT?

- HAVE YOU HIRED AN ARCHITECT?

In my opinion, the correct answers to these three questions are yes, yes, and no, respectively.

Last year, I visited an independent school in Atlanta, Georgia, to consult with the school principal about developing a new set of classrooms to house a middle school for about 300 students. The project entailed remodeling an existing structure currently used as office space. This meeting was in July, and the principal thought that a good time to move into the new set of classrooms would be August of the following year. As a consultant, I told her that I would set up a schedule and attach cost estimates, knowing how close to impossible the target date of August would actually be, but knowing that part of consulting is to educate the client. When I submitted the work breakdown schedule (WBS) one week later, and attached the planning and concept design costs, her enthusiasm turned to gloom. Similar situations happen all the time and there is no one individual to fault. However, if we commit to planning, first by setting aside a planning budget, the job will be made much more efficient and our natural enthusiasm for a new project will return.

HAVE YOU SET ASIDE A BUDGET FOR PLANNING?

Setting aside such a budget shows commitment to the goal of building a new school or modifying an existing facility. A minimum of 1% to 3% of the expected cost of the building and grounds should be set aside for planning—not necessarily all of these funds will be spent in the beginning, but when the project is completed, 3% of the total is the likely end cost. If an organization is contemplating a $10 million project, it is reasonable to set aside at least $100,000 for pre-planning

and pre-design activities. This is the 1%. Now, expect to spend an additional 2% before an architect is even contacted. I emphasize educational planning, rather than architectural planning, because the design of the space is ultimately driven by the school's mission and goals.

DO YOU HAVE A TIMELINE FOR THE PLANNING AND CONSTRUCTION OF AN EDUCATIONAL LEARNING ENVIRONMENT?

If an organization has set aside 1% of an estimated budget for pre-planning and design activities, a rough timetable surely exists in the minds of the people interested in building the educational learning environment. I consider a reasonable timeline to be one year for planning and design, two years for construction and occupancy. Three years from the day you start pre-planning is when you can expect to move into a new educational facility.

Given that an organization has a budget and a rough timeline in mind, it is time to consider the development of a work breakdown schedule. This is similar to a Gantt Chart, a PERT network, or the Critical Path Method of planning. I will leave it to the reader to explore these concepts more completely online. For more general information on educational planning procedures, see "A Review of Educational Planning Procedures" in Tanner and Lackney (2006).

HAVE YOU HIRED AN ARCHITECT?

I strongly recommend hiring a qualified educational planner, not an architect, in the beginning. The REFP (Recognized Educational Facility

Professional) designation endorsed by the Council of Educational Facility Planners, International, is a good place to start looking. You can also investigate the resources of regional colleges and universities that teach educational facilities planning courses and state educational planning organizations. Additionally, there are several websites devoted to planning and several good independent planners that can get an organization up to the point at which an architect should be hired. Look for planners that are independent of architectural firms; as a leader of an independent school, you do not want bias built into the planning process.

FOCUSED PRE-PLANNING ACTIVITIES FOR EDUCATIONAL FACILITIES

FIVE STEPS

This section assists in the development of a facilities plan for independent schools. Reformulated for independent schools, the adjusted model presented here is based on Chapter 16 in Tanner and Lackney (2006). The Focused Strategic Planning (FSP) model, as used here, is a modified version of traditional, generic strategic planning. Intended to generate focused goals for the development of educational specifications and concept design, FSP enhances the process for achieving a school facilities plan by relying on educationally desirable design principles. We wish to avoid the selection of many of the educational specifications already catalogued by the architect (and stored for instant retrieval) because they may be irrelevant to critical, unique program demands. Once the

goals for educational specifications clearly represent a unique setting, the task of completing them may be administered under architectural supervision.

Once the educational plan has been completed (i.e., the goals for educational specifications and concept design are written and approved), it is time to select the architect. This chapter stops short of developing written educational specifications because it is desirable to complete them with the assistance of the architectural team. These specifications, including code requirements, guide the structural plans of the school facility, making way for bidding and construction.

STEP 1:
WHO SHOULD BE INVOLVED IN PLANNING?

Allow one month to formulate the FSP teams. These teams should be selected carefully because the individuals comprising them will be working together for a very long time. Usually, a "leadership team" of 15-25 members who represent a cross section of "stakeholders" is ideal to complete "real-time" planning, programming, and concept design. I recommend the inclusion of an outside facilitator, two or three members of each "activity team," representing various program elements (English, mathematics, music, art, etc.), and a professional planner and designer. The leadership team must be composed of members who are energetic, dependable, knowledgeable, and compatible. Ideally, the facilitator of the smaller activity teams is also a member of the leadership team. Typically, the school system's educational planner has the job of identifying, inviting, and selecting people who will participate in the FSP process. Often, builders and subcontractors are not seen as stakeholders, but representatives from this vital component of the community might be included to add balance as various initial ideas are discussed.

Activity teams should involve no more than 15 individuals and should include at least two members who also work on the leadership team. The leadership team and the activity teams should meet together, first, for orientation. Thereafter, all activity teams should meet before the next meeting of the leadership team. Once the teams hold their first meeting, the flow of information from the bottom up helps to shape the FSP, which includes vision, mission, goals, strategies, and concept design.

The importance of having a good cross section of the school's community of supporters within the teams cannot be overemphasized. Civic clubs and volunteer organizations are key places to start looking for members.

It is a good public relations tactic to develop a website devoted to this specific FSP process before holding the orientation meeting. This website can be used as a source of information for the media and others, and as an internal communication tool to announce meeting dates and times. After each activity has been completed and approved by the board, it may be useful to post it online so the leadership and activity teams can view the results. Even allowing a chat room and bulletin board for the participants to use in discussing

planning and design issues may prove to be worthwhile. A system such as FirstClass may be appropriate.

STEP 2:
DEVELOP A FOCUSED MISSION STATEMENT FOR EDUCATIONAL FACILITIES

First, determine the number of students for whom you are developing the facility. Then, start to develop a mission statement that will complement a school design that facilitates the curriculum (program). This mission will be a complementary part of the larger vision and mission already established by the school, but should focus specifically on the physical environment.

Given clearly articulated values and beliefs about learning environments, approximately three hours should be sufficient to establish a mission statement for both the activity and leadership teams.

The mission is a "belief" statement around which the school and its clients can organize their energies and efforts. It is what your school believes about how its educational learning environments should facilitate its curriculum, which forms the foundation for the remaining FSP activities. It is a description of why the physical learning environments exist, and is the benchmark statement against which all planning steps can be tested for relevance. I suggest following the model of Clay, Lake, and Termain (1989) that indicates "the mission should be developed before the goals and objectives." This approach hinges on the fact that the future of our school facilities is based on our values, including our aesthetic values (as reflected in architecture), as well as the design principles that distinguish our facilities from those of neighboring schools. The basic "identities" (such as minimum safety requirements) are going to be dictated from sources outside the FSP teams' assignment because they are legally binding codes. Ultimately, the development of a mission statement comes between the clarification of beliefs and values and the steps involving scanning the environment (school and community context) in which the school exists.

Sample Questions To Pose to Each Person on a Team

- What is the basic purpose for the physical learning environment?

- Who are the clients of the physical learning environment?

- What are the various types of learning spaces that will be needed?

- What are the major activities to be performed in the learning spaces?

- What goals for educational specifications and design features will best enhance student learning?

To reach consensus, the use of a facilitator is strongly recommended for this activity. Then, place the team's answers on poster paper for viewing, and begin drafting the mission statement. I recommend that the mission statement contain no more than 100 words.

STEP 3:
CONSTRUCT FACTUAL STATEMENTS THAT SUPPORT THE DESIGN OF THE SCHOOL AND EDUCATIONAL

SPECIFICATIONS

Using environmental scans (school and community data) as a jumping-off point, develop a list of assumptions about what the school should look like in 5, 10, and 20 years. One 3-4 hour meeting should be sufficient to generate these scenarios.

It is impossible to predict the future accurately, but it is necessary to make some assumptions about it. This type of thinking supports what Clay et al (1989) refers to as "surprise-free" scenarios. Surprise-free scenarios depend on sound, factual information. They are assumptions about the future based on past trends, current data, and best estimates of experts.

Sample Surprise-Free Scenario Statements

School

- The school that we want will be a (small, large) organization.

- The teaching and learning philosophy will be (teacher-centered, student-centered, etc.).

- The curriculum will be delivered through (traditional scheduling, modular scheduling, parallel block scheduling, etc.).

- Natural light (will, will not) be plentiful in every classroom.

- The school (will, will not) be technology-driven. (Internet ports and/ or wireless capability) will be located in all learning areas, including the cafeteria.

- Aesthetics (will, will not) be of great importance.

- Each classroom (will, will not) have a door leading to an outside learning environment.

- Each student (will, will not) be provided with ample space for learning. (From 39 to 49 square feet will be provided for each student and teacher in classrooms.)

Community of Stakeholders

- The majority of parents (both parents) (will, will not) hold jobs outside the home.

- The majority of students served by the school (will, will not) attend four-year colleges.

- Safety (will, will not) be an issue in this school.

- The school population, within 10 years, will (increase, decrease) by __%.

- Funding for school facilities (will, will not) be a priority of the school.

- Religious values of the stakeholders (will, will not) be significant influences on students.

These scenarios are vital to the planning project, since they set the stage for what the school should look like 5, 10, or 20 years into the future. These are the basic assumptions that guide the design goals and infer the educational specifications. It is now time to encourage the team members to search online, etc. for examples of school design. At this point, the FSP team should know the number of students to be served and the expected program of study (such a study could be completed by some of the FSP team members, but might best be commissioned to an independent team early in the process). The types of scheduling to be used in the school must be known before step 4 begins.

DEVELOP GOALS FOR SCHOOL DESIGN AND EDUCATIONAL SPECIFICATIONS

The development of concept design may parallel the development of goals for specifications, since almost nothing in the "real world" is accomplished in a linear manner. As many as three (or more) half-day meetings, spread out over a month, may be required to develop the detailed documents. Given that the school environment is assumed to influence student outcomes, the purposes of goals for concept design and educational specifications are to facilitate a comprehensive description of the spaces needed to facilitate the school program and further the teaching and learning philosophies of the school.

Context

- Decide on the size of the facility in estimated square feet.

- Determine class size (taking into account scheduling and type of program).

Develop Strategic Goals

The team should review the values expressed in the surprise-free scenarios, the mission statement, the results of the internal and external scans, and the vision of an ideal school. This activity may be expedited through media presentations or flip charts. Each team member may view these before attempting to write the strategic goals.

Sample Goals for Educational Specifications

- To provide a program that will

accommodate more than one teaching and learning philosophy.

- To provide ample usable space (39 to 49 square feet) for each student and teacher within each classroom.

- To provide for natural light on at least two sides of each learning space.

- To ensure ample circulation patterns within classrooms and within the school.

- To guarantee that each learning area has one interior wall that is slightly darker than the other walls.

- To provide appropriate teacher workstations near the places where teaching takes place.

- To provide toilets in each classroom for safety, convenience, and security.

After writing each set of goals, perform a reality check: Does the goal fit the school philosophy and mission statements? Is it based on sound design principles? Does it address one of the needs, problems, or opportunities identified through the scenarios? Can it be accomplished? Is it something worth doing?

Also examine the goals in relation to each other. Does one goal conflict with or prevent the realization of another goal? If so, drop it or find a compromise. Can all goals be reasonably converted to educational specifications? At this point in the "real world" it is advisable to get personnel other than those on the FSP teams to review the goals, and to help the team to write the goals in standard form: i.e., in units, delegated per topic area to members.

STEP 5:
CONCEPT DRAWINGS & SKETCHES

It is time to translate the strategic design goals in Step 4 into a concept drawing. The concept drawings and sketches are direct outgrowths of the overall values, philosophy, vision, environmental information, and surprise-free scenarios.

The concept drawing in Figure 1 (below) was inspired by a schematic illustration of Crow Island School, shown by Roger Shepard, and is available at ***www.coe.uga.edu***.

FIGURE 1

Goals:

- Learning spaces with views on two sides
- Ample circulation
- Green outdoor learning area
- Views overlooking life
- Toilets in each classroom
- 1029 square feet for 20 students and one teacher

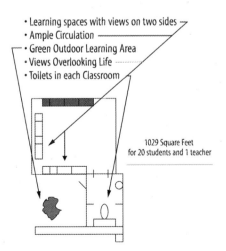

- Learning spaces with views on two sides
- Ample Circulation
- Green Outdoor Learning Area
- Views Overlooking Life
- Toilets in each Classroom

1029 Square Feet for 20 students and 1 teacher

FIGURE 2

Figure 2 (below) illustrates fictitious Sunny River Elementary School.

Each classroom in Figure 2 is an "L" shape similar to classrooms at Crow Island School. There are numerous deisgn features, not necessarily mentioned in the above steps, that may be found in this school. Most are explained in Tanner and Lackney (2006). I have recently validated that these design features influence student achievement (Tanner, In Press).

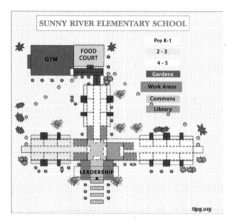

MOVEMENT AND CIRCULATION

Outside Walkways:
Paths or promenades linking main areas, ideally placing major activity centers at the extremes.

Pathways:
Clear and comfortable passages allowing for freedom of movement and orientation, with signage, among and within structures.

Public Areas:
Spaces that foster a sense of community (unity and belonging). They are inviting and comfortable settings and include ample lighting.

Reference:
The main building has an obvious point of reference among the school's buildings in which paths and buildings connect.

Outdoor Spaces:
Defined as learning areas, these places may be surrounded by wings of buildings, trees, hedges, fences, fields, arcades, or walkways.

DAYLIGHTING

Natural Light in Classrooms:
Light in classrooms from windows, skylights, borrowed light, and reflected light.

Sources of Light:
Artificial light plus natural light from the outside, preferably on two sides of every room.

VIEWS

Views Overlooking Life:
Vistas for students to the outside world (not overlooking a wall or parking lot).

Unrestricted Views:
Windows in use, when glare is not a problem, without obstructions such as posters and curtains.

Living Views:
Views of indoor and outdoor spaces (gardens, wildlife, fountains, mountains, etc.).

Functional Views:
Doors and windows that allow the student to easily see at least 50 feet outside the classroom.

Green Areas:
Outside spaces, close to the school building, where trees, grass, or gardens may be seen (few views of parking lots and roads).

CONCLUSION

When the above activities are completed, the team is ready to communicate with an architect, who will then work with the team to develop educational specifications, drawn up according to the concept design and goals; the architect will use all of this material to complete the final drawings. *A set of 32 detailed milestones for planning, programming, and design of educational environments can be found in Tanner and Lackney (2006). Myers and Robertson (2004) have also developed a comprehensive set of steps.*

When followed consciously, this process results in true "buy-in" by all stakeholders, and promotes clear understanding of the intention of every school facility. It is a way to chart your campus's course thoughtfully, democratically, and strategically.

NB A

Tanner, C. K. (In Press), "Effects of School Design on Student Outcomes." *Journal of Educational Administration.*

REFERENCES

Clay, K., Lake, S., & Tremain, K. (1989), *How to Build a Strategic Plan.* Ventures for Public Awareness, San Carlos, CA.

Myers, N., & Robertson, S. (2004), *Creating Connections: The CEFPI Guide for Educational Facility Planning.* CEFPI, Scottsdale, AZ.

Tanner, C. K., & Lackney, J. A. (2006), *Educational Facilities Planning: Leadership, Architecture, and Management.* Allyn & Bacon, Boston, MA.

Al Allen
President, Sodexo Education Facilities Management

Al Allen has provided support to independent schools, colleges, universities, and public school districts in their efforts to maintain their campus facilities since he joined Sodexo in 1978. As president of the facilities management division, Al directs the activities of a team providing services for 221 schools, colleges, and universities, including facility planning, construction management, project management, facility renewal, energy conservation and management, plant operations, maintenance, cleaning, event support, landscaping, and athletic fields maintenance. Al's professional expertise has been enhanced by his experience as an independent school parent and board member; he served for six years on the board of trustees of Pace Brantley Hall School. Sodexo supports the efforts of the Association of Physical Plant Administrators through membership and contribution to the Innovation Awards and Center for Facilities Research. Al was honored to receive the Association's Eagle Award for leadership, vision, and dedication in August 2005.

FACILITIES: OPERATIONS

Supporting Your Structures & Structuring Your Support

Second only to your school's academic reputation, the appearance of your campus plays a critical role in recruitment decisions of potential students and their parents. Parents making substantial investments in their child's future expect campus facilities to be safe, attractive, and well maintained. Since prospective families visit throughout the year, it is imperative that your campus presents an inviting appearance in every season.

Campus facilities are often the greatest financial asset of the school, and few institutions are fortunate enough to enjoy endowments that exceed the replacement value of the facilities. Campus appearance is a visible expression of planning, design, maintenance, and funding. Unless your school has the resources to have both a CFO and a COO, you, as the business officer, will likely be involved in every aspect of your facilities, including master planning sessions with your board of trustees, design approval, construction management, facilities management, and renewal and renovation.

> *Your responsibilities will require your daily attention.*

Most business officers start their careers by acquiring training and experience in the areas of finance and administration. Successful business officers also develop expertise in every facet of facilities planning, maintenance, and operations, all of which require skills, commitment, and resources. The financial resources required for routine maintenance and operations range from 10% to 12% of the school's operating budget. Additional funding is required for effective plant renewal. The combination of funding for these two sectors (routine maintenance and physical plant renewal) makes facilities operations an expense second only to faculty and staff compensation.

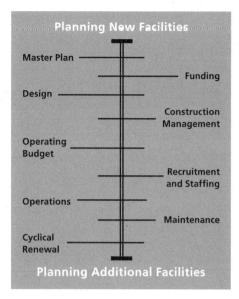

Planning New Facilities

Master Plan
Funding
Design
Construction Management
Operating Budget
Recruitment and Staffing
Operations
Maintenance
Cyclical Renewal

Planning Additional Facilities

You are not expected to be an expert in all of these areas, and it is certain that your expertise will develop throughout the process. Expect that each of the activities on the continuum will be annual and ongoing.

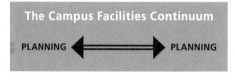

The Campus Facilities Continuum

PLANNING ◄──────► PLANNING

Campus facilities operations, maintenance, and construction are best represented as lying along a continuum that begins and ends with planning.

Business officers must be involved in all facets of planning, including the master plan, funding, facility design, construction management, budgeting, staffing, operations, maintenance, renewal of existing facilities, and planning for new facilities.

PLANNING

The master plan affects every aspect of your campus community experience and must address such daily school activities as student arrival, staff parking, academics, administration, food service, athletics, fine arts, and performing arts. It must also address functional elements such as the sense of arrival projected by your main entrance, the size of your classrooms, how you heat your swimming pool, and the efficient lighting of your fields.

Facilities planning should support the master plan; available funding should lead that planning. Funding considerations should include annual operating and maintenance expenses as well as the initial cost of construction. As new facilities are developed and opened, additional expense is incurred; therefore, annual operating cost and funding for renewal must be included when calculating the total cost of each project. These additional expenses may be covered by current revenues or earnings from endowed funds.

Both design and materials selected to construct facilities such as buildings, roads, swimming pools, tennis courts, and playing fields will impact the expense associated with operating and maintaining these facilities. Operating expenses are a function of size, materials, and design. All schools are encouraged to consider environmental impact and sustainability in planning for their campuses. The planning phase offers the greatest opportunity for implementing decisions that can maximize the benefits of sustainable design features. *A complete discussion of environmentally sustainable design for independent schools is in Chapter 14.*

DAILY SERVICES

Daily or routine cleaning, repairs, maintenance, grounds care, support for athletic events, and special event setups are important support functions and should reflect positively on your school. These labor-intensive tasks are often performed by staff members with limited skill sets and modest compensation who interact daily with your faculty, staff, students, and parents. In view of today's heightened security concerns, service staff should be carefully selected based on comprehensive interviews and thorough background checks. Paying a fair wage and benefits, combined with comprehensive training, encourages retention—a vital element in providing consistent service, quality results, and customer satisfaction.

The Cleaning Services Staff is largest in number and can perform most effectively in the evenings. While some cleaning staff is required during the school day, a split shift beginning at 4:30am and ending at noon can also be effective in maintaining high customer satisfaction and allowing interaction with various customers. This shift usually results in lower staff turnover, reduced security concerns, and savings in electric consumption. Cleaning services can be effectively contracted to private firms. As with any service contract, you must establish clear service specifications before requesting proposals. Effective communication with the management of the contracted firm is very important for consistent good service.

Grounds Care includes the maintenance of your common landscape, parking areas, roadways, and athletic fields. These services require skilled supervisory staff who are knowledgeable and trained in turf maintenance, tree and shrub care, irrigation system operations and repair, equipment maintenance, and application of fertilizers, herbicides, and pesticides. Training in sports turf care and game-day field preparation is critical. At most schools, significant funds have been invested in playing fields, and coaches, athletes, and parents have high expectations for safe, well prepared fields and facilities.

Care of grounds maintenance equipment is intensive and ongoing. Replacement and maintenance of this expensive equipment requires annual budgeting consideration because the value of your grounds equipment inventory can easily exceed $70,000, with the majority of that equipment requiring replacement based on a five-year cycle.

This service can be successfully contracted to private firms once clear service specifications are established and input from your coaching staff and head of school is incorporated. In a contract scenario, the school will still require daily staff to assure a neat appearance, provide setup support, and assist in game-day preparation.

Plant Maintenance and repair functions require talented staff support provided by specialized service contractors. Maintenance staff skill needs range from professional to modest. Maintenance of your heating, air conditioning, plumbing, and electrical systems require staff who have completed specialized training, earned certifications, and preferably acquired licenses to perform maintenance and operate these expensive and critical systems. If highly skilled staff are not available, it is recommended that these services be provided by a contractor based on pre-determined service intervals, combined with time and material agreements for repairs. Proper maintenance of these systems, as well as your swimming pool systems, is imperative to ensure their intended utility and planned asset life.

Routine repairs and service support can be adequately performed by staff members with more modest training. These staff members will often be required to work weekends, supporting school functions and parent-led activities.

STAFFING

Staffing is a function of your school's size, type (day, boarding, etc.), and the extent of its weekend activities. The following chart indicates the physical extent of responsibility your full-time employees (FTEs) will likely have:

Function	Day School	Boarding School
Cleaning	18,000 sq. ft. per FTE	25,000 sq. ft. per FTE
Plant Operations & Maintenance	70,000 sq. ft. per FTE	70,000 sq. ft. per FTE
Grounds	10 acres/ FTE	10 acres/FTE

SAFETY AND SECURITY

The business officer is responsible for personal safety and property security. The risk associated with both is significant. Recent violent events at schools make personal safety a pressing concern for all involved in school administration.

Personal safety involves physical facilities, such as entrances, gates, exterior lighting, video monitors, etc. In addition, personal safety requires the presence of trained personnel during times of campus activities. Your security personnel will be very involved in directing traffic as parents drop off and pick up their children. The entire security standard operating system should be managed by individuals with training, who can evaluate your current situation and provide a risk assessment. Consulting firms are also available to assist the business officer on this front. Note: the expense associated with school safety is not included in the budget figures provided earlier.

FLEET MAINTENANCE

Your school's transportation fleet will fall into three categories:

- ACTIVITY VANS AND BUSES
- SERVICE VEHICLES
- SCHOOL BUSES

Most schools have activity vans and service vehicles, but not all schools use school buses. Regardless of the types of vehicles owned by the school, the business officer will need to decide:

- PURCHASE OR LEASE
- SIZE AND NUMBER OF ACTIVITY BUSES (your insurance carrier should be consulted)
- FLEET MAINTENANCE TYPE:
  - Self-performing
  - Dealer-provided maintenance (recommended)
- FUELING
- CREDIT CARDS
- DRIVERS (consult your insurance carrier)

Your service vehicle fleet will require at least one vehicle that is road-licensed with some hauling capabilities. The balance should be campus-only utility vehicles. The campus-only vehicles can run on electrical power to create a more sustainable campus. These vehicles also restrict staff from making numerous trips for supplies. The campus-only vehicles will cause less damage to your lawns and sidewalks than traditional pickup trucks. Your service vehicles, along with your grounds, maintenance, and cleaning equipment will require a secured, lighted facility similar to a pre-fabricated utility building, or "Butler Building."

A word about vans: most independent schools have stopped using 12- or 15-passenger vans to transport students.

A federal law adopted in 1999 requires that any vehicle that carries 10 or more passengers meet federal safety standards for school buses. The law prohibits the sale or lease to a school of any vehicle that does not meet these standards. In addition, most states have prohibited the use of 12- and 15-passenger vans to transport students. The recommended vehicle for transporting students is therefore an activity van, which looks like a miniature school bus and meets all of the federal safety standards. These activity vans are a little more expensive than passenger vans, and in many states, drivers are required to obtain a special license to drive them, but the safety to students and the reduced risk for the school are reason enough to use them. *School transportation is covered in more depth in Chapter 13.*

FIRE ALARMS AND SUPPRESSION SYSTEMS

Protection of your staff and property is a primary concern. All new construction should have fire monitoring and fire suppression systems. Adding these systems to older facilities is recommended. It is advised that all facilities have fire alarms connected to your fire department and fire suppression. These systems should be maintained by a licensed service contractor.

DEPARTMENT MANAGEMENT

Your director of facilities is a key member of your team. In addition to technical training, this person must be an experienced manager and excellent communicator. Your director will interact with every member of your campus community, including the board of trustees, and must have a comprehensive understanding of construction, renovations, plant operations, cleaning, and grounds. Because it is unusual for a single individual to possess experience in all areas, supervisors for cleaning and grounds care are often recruited to manage these operations. Because the director of campus facilities is responsible for managing one of the largest budgets and numbers of staff, their understanding of budgeting, financial controls, reporting, and human resource policies is essential. Recruitment and retention of these key managers is a challenge, and many independent schools have enlisted the support of outside companies to provide comprehensive campus facilities services.

Typical organizational hierarchy in this department is as follows:

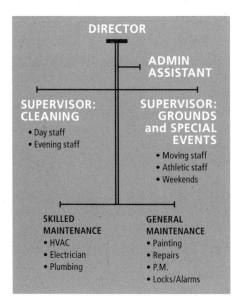

COMPUTERIZED MAINTENANCE MANAGEMENT SYSTEM (CMMS)

The department will need to develop standard operating procedures for training, plant operations, contracts, physical safety, and summer projects. CMMS is a necessary system for scheduling planned maintenance, service requests, and summer projects. These systems also track cost by building, equipment, and department; they are usually operated by an administrative assistant. The expense associated with these systems (including licenses, hardware, training, and implementation) can exceed $50,000. There are web-based CMMS products that are much less expensive than stand-alone programs. The challenges with any CMMS are implementation and training. Often facilities managers and administrators underestimate the complexity of these systems and thus the expense involved: the software and hardware cost may be the least expensive components.

FACILITY RENEWAL

Your physical facilities have an expected life span, and renewal and replacement should be budgeted and scheduled as such. Even with appropriate routine maintenance and proper operations, your buildings, roads, sidewalks, heating, cooling, plumbing, and electrical equipment will require renewal and/or replacement. These expenses are usually referred to as capital items and are budgeted separately from the annual operating budget. The Association of Physical Plant Administrators (APPA) recommends that 4% of your physical facilities' current replacement value (CRV) be budgeted annually, assuring that funding is available and preventing an accumulation of deferred maintenance.

Many independent schools use a system referred to as Provision for Plant Replacement, Renewal, and Special Maintenance (PPRRSM) to budget and plan for cyclical renewal and to prevent accumulation of deferred maintenance. This management and budgeting tool includes a list of your physical facilities, systems such as roofs, electrical, heating, cooling, etc., and projects dates when the school can anticipate the need to fund the renewal or replacement of each system. This system enables your administration to be good stewards of your campus facilities. These plans can be developed utilizing the services of consulting engineering firms at a customary cost average of 12 cents per square foot of building space. Maintenance of these plans is usually the responsibility of the director of facilities. In addition to being a fund-planning tool, they help the business officer keep the board and senior administrative team apprised of future needs and real expense projections associated with providing a quality education.

ENERGY MANAGEMENT AND CONSERVATION

Every school consumes large amounts of energy, such as electricity, natural gas, oil, and water; utility expense can represent fully one-third of your facilities operating budget. The increased costs of electricity, gas, oil, and, in some states, water, mean that conservation of these resources has become increasingly important. In addition to financial concerns, your board members, faculty, students, and parents expect the school to be a good steward of natural resources and the environment. Schools are in a unique position to impact the environment through educating and involving students and staff in conservation initiatives. The students of today are the voters and policy-makers of the future.

Energy management and conservation programs should include:

Data Collection and Monitoring: Understand which facilities consume the largest amount of utilities. The largest consumers are often science facilities, food service, and your swimming pool. Ensure your local utility is charging you appropriately. Mistakes in billing rate can result in large overpayments by the school.

Purchasing at the Best Rate: The deregulation of the electrical and natural gas industries has presented many schools with the opportunity to purchase at more attractive rates. While your local utility representative can assist the school, there are also firms that can advise you and some that will act as your agent. The advisory firms work for a set fee, while agents receive their compensation from the utility that provides you with the commodity. With the advent of deregulation this area has become more complex—yet it is worth the business officer's time.

Conservation Opportunities: Here are four ways to audit your campus facilities to reduce consumption through operations or capital expenditures:

Work with your local utility. The utility has a vested interest in reducing your consumption as it can serve additional customers without further capital investment in generating plants. The local utility can provide advice, and, at times, financing, to make capital improvements. With such proposals, a Return on Investment (ROI) will be calculated. At today's utility rates, with almost certain increases for the foreseeable future, these initiatives can have attractive returns for the school.

Hire a consulting firm. For a set fee, consulting firms will provide an audit. The resulting report will indicate what activities, initiatives, or investments will allow the school to reduce consumption, and will include an ROI. Any financing required will be the responsibility of the school. The advantage of this method is the objectivity provided by a third-party consulting firm, as well as the return on investment. The consulting firms make their profit from their stated fee for the study.

Use performance contracting. With this plan, equipment and building controls companies will conduct the study of your campus, install equipment, and provide financing under a long-term contract. The cost of the study, equipment, controls, and financing will be paid back by the school to the firm over a ten-year period through the pro forma annual savings. While this approach is almost always effective in reducing consumption and should be considered, it is based on complicated methods of measurement and verification. This approach requires great diligence and a sense of "buyer beware" on the part of the business officer.

Contract with a firm that has the experience and the resources to provide all three components:

- Data collection and monitoring
- Purchasing or risk mitigation
- Conservation

SUSTAINABILITY

Conservation brings with it both financial and social returns on investment. An informed and committed campus community is critical to efficient, financially prudent, and socially responsible management of your infrastructure. Each campus creates a "carbon footprint": the amount of carbon dioxide (CO_2) emissions released into the atmosphere due to heating, lighting, and cooling school facilities, as well as the daily commute of students, faculty, and staff. The electricity and natural gas consumed for heating, and the gasoline burned in the automobiles of your staff, students, and parents all contribute to your school's carbon footprint. *Further information on creating a more sustainable campus, from the business officer's perspective, is discussed in detail in Chapter 14.*

CONCLUSION

As the business officer, you are the primary steward of your school's first impression—your campus facilities. Yet it is also, in many ways, the "last" or "lasting" impression: when alumni think back to their experience at school they remember their friends, teachers…and campus. You have the opportunity to help make their experience truly exceptional.

NBOA

Chapter Four

ETHICS

*Establishing A Moral Compass
for Yourself and Your School*

IN THIS CHAPTER:

- Your unique ethical role

- "Right vs. wrong" and "right vs. right"

- Compliance issues: how to be realistic yet stay prudent

- Sarbanes Oxley & you

- Real-life ethical dilemmas

by **Mari Brown**

Mari Brown
Contributing Writer and Editor, National Business Officers Association

Mari Brown is a freelance writer and editor based in New York City. Prior to her time at the National Business Officers Association, she wrote and edited articles for various print publications, including *Departures* magazine. Mari has taught numerous classes in copyediting, editing, and nonfiction writing in schools and literary centers in New York and Wisconsin. She has also worked as a litigation paralegal for the law firm of Richards Spears Kibbe & Orbe and as a fundraising associate for the Lower East Side Tenement Museum. Mari has co-edited NBOA's quarterly publication, *Net Assets*, since 2007, contributing numerous articles on forward-thinking solutions to emerging issues in the independent school field. She has written about financial sustainability in uncertain economic times, technology trends, "going green," and endowment management. Mari's passion for interviewing extends to her creative life, in which she writes and produces documentary theater (interview-based plays) about current events.

ETHICS

Establishing A Moral Compass for Yourself and Your School

> 66
>
> *Relativity applies to physics, not ethics.*
>
> — Albert Einstein
>
> 99

No person of honorable character lives without a system of moral values, and no institution with integrity lacks one. Most schools have a mission statement that expresses the values of the institution and gives it an ethical compass. Yet it is the ethical *culture* of a school that is much more difficult to codify, as it is a fluid, living thing. The difficulty (and the opportunity) is precisely in the "living" of a code of ethics. Ethical dilemmas come down to individual situations that create their own tapestry for the institution, revealing its own off-the-record history (which is more "on-the-record" to everyone involved, no matter how spotless the laundry hung out in public is). As the business officer, you are responsible for many areas of school operations that require ethical behavior, necessitate ethical decision-making, and create ethical dilemmas. It is essential that you understand your own code of ethics and the ethical standards of your school, and become comfortable standing in the ethical spotlight.

"Have you taken the mandatory training for business ethics?" Dilbert's manager asks Dilbert in the syndicated comic strip. Without hesitating, Dilbert turns from his cubicle's computer and replies, "No, but if you say I did, then you'll save some money on training, which you can spend to decorate your office." Pleased with this idea, the manager says, "Luckily, I haven't taken the training myself." Dilbert says, "I hear it's mostly common sense anyway."

Leave it to Dilbert (and satire) to hit the nail on the head. There's often a tension in professional development between the desire to learn something new and the fear of wasting one's time. Ethics is an area business officers frequently avoid exploring, because a) they don't think it's relevant, b) they believe they already understand it and don't need to "improve," c) they're interested but can't justify spending time on it, or d) they haven't found adequate resources or training programs. Yet nearly every business officer agrees that dealing with ethical issues is a part of the job. A recent national study of nonprofit, private sector, and government employees conducted by the Ethics Resource Center (***www.ethics. org***) revealed that a staggeringly small percentage of employee evaluations asked questions about ethical issues, yet one out of every two people said there were ethical issues in their job.

In defining what ethics *is,* it's helpful to define what ethics is *not.*

Here, the Markkula Center for Applied Ethics at Santa Clara Univeristy (***www.scu. edu/ethics***) gives some helpful guidelines[1]:

"Ethics is not following the law. A good system of law does incorporate many ethical standards, but law can deviate from what is ethical. Law can even become ethically corrupt.

"Ethics is not the same as feelings. Feelings provide important information for our ethical choices, but many people feel good even though they are doing something wrong, and often our feelings will tell us it is uncomfortable to do the right thing if it is hard.

"Ethics is not religion. Many people are not religious, but ethics applies to everyone. Most religions do advocate high ethical standards but sometimes do not address all the types of problems we face.

"Ethics is not following culturally accepted norms. 'When in Rome, do as the Romans do' is not a satisfactory ethical standard.

"Ethics is not science. Science may provide an explanation for what humans are *like,* but ethics provides reasons for how humans ought to *act.*"

---

1. Markkula Center for Applied Ethics, Issues in Ethics, v.1, N.2 (Winter 1988).

So what *is* ethics?

A good working definition comes from Ronald and Brenda Duska's <u>Accounting Ethics</u>: "A set of principles by which a person or social group analyzes and evaluates *intentional* human actions, judgments, and practices that benefit or harm human beings."

RIGHT VS. WRONG AND RIGHT VS. RIGHT

Yet if ethics were simply about benefiting or harming human beings, you'd have a much easier job. Let's say Sophie, a food service worker at your school, *intentionally* served undercooked chicken to give Nathan, a student, food poisoning, and then confessed the act to you. Terminating Sophie's employment (and pressing charges) would be a no-brainer. It is obvious that someone is being harmed in this situation; there's a right thing to do and a wrong thing to do. But this situation becomes more complicated when you can't prove that Sophie is the one responsible for the error, or if Nathan has a history of lying, or if Nathan's teacher told you she saw him eating expired mayonnaise out of a jar before lunch. Now let's compound this by saying that Nathan's parents have had a problem with the food service under Sophie's direction for years, and now threaten to withdraw their financial support for the school if Sophie is not fired. Let's say their contribution to the school is 1/3 of the school's operating budget, and that without the support of this key donation the school will be forced to declare bankruptcy. You are then faced with a decision that will either harm one person (Sophie) or several hundred (the students who will be without a school, the faculty who will be without jobs, etc.). Is this a case of right vs. wrong or right vs. right?

For some, that situation might be a no-brainer—in two completely different ways. Ted, whose personal code of ethics says that condemning anyone who has not been proven of a crime is unacceptable, no matter what the consequences are, will let the school go under. Leah, whose code of ethics says that the magnitude of the consequences should determine the action, will fire Sophie and keep the donors (and hundreds of others) happy.

Ted and Leah's codes of ethics are more formally known as the "Kantian Approach" and the "Utilitarian Approach."[2]

The Kantian Approach:

Decisions are made based on principles. Act in such a way that nothing is relative; your actions are a universal standard, determined by what the world would be like if everyone followed the same principles. "Even though I am visiting a city without a recycling program, my hometown recycles. If everyone recycled, we would protect the planet, therefore, I should recycle, and take this soda can home with me on the plane."

The Utilitarian Approach:

Decisions are made based on potential

---

2. Kidder, Rushworth. <u>How Good People Make Tough Choices: Resolving the Dilemmas of Ethical Living</u>. New York: Harper Collins, 2003.

benefit vs. potential harm. Do whatever produces the greatest good, and/or the least harm, for the greatest number of people. "The IRS would frown on me recording this pledge as a donation, but accepting the money this way means we can educate 150 more kids and build a new football stadium."

The Institute for Global Ethics (*www.globalethics.org*) offers other "tests" for making a decision, including:

New York Times **Headline Test:** How would I feel if the results of this decision were put on the front page of tomorrow's paper?

My Own Children Test: Would I advise my own children to do this?

"Golden Rule" Test: Would I want someone to do this to me?

Many ethicists recommend looking at a situation from as many angles and approaches as possible to make the best decision possible. In other words, utilize all available ethical systems and tests to help you (and your team) take action. However, in your job, there are three major documents that can help you and your school resolve an ethical dilemma: your school's mission statement, employee handbook, and code of ethics.

THE MISSION STATEMENT & YOU

Let's say your school is deciding between admitting Miriam, a student whose academic performance is poor, but whose family donates significant funds

to the school, and Jason, an excellent student who will need significant financial aid. If your school's mission includes a commitment to socioeconomic diversity, you may choose to admit Jason. However, if your school's livelihood depends on the admittance of Miriam, the decision becomes more complicated. If you rely on the mission statement as the standard by which your school adheres, you will likely need to find another financial solution that will allow you to admit Jason without harming the financial health of the school.

Here, it is clear where the business officer comes in. You are the person at your school who has the single clearest picture of the school's finances and can make the best diagnosis of its financial viability. This is why you are not a "numbers-cruncher," but rather, a strategic partner. When your head of school asks, "how can we afford to live within our mission and stay afloat financially?" *you* are the one who turns that from an abstract conversation to one based on real numbers, real data history, and real projections.

THE CODE OF ETHICS & YOU

Some schools do not have a code of ethics. Sometimes this is because they simply have not taken the time and energy to focus on creating one, but often it is because they don't consider the code of ethics something that is actually relevant. However, schools that *have* created a code that is relevant and real confirm that it can be crucial in resolving ethical dilemmas. For example, one school consulted for this book had a code of ethics that included "bullying" as an example of "unacceptable behavior" at the school. When the school moved into the digital age, it was initially overwhelmed by the problem of policing "unacceptable behavior" online. The school rewrote its code of ethics so that it included a Technology Acceptable Use Policy, and updated its definition of "bullying" to include "cyberbullying." This Policy is signed, at admission or hiring, by every student, faculty, and staff member, and can then exist as a document that creates a system of rules for the community.

If your school does not have a code of ethics, you can suggest that one be drafted. Essentially, the code is a public document that sets clear expectations of acceptable and unacceptable behavior by all persons in the school community. Like the mission statement, it should speak to the core values of your school. The code of ethics is not a legal document, and should be carefully written so as not to unintentionally create legal obligations. However, it is a document that can prove that the person who signed the document understood and agreed to adhere to the values, boundaries, and principles of acceptable behavior at the school. Your code should be signed by all who join your campus. If you are responsible for the human resources function at your school, you will likely be the person who acquires and keeps these signatures on file.

THE EMPLOYEE HANDBOOK & YOU

As described by attorney Benjamin Hahn in Chapter 5 of this book, a well designed handbook can be a great resource for your school, faculty, and staff—eliminating ambiguities in policy, encouraging open communication, and preventing misunderstandings before they arise. "As with your code of ethics," Hahn says, "language used may unintentionally create legal rights and obligations. It is essential, therefore, that handbooks be carefully worded to reflect accurately, in a clear and concise manner, the actual policies of the school."

It is essential that you understand what is in your employee handbook, since you, as the business officer, will frequently be asked to explain or enforce school policies. You should also take care to evaluate your handbook to make sure it protects your school adequately from risk; if not, it needs to be updated. In redrafting handbooks, consider the reasonableness of your school's policies. One way to create reasonable policies is to combine the Kantian and Utilitarian approaches. For example, creating a rule that says, "No employee shall ever be late to work" is not realistic. An alternative might be something like, "Employees are expected to come to work on time, all the time. However, the administration recognizes that unforeseen obstacles may occur. Thus, an employee may be late twice without censure. Any tardiness beyond this may require disciplinary action." Then, lay out exactly what the disciplinary action can entail, so that there is no confusion when the issue actually arises.

Every employee should sign a form acknowledging receipt of the handbook. Again, if you oversee (or perform) the human resources function at your school, the collection and maintenance of these

BEYOND COMPLIANCE

As the business officer, you must keep your school in compliance with a host of institutions, from the IRS to OSHA. *How* to stay in compliance is covered in Chapter 6. You must also report financial information accurately and punctually to a host of people who serve the school: from donors to trustees to staff. More on financial reporting, macro and micro, is covered in Chapter 2.

Ethics and compliance overlap because every decision to be compliant or not compliant involves a human being making a judgment call that involves weighing "what is right" against "what is practical" and "what it will cost" against "what we can afford." Almost every business officer interviewed for this piece discussed a moment when she or he was told, "Your _____ (stairwell, fire escape, etc.) is not in compliance." And often, when the business officer went to look for the record of the stairwell or the fire escape, there was no record of it ever having *been* in compliance. With almost every example, bringing the school into compliance meant engaging in a time-consuming and costly process. No business officer has extra time. No school has money to burn. Therefore, the temptation almost everyone we talked to described was this: "We didn't *have* to fix anything, but once we became aware of the situation, we felt we *should*."

How to solve this dilemma?

It is, again, a case of right vs. right: "It's right to keep the school in compliance,

signatures will be your responsibility.

but if we spend the money to do it, our teachers' salaries/extracurricular activities/ marketing materials will suffer. What's more important?" One business officer with whom we spoke recommended consulting a lawyer to ascertain how exposed to risk the school really is—if you're exposed, you need to make compliance the number one priority. If the risk is not significant, you can compromise by developing a prioritized action plan that proves you will take the necessary steps to bring your school into compliance, but that you won't do so at an unreasonable pace that would harm the institution or its resources.

SARBANES-OXLEY

The Sarbanes-Oxley Act of 2002, also known as the Public Company Accounting Reform and Investor Protection Act of 2002 and commonly called SOX or Sarbox, is a United States federal law that was enacted in response to a number of "big-league" accounting scandals, especially those related to Enron, Adelphia, and WorldCom. The 11 titles, or sections, of the legislation aim to strengthen corporate accounting controls by establishing standards for all U.S. public company boards, management, and accounting firms. SOX also established the Public Company Accounting Oversight Board (PCAOB), which is charged with overseeing, regulating, inspecting, and disciplining accounting firms in their roles as auditors of public companies.

Despite some belief to the contrary, Sarbanes-Oxley does indeed apply to nonprofit organizations, and therefore, most independent schools. Recently, Venable, LLC, commissioned by the National Association of Independent Schools, recommended eight actions independent schools should consider taking in order to achieve voluntary compliance with certain key provisions of Sarbanes-Oxley. Two of these are legal requirements ("REQ"), the rest are suggested best practices ("BP"). Business officer James Kirkpatrick condensed them into a memo, while at The Hill School, as follows:

1. ESTABLISH AN AUDIT COMMITTEE (BP)

- Establish a separate audit committee or create one as a subcommittee of the board finance committee.

- Make certain that a majority of the members are independent of school management.

- Have at least one member be a "financial expert."

- Committee should be responsible for appointing, recommending compensation for, and holding accountable the auditors.

- Committee should set up internal procedures for complaints regarding accounting or auditing matters.

2. ESTABLISH CODE OF ETHICS FOR FINANCIAL MATTERS (BP)

- School should adopt a code of ethics for senior financial officer, head of school, and board.

- Code should include the basic provision that it is unethical for any officer or trustee to fraudulently influence auditor in performance or audit for

purpose of rendering financial statements as misleading.

3. ESTABLISH DOCUMENT MANAGEMENT POLICY (REQ)

- Policy should guide staff in handling and disposing of documents, focusing on documents relating to "matters within the jurisdiction of any agency" of the federal government (e.g., tax matter of interest to IRS, employment matter of interest to EEOC, or any grants or loans from federal agency).

4. ESTABLISH WHISTLEBLOWER PROTECTION POLICY (REQ)

- Policy should prevent retaliation against employees who report problems or raise questions regarding school financial matters.

- Policy should provide specific procedures for handling such individuals to ensure that both the school's and the individual's rights are protected. Schools should work with counsel in drafting this provision.

5. REVIEW CORPORATE BYLAWS (BP)

- Board must operate under a clear and up-to-date set of bylaws.

- Board committees must be compliant with bylaw regulations, and should be reviewed to ensure they are functioning properly, are constituted properly, and that they have appropriate charges and descriptions.

- Bylaws should be revised, as necessary, with counsel.

6. EDUCATE BOARD (BP)

- Review "duty of care" with board: act with the care an ordinary person would exercise under similar circumstances.

- Review "duty of loyalty" with board: act with undivided allegiance to school's purpose and prohibit conflict of interest or self-dealing with school (often arises when director has independent financial interest in proposed transaction).

- Review and update conflict of interest policy to ensure that individuals serving the school know that they must act, at all times, in a manner consistent with their fiduciary duties, and that if an individual believes that he or she has a conflict of interest, it must be fully disclosed to the finance committee, and all participation in it ceased until resolved by the committee.

7. REVIEW DIRECTORS & OFFICERS LIABILITY INSURANCE (BP)

- Review your coverage, make sure you still have it, and update it if necessary.

- Understand the limitations and exclusions and ensure that all of the trustees and officers understand the coverage with which they are provided.

- Compare carriers and prices.

8. REVIEW COMPLIANCE WITH INTERMEDIATE SANCTIONS PROHIBITIONS (BP)

- Intermediate sanctions by the IRS are designed to penalize people who receive unreasonable compensation or other disproportionate benefits.

- The policy imposes a 25% tax on any disqualified person (who exercised substantial influence) who received excess benefit from the school.

- Comply with three-step safe harbor whereby a governing board or a committee thereof is entirely independent, relies on comparable data, and adequately documents the basis for its decisions.

REAL-LIFE EXAMPLES

Here are just a few examples of ethical dilemmas business officers across the country have faced during their careers. Names have been omitted to protect confidentiality.

The Case of the Forfeited Tuition

"When I was a young business officer working at my very first school, a parent came to me and said, 'We're moving. Will you convert the forfeited tuition for our son into a donation to the school?' I didn't know the answer, so I told her I would get back to her. I happened to mention to my head of school, while we were in the teacher's lounge getting coffee, that I was investigating the answer to this question. My head looked at me and said, 'We need the money. The IRS won't catch this. No one needs to know.' I was uncomfortable with this answer, but I didn't want to go against my boss's wishes for fear of being fired—and I also understood what he was saying: was it more important to uphold this procedure than to take what was being offered as a gift to the school? I consulted a few other business officers for perspective, and got conflicting responses. By and large, older business officers advised me to follow the head, while younger business officers told me to follow the IRS—so now I was really confused. Finally, I decided to calculate the worst-case-scenario risk: what would happen if we were caught? The worst-case scenario was that our 501(c)3 status would be revoked. That seemed to me to be a chance that was too scary to take, so I went back to the head of school and explained that I didn't feel it was worth the risk. He was upset, but I refused to budge. It took several awkward weeks, but he finally came into my office one day and said, 'You did the right thing.' Which, of course, I already knew!"

The Case of the Discriminatory Termination

"My head of school called in our senior science teacher to tell her that her contract was not going to be renewed, and then told me—afterward—that he had done it. This science teacher was a lesbian, and my head was incredibly homophobic. He also didn't even look at her file, so he didn't realize that he had fired her on her birthday. If he had talked to me before going ahead and firing her, I would have instantly looked into all the ways that she could come after us and sue us before even thinking about having the conversation that would terminate her. There was nothing in her file, in eight years of teaching, which indicated that she had performed poorly. Well, she hired a lawyer and filed suit against the school. I was told that I was going to be deposed. The head called me into his office and said, 'You know, you have to tell the truth up on that stand, but remember, she is trying to hurt the school, and your duty is to protect the school.' I knew that if I told the truth, it would reflect poorly on the head, but I absolutely knew that this science teacher had been discriminated against. I called a fellow business officer, who then told me to call an employment lawyer, who then told me to call the school's attorney. I said to our lawyer,

'Look, I need to have a clear conversation with you. It is likely that I am going to have to say something in this deposition that will make you flinch. I understand my rights not to be retaliated against for telling the truth in a deposition, but I don't think my head understands these rights, and I'm worried he's going to go after me.' My lawyer said that the law would protect me. Well, it did, but it didn't protect me from the head's wrath. I testified truthfully and the next day my head came storming down to my office, steam coming out of his ears, and yelled, 'You've betrayed me, and you've betrayed the school!' I said, 'Yes, I betrayed you, but I did *not* betray the school. In the long term, if this makes you change the way you hire and fire, this is the best thing *for* the school.' And it did change. He ended up, later, buying out a long-term employee, rather than firing him. But working with him was very awkward. Finally, serendipitously, I found a new job, with a head of school whom I respected, and I left."

The Case of the Nonexistent Asbestos Management Plan

"Monday morning, 9am, I walk into my office and the phone is ringing, and it's the state inspector saying that they're going to be doing a random inspection on us sometime soon to make sure our asbestos management plan is up to date. I said, 'What asbestos management plan?' Well...I did some digging and found out that we had an asbestos management plan that was 20 years out of date! And the state hadn't been up to date, either, by the way—they were supposed to make a visit every 3 years and I couldn't find a record of the last visit. I got together as much documentation as I could and when the state inspector came, we were able to come to a resolution about a prioritized action plan to get into compliance that wouldn't bankrupt the school—but it took about 18 months. Luckily, we were able to use PPRRSM dollars. Why did I get that nasty surprise? Well, my predecessor hadn't told me about updating any asbestos management plan! And it was really likely that his predecessor hadn't told him! When I arrived on the job, there were tons and tons of files that I would have loved to have gone through to get a handle on the school's compliance situation, not to mention its basic record-keeping situation, but there wasn't any time! It took me literally 5 years to get through most of the files in the office, so I'd look for things only when something would come up. That's the challenge in the work—you don't know what you don't know, and you don't get real overlap time with your predecessor. You know, your new school has a pool and your old one didn't—do you know what all the compliance issues are? Your new school's got a wastewater treatment plant and your old one didn't, etc. This is why I think the old model of the business officer doesn't work: there really needs to be one CFO and one COO/Facilities Manager. The idea that one person has both the skill sets and the time and the energy to do both sides is unrealistic. But it's of course a financial problem—how do you hire two people at the salaries you need to do that? Personally, I think it's a problem worth solving."

CONCLUSION

As your job becomes more and more complex, it becomes more and more important for you to know where you stand—and to know, to the extent possible, where your school stands. Your first resource is always yourself. Trust your innate power to critically evaluate a dilemma. Your second resource is your immediate community of business officers who have dealt with many of the same issues you are now facing. NBOA's online members' forum (*www.nboa.net*) exists so that just these kinds of conversations can take place—"Has this ever happened to you? What did you do? What should I do?"

As you go forward in your career, you will become more skilled at spotting and resolving ethical dilemmas. While the dilemmas themselves may not get easier, your ability to work through them will build muscle. As Aristotle said, "Moral excellence comes about as a result of habit. We become just by doing just acts, temperate by doing temperate acts, and brave by doing brave acts."

NBOA

Chapter Five

HUMAN RESOURCES AND EMPLOYMENT LAW

The Attorney's Guide to Dealing Effectively with Your Employees

IN THIS CHAPTER:

- Informed hiring & firing

- De-thorning grievance issues

- The legal lifespan of your HR documents

- Casual employees vs. independent contractors

- ADA & FMLA: what you need to know

by Benjamin W. Hahn

Benjamin W. Hahn

Partner, Schnader Harrison Segal & Lewis LLP

Benjamin Hahn is an experienced employment and litigation attorney who has represented a range of private and public sector employers in court and before administrative agencies. He has provided extensive counseling to clients with employment and workplace issues, successfully representing school systems, boards of education, boards of trustees, administrators, and faculty members in various contexts for more than 20 years. Ben has been lead trial counsel in employment discrimination, harassment litigation, and has represented private and public schools in disability discrimination, educational malpractice, and failure-to-accommodate matters. He has also written and revised many tuition and faculty agreements, employee handbooks, and parent guides. The scope of his work has recently included counseling school administrators in dealing with violence in the workplace, risk management, and constitutional issues arising out of the use of school facilities by outside organizations. Ben is a graduate of Stanford Law School (J.D., 1979) and Stanford University (B.A., Economics with Distinction, 1975).

HUMAN RESOURCES AND EMPLOYMENT LAW

The Attorney's Guide to Dealing Effectively with Your Employees

An independent school must always maintain as its central focus and mission the growth and development of its students—whether they are pre-K "little people," young adults, or students with disabilities receiving specially designed educational services. That said, the business officer has the essential task of running the school as a business entity providing a service to consumers, who in this case are the parents and students. For this reason, it is critical that the business office understand how to deal effectively and consistently with the employees who deliver the school's educational and other services. This chapter provides information on legal and contractual issues arising from the employment relationship. Its purpose is to better equip the business officer to handle the myriad issues, disputes, questions, and dramatic episodes that attend dealing with employees in the independent school context.

SCHOOL EMPLOYMENT RELATIONSHIP OVERVIEW: ORGANIZATIONAL

The various members of the school's leadership team have different roles. Unfortunately, those roles are often either misunderstood or not honored. This leads not only to unnecessary clashes, but also to potential legal problems. A frequent and most unfortunate example is when a board member—often with "good intentions"—feels compelled to get involved in a teacher discipline issue. Understanding the roles of the board, the administration, and the business office in particular are important topics in the employment arena.

Board of Trustees Role

The board of trustees exists to design and perpetuate a school's organizational mission and philosophy, its "master plan." When first formed, it develops this mission and designs a school to achieve it—developing the school's governance and administrative structure, its general educational plan, and its budget; it also locates and constructs appropriate facilities.

Once a school is underway, the board of trustees steps back to handle only "big picture" matters. It gives strategic direction in the areas of finance, physical plant, and long-range planning and development; engages in fundraising; and holds in trust the school's assets, whether in the form of funds or property.

The board of trustees also oversees the employment and evaluation of the head of school, and should serve as a resource or sounding board for the head as needed throughout the year. The board does not get involved in day-to-day school management, student, or staff matters. As a matter of general policy, therefore, board members should direct all inquiries and concerns to the head of school and staff. For example, when parents complain about a teacher or a school policy, the board should direct the parents to their child's teacher or the head of school first, where appropriate, and should not engage the parents on the issue. The board's purview should remain the "big picture."

Head of School Role

The head of school's role is much like that of a CEO of a company. He or she is the highest-ranking administrator at a school and typically the only one to report directly to the board of trustees.

From an operations standpoint, a head of school acts much like a traditional principal who monitors the daily operations of the school. The head guarantees educational policies are adopted and implemented in accordance with pedagogy; oversees staff and faculty; adheres to budget; maintains enrollment at full capacity; ensures constituent relations and institutional image are positive; and creates a strong management team, to whom the head is comfortable delegating responsibilities. At all times, the head is responsible for ensuring not only that the school runs smoothly and efficiently but that operations are continually improved. In the independent school context, the head of school may also engage in fundraising. In addition, depending on the size of the school, he or she may be involved in curricula development and/or discipline, but often these matters are delegated to others.

Finally, the head of school must maintain a positive relationship with the board of trustees. He or she must keep the board of trustees abreast of all matters and information as appropriate and may rely on the board for advice when needed. The head also serves as the chief communicator between faculty and staff and the board of trustees.

Business Office Role

The role of a school's business office will vary depending on the size of the school. At a minimum, the office will handle all financial matters related to money in (e.g., tuitions and donations) and money out (e.g., salary and other expenditures) and create and monitor the budget throughout the process. The business office will keep and monitor contracts, such as those with third-party vendors of food, supplies, or services (as in janitorial or groundskeeping). School insurance issues are also handled by the business office. In addition, in most independent schools, especially small- to medium-sized schools, the business office is in charge of human resources, including payroll, employee benefits, paid and unpaid leaves, discipline, faculty and staff contracts, and post-employment disputes, such as discrimination claims or wage actions.

Human Resources Role

For purposes of the employment relationship, the human resources

function deserves individual attention. As noted above, it is commonly overseen directly by the head of the business office. But whether there is a separate individual responsible for human resources, or the duties are rolled into the position of business officer or chief administrative officer, someone must handle these duties at even the smallest of schools. Most of the obligations—and the headaches—come into existence with the hiring of the first employee.

The scope of responsibilities within the human resources function varies with the school. Generally, the human resources function fulfills the administrative aspects of all personnel transactions—including hiring, firing, salary adjustments, transfers, and classification of positions within a school-wide scheme—at the direction of the head of school. This function will usually handle verification of required background checking, certification and credentialing, fingerprinting, and other pre-employment and post-employment requirements.

The human resources function may also implement and maintain training programs and oversee performance evaluations. In addition, it administers employee insurance and benefits transactions and, in some instances, offers confidential advice to staff on work-related issues. The human resources function is the chief document manager for all personnel files and also is responsible, therefore, for maintaining a requisite degree of confidentiality and discretion.

Depending on the size of the school, the human resources function may also administer and coordinate payroll, pensions, bonuses, leave, and attendance or, at a minimum, serve as liaison to a payroll department on these matters. Unemployment and workers' compensation claims are also included in this function.

Given these many responsibilities, many of which are sensitive in nature, whoever is ultimately placed in charge must have a certain level of experience and comfort with recruiting and screening potential employees; engaging in confidential, internal investigations; evaluating and disciplining employees as needed; and, if in charge of benefits, understanding personally (and being able to convey) the types of benefits offered by the employer. Perhaps most importantly, the individual in charge must have the capacity to exercise good judgment as most disputes that end in legal liability could have been avoided if sound judgment was exercised earlier in the process, often as early as hiring (or declining to hire).

SCHOOL EMPLOYMENT RELATIONSHIP OVERVIEW: NATURE OF EMPLOYMENT

A school employs individuals under a host of different circumstances. Most employees at a school are either "at will" or under contract, whether single-year or multi-year. Independent schools are not usually unionized. A school, from time to time, may also employ individuals on a "casual" basis, or contract for services from independent contractors. Each of these employment or contractual arrangements imposes distinct rights and obligations on both the school and the employee, with potentially costly consequences if violated. It is important, therefore, to communicate clearly with an employee about his or her employment status, and to ensure that an employee's classification and treatment comport with the nature of his or her working arrangement.

Employment At Will

An employee is an "at will" employee if neither the employee nor the school has entered into a contract regarding the duration of the employment. The chief benefit (and drawback) of at will status is the freedom it affords both employer and employee. A school may terminate, transfer, or demote an at will employee at any time for any *legal* reason, with or without notice, but an at will employee may also resign at any time for *any reason*, with or without notice.* If an employer intends to employ an individual at will, at will language should be included in the offer letter, the employment agreement (if one is used), and the employee handbook. Employees hired at will should sign an acknowledgment that the employee understands the meaning of at will with respect to the employment relationship.

---

* While "at will" employees may quit for any reason whatsoever, or no reason at all, an employer can only terminate an at will employee for a legally valid reason. What constitutes a legally valid reason, however, will vary widely from state to state. In most states, a legally valid reason encompasses a wide range of motivations with the exception of those in violation of "public policy." Thus, an employer may not fire an at will employee in violation of anti-discrimination, anti-retaliation, or similar laws. A few states, however, also recognize an implied covenant of good faith and fair dealing in the employment relationship, even one defined as at will. In some instances, this covenant has been understood as imposing a de facto "just cause" requirement on termination, but in others it is understood merely as outlawing terminations motivated by bad faith or malice. Whether and to what extent these restrictions will play out in a particular jurisdiction will depend on the jurisdiction and require more detailed analysis than is relevant here.

For example, a typical employment clause defining at will employment may read:

Employee's employment with the Company pursuant to this Agreement is at will employment. Either party may terminate this Agreement and the employment relationship at any time, for any reason or no reason, with or without cause and/or notice.

A school can inadvertently eliminate or modify an employee's at will status, however, and thereby restrict its ability to terminate an employee when, for example:

- An employer agrees with an employee (orally or in writing) that employment will be for a certain duration.

- An employee handbook limits the circumstances in which the employer can terminate an employee's employment. Careful drafting of handbooks will prevent this inadvertent consequence.

- An employer makes certain promises to an employee on which the employee relies. For example, if an employer induces an employee to take a different assignment (e.g., a fourth- instead of a sixth-grade classroom) promising "this reassignment will only last a year," and the employee takes the fourth-grade class, the employer may have destroyed the at will relationship for the "promised" year.

Annual Contract for Employment

An employee is a contract-based employee if the employee and the school have entered into an agreement regarding the duration of the employee's employment. In the school context, employee contracts are typically "annual" 10-month or 12-month contracts based on the academic year. The terms of the employment—including the grounds for termination, transfer, demotion, and resignation, and related requirements— should be spelled out in the contract, which is done in writing.

In general, an employee enjoys no automatic expectation of renewal at the end of the contract term. As in the at will context, however, an employer by its actions may create an expectation of renewal and, if the employee relies on the school's actions, the school, nevertheless, may bind itself to renew the relationship, at least for the next academic year and absent legal cause to terminate.

Multi-Year Employment Contract

Multi-year contracts, like annual contracts, individually govern an employee's relationship with an employer and are not subject to automatic renewal, absent provision otherwise. Multi-year employment contracts differ from annual contracts only in the length of the term of employment, extending beyond one 10-month or 12-month term.

Casual Employment and Independent Contractor Relationship

"Casual" employees are individuals hired on an irregular "as needed" basis, with no expectation of regular or ongoing employment or set routine. The length of their employment is usually determined by the services to be rendered, rather than by the calendar. They can work for any period—e.g., an hour, a day, a week, or a season. For example, a school may hire a substitute teacher or a soccer coach on a casual basis. In most cases, casual employees do not receive sick leave or vacation, and are paid by the hour or by the project (such as the soccer season).

Casual employees should not be confused with independent contractors, who are third parties engaged to provide ongoing services to a school either at will or for a term, but whose services are compensated based on a fee rather than a wage or salary. Independent contractors are typically retained to perform a job, but the method of completion is left to them. They run their own businesses, control their own work, and supply their own equipment, materials, transportation, and tools. They also pay their own expenses. They usually do not work exclusively for a single client or customer (here, a school).

Independent contractors may also be confused with (or converted to) at will or term employees if and when their engagement begins to resemble regular work. A school must remain cognizant of this possibility because at will employees are entitled to numerous benefits not otherwise available to independent contractors, such as insurance coverage, sick leave, and vacation. In addition, the school does not pay employment taxes on fees to independent contractors, nor does it withhold wages. Independent contractors are not entitled to unemployment compensation or workers' compensation benefits. Preserving the independent contractor relationship requires vigilance and careful administration, as it is easy to take shortcuts and wind up with a contractor being deemed an employee.

EMPLOYMENT CONTRACTS

The Head of School Agreement

A head of school negotiates his or her employment contract directly with the board of trustees. A head of school's employment contract is typically for a multi-year term, i.e., more than one academic year.

The following are items that are commonly addressed in a formal, multi-year employment contract with a head of school:

1. The title, role, and reporting duty of the head

2. The term of the contract

3. The duties, including whether the head also holds a position on the board; a job description may also be attached

4. Compensation and benefits, including salary, moving expenses, vacation/sick leave, perquisites (such as cell phone), insurance, and pension

5. Professional growth activities, whether mandatory or expectational, including professional meetings, memberships, and discretionary allowances

6. Insurance, indemnification and provision of counsel (in the event the head is sued by a third party)

7. Expenses, reimbursable and not

8. Termination and renewal (including with/without cause termination and automatic or negotiated renewal)

9. Evaluation procedures by the board

10. Dispute resolution

The contracts with heads of schools are almost always individually negotiated between the parties, usually the board chair on behalf of the school and the prospective head. Legal counsel is advised for both parties.

Faculty Agreements

Schools may employ faculty under contract or at will, but typically opt to employ faculty under contract to maximize continuity in the classroom for the year's term. Legal counsel is consulted as to the form of a school's template faculty agreement, but not usually in regards to individual executions of the document. Contract terms, therefore, are standard for all faculty. Room to negotiate between school and faculty member is only within a narrow range (such as specific salary, ancillary duties such as coaching or after-school duties, and the like).

Faculty contracts are typically for one academic year, often September to June (10-month), or July to June (12-month). They may be renewed but, by their terms, do not renew automatically. Rather, new contracts are offered to faculty members in the late winter or early spring for the next academic year. If a teacher does not receive a new contract, he or she leaves at the end of the school year. Thus, technically, a teacher who is not being renewed is not being terminated. Rather, the employment relationship simply ends by operation of the contract's expiration.

Standard provisions in a faculty employment agreement address the following:

1. Job title and duties (job description may be attached)

2. Term

3. Compensation

4. Benefits, including medical insurance and pension plans

5. Vacation/sick days, leaves, holidays

6. Additional duties

7. Renewal/non-renewal

8. Adherence to school policies

9. Dispute resolution

Teacher contracts, as noted above, are almost always based on a standard form of agreement. This agreement form may have board approval or it may be developed by the business officer with the approval of the head of school.

Administrative, Staff & Specialist Positions

Administrative and other staff positions vary widely. Individuals employed in any of these positions may be at will or under contract, depending on the needs of an employer. Where possible, it is advisable to have these employees be employed at will. Upper-level staff, such as directors of departments or division heads, are usually employed under contracts comparable either to a faculty agreement or a multi-year contract, usually depending on the level of responsibility of the employee and the common practice in the geographic area in which the school is located. Specialists, as in speech, occupational therapy, or psychology, are often treated like faculty and thus subject to annual contract, or they may be independent contractors or casual employees. Legal counsel would be consulted as needed.

Auxiliary Responsibilities, Coaching & Special Events

Employment for specialty tasks may be governed either by an "add-on" to a faculty or staff contract (if it governs auxiliary responsibilities), or by a short agreement with a non-faculty member (if the individual is under no other agreement with a school). For example, a teacher who also serves as a coach after school might have a coaching agreement added on to his or her teacher's contract, or an at will staff member who coaches may enter into a short coaching agreement with the school even though his or her regular employment is not under contract.

Contracts for auxiliary or other special responsibilities preferably are *not* incorporated into an employee's primary contract. A teacher who is also an after-school coach might injure himself mid-year and be able to teach but not to coach. Separate agreements make it easy, from a contract administration standpoint, to address the distinct duties and adjust compensation accordingly. By keeping the contract for auxiliary or other special responsibilities as an add-on to a primary contract, or entirely separate, the school and the employee can avoid unnecessary ambiguities if a problem arises in or out of the classroom.

Consultants & Independent Contractors

A school may hire a third party to perform certain services if a school either cannot, or does not wish to, provide these services for itself. For example, schools often hire search firms to find qualified applicants for employment; auditors or accountants to maintain or review school books or file taxes; and attorneys to provide legal counsel and representation in litigation or administrative proceedings. Schools may also hire third parties for in-school services like janitorial work, groundskeeping, food service, or busing.

These third parties are typically considered "consultants" or "independent contractors." They should be engaged under individually negotiated written agreements that are specific to the party and type of service to be rendered. Schools should *not* use or attempt to modify the standard form faculty or staff contract to apply to a consultant or independent contractor. Both the school and the consultant/independent contractor are well-advised to seek advice from legal counsel.

POLICIES AND PROCEDURES

Independent schools should adopt and maintain personnel policies and procedures on a wide variety of subjects paralleling those of other private employers, but augmenting them to address issues peculiar to the school environment. These policies are usually adopted by the board of trustees and kept by a custodian on the board or in the school who is responsible for tracking changes and ensuring that the most up-to-date versions are disseminated and followed.

Careful wording of these policies and procedures is essential as they must conform to law. In addition, policy language may unintentionally create rights and obligations on the school and employee if they are not carefully worded. Moreover, to the extent a policy misstates a school's position or is ambiguous, and an employee relies on it in a manner adverse to the school, the language is likely to be construed against the school as the author of the language.

Legal counsel experienced in education issues can help a school articulate a set of policies that is encompassing, in accordance with law, and accurately reflective of a school's position.

Employee Handbooks

Employee handbooks are a good way to communicate a school's policies and procedures to faculty and staff. Handbooks should set forth the school's expectations of its employees and describe what employees may expect from the school. A well-designed handbook can be a great resource for the school, faculty, and staff—eliminating ambiguities in policy, encouraging open communication, and preventing misunderstandings before they arise. As mentioned above, language in handbooks, however, may intentionally and unintentionally create legal rights and obligations. It is essential, therefore, that handbooks be carefully worded to reflect accurately, in a clear and concise manner, the actual policies of the school.

The scope of an employee handbook will vary by school. In a nutshell, this handbook should be the equivalent of "ask.com." However, it should also walk

a fine line between providing enough detail to be helpful, but not so much as to overwhelm. At a minimum, employee handbooks usually describe policies in the following areas:

1. General employment (e.g., categories of employment, types of employment, non-discrimination and harassment policies, equal opportunity statements, approach to disability accommodation)

2. Payroll and benefits

3. Attendance, holiday, vacation, medical, and sick leave, including FMLA when applicable

4. Discipline and grievances

5. Separation and termination

6. Code of conduct

Schools should also lay out their policies related to students, including approach to in-school discipline, child abuse and neglect reporting requirements, special education services, etc. These student-related policies may be included in the employee handbook described above, or detailed in a separate handbook that may also be made available to parents.

Finally, schools should always have employees sign a form acknowledging receipt of any handbook(s) or other policies distributed for their review.

EMPLOYMENT RECORDS

Personnel Files

Schools must maintain up-to-date personnel files on all current and former employees. Documents in a personnel file should fall broadly into four or five categories: (1) hiring material, including resumé and references, if submitted, background check(s), and executed contract(s) for employment; (2) payroll, including annual notices of wage change; (3) personnel actions, including evaluations, promotions, demotions, transfers, pay raises, complaints, and disciplinary actions; and (4) exit information in the event an employee separates from the school, voluntarily or involuntarily. Personnel records may also include limited medical information, such as an employee's letter of good health from a physician, tuberculosis test results, etc., which are discussed in more detail below.

All personnel files must be kept in strict confidence. Generally, they should be in locked files and password-protected computer databases. Access should be restricted to persons with a need-to-know within the confines of state.

Medical Records

School employees may be required to have a medical examination prior to employment or at regular intervals while employed, and to obtain letters of good health from a physician as a prerequisite to work. School employees may also be required to comply, and aid a school in complying, with tuberculosis and other disease testing and result reporting, as required by applicable law.

Medical prerequisites will vary by jurisdiction. They may apply to *all* individuals working in a school (faculty *and* staff) and also may extend to temporary or casual employees, or independent contractors, as well.

All medical records, like general personnel records, are to be kept in strict confidence. Medical records may not be included in an employee's general personnel folder. They should be maintained as separate files and kept in a secure place under lock and key, accessible only to those with a need to know, as defined and limited by law.

Employment Verification Forms

Finally, employers must maintain copies of their employees' federal employment eligibility verification forms, also known as "I-9 Forms." These forms must be kept separately from other personnel and medical records and in strict confidence as well. The best practice is for employers to make copies of the documentation provided by the employee (such as social security card, driver's license, passport) and maintain the copies with the I-9 form.

HIRING: RECRUITMENT, APPLICATION, AND SELECTION

Recruitment

Depending on the size of the school, the head of school and/or department or division chairs have primary responsibility for recruitment and selection of applicants to employment. Typically, one or more individuals are delegated with authority to narrow a list of candidates to a group of "finalists" from which the school's leader(s) will draw interviewees and ultimately select an employee.

To maximize quality applications, schools should view recruitment as part of their ongoing strategic planning. First, it is essential that a school maintains a sensible timetable for evaluating current employees, making offers of employment for the next academic year, and setting and enforcing a deadline for signing next-year contracts relatively early in the prior year. This will enable school leaders to anticipate vacancies and to fill them in a timely fashion, while staying ahead of, or at least keeping in step with, recruitment efforts by competitors.

Application

The process and procedures for selecting employees should be established before posting any job openings. A school should be sure to follow the process and procedures uniformly and consistently in *all* employment and hiring decisions. Some schools establish a diverse hiring/selection committee of three or more staff, including administrators, faculty, or other appropriate staff of school, to review all resumés and applications submitted, and to interview applicants. Each committee member should be knowledgeable concerning appropriate guidelines for the hiring process and the posted position.

Interviewers should be trained in the legal restrictions attending the interview process, such as what questions are lawful and what ones are not. To the extent feasible, the selection process should be transparent. If records are created in connection with the selection process, they should be preserved for one year from the date an applicant is rejected or one year from the date an employee, once hired, is terminated.

A useful resource is the *Title VII Guide to Pre-Employment Inquiries*. This document can be found on the website of the U.S. Equal Employment Opportunity Commission (EEOC), ***www.eeoc.gov***.

Selection

Once a pool of qualified candidates has been identified, a school's leader(s) should have in-depth conversations with at least two references for each of the finalists and observe the finalists teaching in the classroom at the school. They may also be required by state and federal law to order background checks, fingerprinting, and ensure certifications and licensures are up-to-date and valid. If a school's background check policy includes a credit check, the school must adhere to the federal *Fair Credit Reporting Act (FCRA)* as well as any state laws governing prospective employee credit checks. Such laws will apply any time the school uses a third-party vendor to run the check; thus, even when a school turns to the internet for its check, technically it employs the services of a third-party vendor to secure the information and will be subject to the FCRA.

Throughout this process, a school's leader(s) should create a climate in which key members of the department can feel involved in the recruitment and selection process, and feel free to offer their observations of the finalists. When a candidate is eventually selected, it will then be the result of some consensus.

Finally, schools should exchange as much written material as possible with the finalists, such as the employee handbook and curriculum guides. A good candidate is not sufficient; a school should want a good candidate who will be happy at its particular school. Any serious candidate, therefore, should have a full and fair opportunity to make an informed decision about accepting an offer of employment. All parties need to make sure it's the right fit.

PAY AND BENEFITS

Pay Period

A school must adopt a regular, uniform pay system. Employees should be paid at regular intervals. For example, if a school adopts a semi-monthly policy, it may elect to pay employees on the 15th and 30th of each month. It should also adopt a policy if the pay date falls on a Saturday, Sunday, or holiday, in which case it would promise, for example, to make paychecks available the Friday before or on the day the employee returns to work. Schools should also ensure that their selected pay periods conform with state laws, which are often more restrictive than federal statutes. In addition, schools offering employment contracts that span 10 months may allow employees to elect to receive their salary over the course of 12 months, effectively deferring a portion of their earnings in order to receive a paycheck during their months off. Employees electing to be paid over 12 months must do so in writing prior to the start of the employment term; this arrangement will remain in effect until the employee notifies the school of a change in election.

Insurance-Related Benefits

Depending on the nature of an individual's employment, a school may provide certain insurance-related benefits. These benefits include medical insurance, dental care, vision care, flexible spending, pension (including 403(b) plans), long-term disability, short-term disability, group life insurance, and other benefits. The summary plan description for any such plans must be available in writing for an employee's inspection. The school should *not* create additional documents that describe the plans to employees, unless language is used that makes clear that the language in the actual plans is what controls. Otherwise, a school runs the risk of creating the impression in an employee's mind that a benefit is available on certain terms or with certain coverage when that may not be the case. This is particularly problematic when the school negotiates new agreements with insurance carriers or plan administrators, and the new plans do not have the same terms.

A school would be well-advised to reserve the right to change, add, eliminate, or modify the benefits in accordance with their terms at its sole discretion.

Paid Time Off
(Vacation and Sick Time)

Paid time off, whether vacation or sick time, should be clearly outlined in the employee handbook and itemized in any employment contract, at least by reference to the applicable employee handbook policies. School policy should specify how many days in each category and giving-notice requirements, as well as whether employees must "use it or lose it," may "bank" it, or may contribute unused days to an emergency fund for all employees. If a school opts for a banking system, it should consider whether banked time must be used within a certain timeframe, or if employees may "cash in" unused time at retirement or upon termination.

It is generally advisable to have a cap on the amount of unused leave an employee may accrue. In the independent school context, most teachers have sufficient opportunity for vacation, holiday, and recreation time because of the semester or quarter breaks and summer break. Therefore, allowing teachers or staff to accumulate large amounts of paid time off, to be used during the school year, would be unusual. Most independent schools limit the time periods in which some employees may take vacation to the times that school is not in session.

Employee Leave

A school should adopt and uniformly follow employee leave policies applicable to a host of situations, including the birth or adoption of a child, an employee's own serious illness or the serious illness of one close to the employee, military leaves of absence, bereavement, jury and witness duty, religious accommodation, and voting. Depending on the jurisdiction and the size of the school, some or all of these policies may be defined by state and/or federal law.

Parental leave is a prime example. If a school is large enough, the federal *Family and Medical Leave Act* will define a school's policy with regard to parental leave and leave in the event of an employee's own (or close family member's) serious illness.

The Family and Medical Leave Act (FMLA)

The FMLA provides eligible employees, both male and female, with the right to take unpaid leave in connection with the birth or adoption of a child, the employee's own serious illness, or the serious illness of the employee's spouse, child, or parent. In 2008, the FMLA was amended to include time off for families to care for family members who are members of the armed services. The FMLA applies to employers with 50 or more employees within 75 miles of a work site for 20 or more weeks in the current or prior calendar year. To be eligible for FMLA leave, an employee must have been employed by the employer for at least 12 months and must have worked at least 1,250 hours in the 12-month period preceding the leave.

An eligible employee may take up to 12 weeks of unpaid leave during any 12-month period in conjunction with the birth or adoption/foster care of a child, the employee's own "serious health condition," or the serious illness of a spouse, parent, or minor or incompetent child. FMLA may run concurrently with other leave, such as workers compensation, vacation, sick leave, etc.

If a school or particular employee is not governed by the FMLA, the school must adopt its own policies with regard to parental and serious illness leave, which it may model after or depart from the FMLA. A school employer may nevertheless be subject to other limitations imposed by state and federal law and would be wise to consult an attorney for advice on its policies.

Tuition Remission & Loan Repayment

Independent schools frequently grant tuition remission and/or reduction for one or more dependents of faculty and staff enrolled at the school. Schools may also wish to help new employees pay off educational loans.

There are very important—and sometimes complex—tax issues regarding the treatment of remitted tuition. Many schools provide tuition remission to dependents of faculty and staff as a non-taxed benefit to all employees on an equal basis. It is not permissible, however, to allow employees to remit their portion of tuition due on a pre-tax basis as a setoff against salary.

Treatment of student loans or ongoing education costs for employees should be carefully scrutinized for opportunities to provide help on a non-taxed basis, but, as with tuition remission, employees' payment of educational expenses should not be treated as excluded from an employer's taxable income without consulting applicable Internal Revenue Code sections.

Before- and After-School Care and Costs

If a school offers before- or after-school care, a school may wish to waive or discount care costs for dependent children of faculty and staff. If the children are not also students at the school, however, a school would be well-advised to consult its insurance policy to ensure children not enrolled at the school are still covered while on school grounds.

Professional Development

A school wishing to encourage professional and academic development among its faculty and staff may offer its contribution to the cost of that development as an additional employment benefit. Factors to consider should include: (1) whether a school is willing to contribute to all academic and professional development, or only that which specifically furthers an employee's work in his or her particular position; (2) whether a school will pay up-front or reimburse; (3) what constitutes successful completion of an academic or professional development activity, i.e., unblemished attendance, a grade "B" or higher, etc.; (4) what will be the approval process for an employee interested in taking advantage of the benefit; and (5) the size and frequency of a school's contribution(s).

RETENTION: EVALUATION, CODE OF CONDUCT AND DISCIPLINE

Evaluation

Schools typically adopt a process for evaluation, including an evaluation form. The form and process should be uniform within each category of job or position. Once adopted, it should be followed to the letter and applied uniformly to everyone in each category of job or position. Thus, classroom teachers should all face the same evaluation process; specialists the same process; administrative staff the same process, etc. Evaluations, moreover, should occur on a preset regular basis known to, and anticipated by, the employees.

School administrators enjoy wide latitude and discretion in establishing performance criteria applicable to particular categories of employment, provided that criteria are reasonably related to essential job functions and responsibilities. Just remember to stay within legal boundaries. Regardless of their content, however, performance criteria must be clear, verifiable, and appear as objective as possible from the employees' perspectives. Criteria also should be communicated to employees in advance of evaluation. Ideally, all employees are apprised of evaluation criteria when they are hired and reminded of that criteria in the form of a written policy included in the employee handbook.

Evaluation of all employees by the various administrators, supervisors, and managers should be overseen and monitored by a single manager or administrator to ensure school-wide consistency and fairness in evaluation of employees.

Code of Conduct and Discipline

A school is well-advised to develop a school-wide discipline policy that is uniformly enforced. After all, it is just as important to encourage uniform discipline among employees as it is to encourage it among students, thereby avoiding complaints of unequal treatment, favoritism, etc. This policy should be communicated to all employees as explicitly as possible, ideally in the handbook. It should include a description of the kinds of disciplinary actions that may be taken—e.g., verbal warnings, written warnings, final warnings, transfer, demotion, discharge, etc.

A school also may wish to provide a *nonexhaustive* list of the kind of conduct qualifying an employee for discipline and, where appropriate, specify which of these offenses may be so serious as to warrant immediate suspension with or without notice and regardless of other agreements. Some serious offenses may include physical or verbal assault or abuse of another adult or child, possession of firearms, weapons, or explosives on campus, or possession, distribution, or consumption of intoxicants, narcotics, or any nonprescribed drug while on campus or on duty. Serious infractions may also include some activities that may be less obvious, e.g., harassment, discrimination, improper handling of school funds, insubordination, negligence, or any careless action that endangers the life or safety of another person, etc.

Schools should keep in mind at all times that there are some things that an average private employer might be willing to work with an employee to improve, but that a school may not. In addition, should a school wish to publish a Code of Conduct (as recommended above), it should remind its employee readers that the list of possible infractions is nonexhaustive and provided merely to help the employee conform his or her conduct to the employer's expectations. The school should reserve the right, at its sole discretion, to recognize other grounds for discipline and modify the severity of discipline in accordance with the facts of any particular case.

GRIEVANCE POLICY

Employees at even the most well-run schools are likely to have grievances about their responsibilities, colleagues, supervisors, or school policies from time to time. Schools would be well-advised, therefore, to adopt and communicate to employees both an informal and formal grievance policy. Doing so is likely to discourage faculty and staff from discussing grievances with parents, other employees, or board members, which is not constructive and may damage a school.

Informal grievance channels may include bringing verbal complaints to one's supervisor or the head of school, who in turn (depending on the circumstances) may or may not adopt a proactive response. A school should also offer a formal grievance channel for an employee who prefers the formal route, or who is dissatisfied with the result of an informal grievance previously reported. Formal grievances should be in writing and an employee should be encouraged to be as explicit as possible with regard to the cause and grounds for his or her grievance. A school should promise to respond to an employee's formal grievance, in writing, within a set period of time, and adhere to that promise. Appropriate responses may include meeting with the alleged cause of a grievance (if another employee) and discussing the behavior at issue. If the allegation is substantiated, a school should then impose appropriate discipline (including termination, if warranted). Finally, grievances should be kept as confidential as possible in order to encourage open communication.

SELECTED GROUNDS FOR GRIEVANCE: DISCRIMINATION AND HARASSMENT

Federal and state law and regulations impose a number of obligations on all employers, including schools, which pertain to how individuals should behave in the workplace and be treated by their employer.

Equal Opportunity and Anti-Discrimination

Employers often issue an affirmative statement that they are "equal opportunity employers." An equal opportunity employer promises to provide equal employment opportunities to all job applicants and qualified employees without regard to race, color, gender, religion, creed, national origin or ancestry, age, sexual orientation, marital status, mental or physical disability, pregnancy, veteran status, or political affiliation, and/or similar basis protected by federal and/or state law. Such equal opportunity extends to all terms and conditions of employment including hiring, placement, promotion, termination, compensation, and training.

Anti-Harassment

Every school needs an explicit anti-harassment policy. It should be formally implemented and uniformly and effectively monitored. Harassment may take the form of verbal, physical, or visual abuse, and may be the product of actual animus or just unwanted attention, both intentionally and unintentionally inflicted. Moreover, anyone can be the perpetrator and/or the target of harassment. No harassment should be tolerated at any time, but particularly against employees in protected or semi-protected classes, which include race, color, gender, religion, creed, national origin or ancestry, age, marital status, mental or physical disability, veteran status, or other protected status as defined by law.

Disability

The *Americans with Disabilities Act* (ADA) requires an employer to provide reasonable accommodation to qualified individuals with disabilities who are employees or job applicants, unless doing so would cause undue hardship. It applies to employers with over 15 employees.

The ADA in the employment context protects disabled individuals in the workplace if they are "qualified" to do their job. A "qualified" individual with a disability is one who can perform the essential functions of the job at issue either with or without reasonable accommodation.

The ADA does not define "reasonable accommodation," but it has come to signify the steps that the employer must take to accommodate the physical or mental limitations of a "qualified disabled person" that are actually known (or should have been known) to the employer. Reasonable accommodation may include, but does not necessarily require, the following:

- Making facilities readily accessible to and usable by disabled persons;
- Some job restructuring and

reassignment to vacant positions which the disabled person is qualified to perform (but not creating new positions);

- Modified work schedules (which may include reduced hours, although an employer is not always required to offer part-time work as a reasonable accommodation);
- Acquisition or modification of equipment or devices; and
- Provision of aides on a temporary or periodic basis.

Finally, "undue hardship" under the ADA means "significant difficulty or expense," which depends on the resources and circumstances of a particular employer in relation to the cost or difficulty of providing a specific accommodation. In determining whether an accommodation constitutes an undue hardship, the following factors are considered:

- The overall size of the business, including number of employees and number and type of facilities;
- The type of operation, including the composition and structure of the work force and the number of employees at the location where the employment would occur;
- The nature and cost of the needed accommodation;
- The effect of the accommodation on a collective bargaining agreement or bona fide seniority system;
- The reasonable ability to finance the accommodation at each site; and
- Documented good faith efforts to explore less expensive alternatives, including consultation with the disabled person or with knowledgeable disabled

persons or organizations.

ADA guidance confirms that an employer has no obligation to provide reasonable accommodation until the disabled individual, or his or her representative, informs the employer that he or she needs an adjustment or change at work related to a medical condition. According to the Equal Opportunity Employment Commission (EEOC), this request is supposed to initiate an interactive process between the individual and the employer to determine if there is a reasonable accommodation.

Pregnancy

Pregnancy does not qualify as a "disability" for purposes of protection under the ADA, but pregnancy-related conditions may constitute protected disabilities. Pregnancy is also a circumstance that may give rise to a claim of gender discrimination. A pregnant employee who is unable to work due to pregnancy or childbirth is entitled to the same disability plan benefits available for others for non-pregnancy-related conditions. For example, if an employer pays all benefits for a male employee who suffers a heart attack and must remain at home for three months, the employer also must pay all benefits to a woman confined to bed rest for three months during her pregnancy. Similarly, if the man is restored to his position when he returns to work, so too is the woman entitled to her position upon return.

Race, Ethnicity, National Origin

Race-based discrimination, including discrimination based upon a membership in a particular ethnic group, can be evidenced by the employer conducting or permitting harassing, hostile, or intimidating remarks or behavior to occur; failing to provide equal opportunities in the hiring process; lower wages; fewer opportunities for promotion; or more unfavorable working conditions, all because of the person's race or ethnicity. Be certain that discipline and other work policies are uniformly applied and that work opportunities are provided to all employees, where they are qualified.

Discrimination on the basis of national origin or alien status is similarly prohibited. These types of discrimination involve many of the same issues as race-based discrimination.

Current immigration issues have also brought national origin and alienage-based discrimination to the forefront. Instances often involve the ability of the applicant or employee to communicate in English.

Gender Discrimination

In the independent school setting, particularly at schools where most of the employees, including administrators, have historically been women, it is important to be mindful of the fact that men may claim that they are being discriminated against in favor of women. The business officer should be aware that most of the concepts applicable to discrimination claims by women against men apply in the case of men making claims against women as well.

Religion

Rarely may an employer take an

applicant or employee's religion into account in the workplace. If the employer is a church or other religious organization, and the school's program is directly affiliated with the religious tenets of that organization, an employer may use some religious criteria in making employment-related decisions. Otherwise, employers must not discriminate against applicants or employees based on their religious beliefs or practices, and the employer should also permit employees to practice their religious faith at work to the extent that it does not interfere with job requirements or other employees' job performance.

SEPARATION OF EMPLOYMENT

Forms of Separation

A school and an employee may separate for a variety of reasons, sometimes at the behest of the employer or the employee, or upon mutual agreement. The simplest form of separation occurs at the expiration of a contract term when either the school has decided not to offer a new contract or an employee decides to decline a school's offer to renew.

An employee also may initiate early separation by resigning or abandoning his or her job. An employee resigns, or quits, when he or she voluntarily leaves employment. An employee is said to have abandoned his or her job when absent for a period of time without notifying his or her supervisor or the school. Abandonment is often treated as a form of termination, effective the last day the employee reported to work.

Other forms of termination are initiated by the school as employer. A school may terminate an employee "for cause" if an employee, for example, performs poorly, fails to demonstrate an acceptable attitude in the workplace, or commits an infraction worthy of termination. An employer also may terminate an employee "without cause" if it chooses to lay off an employee. A school may initiate a layoff if an employee's job function is eliminated or the work is no longer needed.

Termination of faculty during a school year is a common but complicated matter. Unless the contract is one for at will employment, a faculty member is usually terminable only for "cause." In the independent school context, a teacher whose performance is marginal but not truly unacceptable will often be retained through the end of the academic year so as not to interfere with the departing faculty member's efforts to obtain new employment. "Cause" should be used sparingly as a justified termination during the term of the employment contract.

Exit

Employees separating from their school employer, for any reason, should have an exit interview with human resources personnel to discuss logistics of insurance conversion, retirement benefits, final paycheck, and similar matters.

The school may also use the exit interview to ensure that a separating employee has returned all school property, including documents, files, computers, electronics, equipment, school credit cards, keys, etc.

This interview is also an opportunity to ascertain whether the employee has any outstanding complaints about the school. If there are such complaints, the interviewer should obtain as much information as possible from the departing employee so that the matters may be properly investigated and resolved.

Clear communication and consistent action, taken after obtaining appropriate advice and considering the school's mission, will result in a strong faculty and administrative team and very few employment law problems!

CONCLUSION

This chapter has provided a brief overview of many employment-related issues faced by the business office of an independent school. Many of the subjects treated seem complicated, difficult, annoying, contradictory, or scary. However, a few simple guidelines will help the harried business officer to keep on an even keel:

1. Remember the mission of the school: if the decision made or the action taken in the employment or personnel matter is in the best interest of the students, it is very likely to be the correct approach.

2. Ask questions and get advice: if it is unclear what action should be taken, seeking legal or tax or regulatory counsel is always the best course, but seek it before taking the action!

3. Be honest, clear, and direct, and, where possible, consistent: a large number of employment problems arise when employees do not understand a policy or practice, do not feel they are getting the real story, or feel that they are being treated differently from other employees in similar circumstances.

Chapter Six

REGULATORY COMPLIANCE

Checking the Box, Avoiding the Shocks

IN THIS CHAPTER:

- Understanding the "Headless Fourth Branch" of the government

- The needs of the IRS

- The larger legal context of regulatory compliance

- Becoming one with F-1 and J-1

- The ties that bind: federal financial assistance

by Debra Wilson

Debra Wilson
Legal Counsel, National Association of Independent Schools

Debra Wilson began her career with independent schools as a student at The Williams School in New London, Connecticut. After college and law school, she joined the Department of Justice in the tax division, serving as a tax litigator. She now serves as legal counsel for the National Association of Independent Schools (NAIS). Through her work with the NAIS Government and Community Relations Team, she reviews legislation, regulations, and cases impacting independent schools. Her numerous publications include *But it's My Space! Independent Schools & the Internet; Bylaws: Your School's Corporate Constitution;* and *Records in Independent Schools: What, How Long, and Why.* Debra has also directed and co-authored the briefs filed by NAIS in a number of cases important to independent schools, including several filed with the Supreme Court on issues relating to school records, school choice, consideration of race in admission, and athletic association rules.

REGULATORY COMPLIANCE

Checking the Box, Avoiding the Shocks

Many heads, business officers, and trustees would love to have one long checklist of all of the regulatory compliance areas that must apply to their school. Given the overlapping state and federal regulatory structures, as well as a school's own self-regulation through its policies and precedents, such a list is virtually impossible to create. However, there are particular agency-regulated areas within schools with which all schools should be accustomed. This chapter addresses those areas, primarily from the federal level, to help you navigate these often confusing waters.

Business officers serve a special role in regard to corporate compliance. In many ways they are the ones who track most areas of compliance: human resources, benefits, tax, and record-keeping, to name just a few. The business office maintains many of the records that are a key to proving school compliance, and as such is often the de facto home of other compliance initiatives.

LEGAL AND REGULATORY STRUCTURE

Although many people talk about regulatory compliance as a stand-alone objective, it really cannot be taken fully out of its larger legal context. Regulations always stem from legislation passed by either the federal Congress or the state-level equivalent (often a state house of representatives and state senate). These bodies generally pass legislation as is appropriate for their level of power, usually delegated to them by the federal or state constitution. This legislation is rarely complete in itself, particularly at the federal level, and the legislation itself often becomes the subject of regulatory actions. In many cases, legislation will specifically delegate authority to an agency to enact regulations on a piece of legislation; in other cases the legislature will order an agency to provide regulations for a particular piece of legislation. In some instances, an agency will have a more overarching authority to enact regulations that clarify specific areas of legislation in general, as is the case with the Internal Revenue Service and the tax code. When tax law is passed on the federal level, the legislation generally falls within Title 26 of the U.S. Code, and is more familiarly known as the Tax Code or the Internal Revenue Code. For a full list of titles of each section of the U.S. Code, see **uscode. house.gov**. For each title, there are vast pieces of legislation governing a broad array of activities in our country. For many, if not most, of these pieces of legislation there are regulations that clarify, explain, and guide their interpretation.

Although the agencies are often known as the Headless Fourth Branch, given the power they have been delegated in interpreting, regulating, and enforcing areas of the law, there are several main checks on their power. The agencies must comply with a variety of orders, legislative checks, and cases that build in limitations on their authority. The agencies can be challenged by individuals or entities if they overstep their bounds. In response to these checks, the agencies are required to follow procedures in most areas, particularly in rulemaking roles. The agencies must first publish proposed rules, give the public an opportunity to comment on them, open the comments up for public review, and consider the public's opinion when enacting final regulations.

Beyond the actual creation of regulation is the enforcement of the regulations and legislation, which the agencies may embrace with great gusto. This is often the element of agency interaction with which most individuals are familiar. Few are those who are thrilled to hear that the Internal Revenue Service, the Environmental Protection Agency, or the Equal Employment Opportunity Commission is requiring submission to an audit. These compliance checks are driven by regulations and legislation, but also by internal agency policies, procedures, manuals, and previous agencies' rulings and findings. These extra pieces of guidance can help schools and others maintain compliance within a certain field, but many times they provide additional confusion for those that are trying to "get it right."

When considering the amount of

regulation out there, as well as the confusion that can result in the actual enforcement of these regulations, it is safe to say that being in absolute regulatory compliance is not necessarily an achievable goal. However, schools should aim to be as near the mark as possible and always keep in mind the particular agencies and regulatory areas within the school that have historically received significant attention.

AGENCIES

While there are any number of agencies with which schools may interact, the following is a list of the major ones. Agency websites are listed at the end of this chapter. Again, these agencies are all federal agencies. That being said, many states have regulatory agencies that are similar to the federal agencies, with many of the same state agencies also being likely regulatory points.

Department of Agriculture (USDA)

The Department of Agriculture administers programs that many independent schools participate in, namely the school milk program, the school lunch program, and the school breakfast program. These programs are administered by the Food and Nutrition Service component of the USDA. While the actual funds for this program are administered at the state level, the program itself is organized through the USDA and has, historically, been one of the more popular federal programs in which independent schools participate. The current interest in childhood obesity

has brought considerable attention to the USDA recently, particularly in the area of school nutrition.

Department of Education (DOE)

The Department of Education does not impact independent schools as much as it might. That being said, there is an Office of Non-Public Education (ONPE) within the DOE that focuses solely on education outside of the public school system. This office acts as a liaison between the DOE and the nonpublic school realm, often fielding questions from schools relating to nonpublic school participation in federal programs that the DOE administers. In addition to the ONPE, schools should also be aware of the Office of Civil Rights (OCR) within the DOE, which enforces federal civil rights laws that are triggered when schools of any kind (including independent, proprietary, religious, vocational, etc.) receive funds or financial assistance from the federal government.

Department of Homeland Security (DHS)

When the Department of Homeland Security was formed after 9/11, it absorbed and created several agencies, the most important of which, from a school standpoint, are likely the U.S. Citizenship and Immigration Services (USCIS), U.S. Immigration and Customs Enforcement (ICE), and the Federal Emergency Management Agency (FEMA). USCIS and ICE provide the structure through which all visas and similar documents are obtained and immigration laws are enforced. As such, ICE is the administrator of the Student and Exchange Visitor Information System

(SEVIS), the main program that handles student visas. It is also the recipient of all applications for visas relating to teachers. FEMA has been in the spotlight for its role in post-Hurricane Katrina efforts as well as the 2008 flooding in the central states. In 2007, independent schools became eligible to receive FEMA relief money, making FEMA an important contact for independent schools in the event of a natural disaster. Finally, ICE has a variety of roles, especially its overseeing of the employment verification form (I-9), which was redrafted in 2007.

Department of Labor (DOL)

The DOL actually contains a large number of agencies that many might recognize more as stand-alone entities. Most well-known to schools are the Employee Benefits Security Administration (enforcing regulations and legislation related to health and other benefit plans), the Employment Standards Administration (enforcing regulations related to worker welfare and rights, particularly the Fair Labor Standards Act [FLSA] and the Family and Medical Leave Act [FMLA], as well as the bulk of the regulations relating to retirement plans in the Employment Retirement Income Security Act [ERISA]), and the Occupational Safety and Health Administration (OSHA), which deals with safe and healthy workplaces.

Department of Treasury

The Department of Treasury has many entities within it, but the most important to independent schools is the Internal Revenue Service (IRS). The IRS is the entity that arbitrates the nonprofit status of most nonprofits in the United States and ensures that, in its opinion, those nonprofit entities continue to operate in manners consistent with that designation. Maintaining this nonprofit status is vital to most organizations as it ensures that any donations are tax-deductible, all mission-related income is nontaxable on often the federal and state levels, and, depending on state law, often exempts the entity from property taxes. The IRS enforces other tax-related laws, including those related to tax-deductible donations, income, and taxable income to nonprofits. The past decade has brought much focus from both the IRS and Congress on the nonprofit sector, so much so that the IRS has created a special sub-website for charities and nonprofits. The IRS website has improved dramatically over time, as have the agency's efforts in making its guidance more user-friendly and digestible.

Environmental Protection Agency (EPA)

The Environmental Protection Agency covers a vast array of laws designed to protect the environment and general health. Many schools have become more familiar than they ever wanted to be with asbestos-related regulations. However, starting in 2008, the EPA began to express an even greater interest in our schools in other key areas.

Equal Employment Opportunity Commission (EEOC)

The Equal Employment Opportunity Commission is the main government venue for enforcing anti-discrimination laws in the workplace. The EEOC covers the waterfront, from equal pay to sexual harassment. The EEOC may conduct its own audits of workplace practices and may choose to follow up on employee-filed complaints in courts of law, on behalf of employees. Over the years the EEOC has served as an employment litigation barometer of sorts, providing routine reports on the kinds of discrimination about which it receives complaints. The EEOC also provides routine guidance on nontraditional areas of discrimination, such as the Questions and Answers about the EEOC's *Enforcement Guidance: the Unlawful Disparate Treatment of Workers with Caregiving Responsibilities* (released in 2007).

Key Compliance Areas

While it is helpful to know who may be enforcing a variety of laws, most schools find it equally or more helpful to know where the key issues are within the school itself. It would go far beyond the scope of this chapter to expound on the length and breadth of all of the laws in play for schools, but the following section is designed to outline key laws that have a particular focus from the agencies. Obviously, this is not a complete list and schools need to be aware that other regulations and legislation may also impact school operations.

EMPLOYMENT-RELATED LAWS

Anti-Discrimination

As noted above, the EEOC is the main agency that focuses on employment-related discrimination complaints. Outside of federal or state courts, employees may turn to the EEOC to file a complaint, and the EEOC itself does

various kinds of audits and investigations in this area. Schools should bear in mind that anti-discrimination includes harassment-related charges. The EEOC requires particular posters related to anti-discrimination laws, links to which are on the EEOC website, and about which schools should be most aware.

The EEOC enforces the main anti-discrimination laws, namely Title VII of the Civil Rights Act of 1964, the Americans with Disabilities Act (ADA), and the Age Discrimination in Employment Act (ADEA). Collectively, these laws cover the categories of race, color, religion, sex/gender, national origin, disability, and age. These laws make it illegal for an employer to discriminate on these grounds in any area of employment, including hiring and firing; compensation, assignment, or classification of employees; transfer, promotion, layoff, or recall; job advertisements; recruitment; testing; use of company facilities; training and apprenticeship programs; fringe benefits; pay, retirement plans, and disability leave; or any other aspect of employment.

Obviously, this list underscores the importance of being aware of all aspects of the employment process. For schools, this can be particularly difficult in the hiring process when so many individuals are involved in the interview and decision phase. As the EEOC website provides, discriminatory practices are somewhat broad on these laws and include:

- Harassment on the basis of race, color, religion, sex, national origin, disability, or age

- Retaliation against an individual

for filing a charge of discrimination, participating in an investigation, or opposing discriminatory practices;

- Employment decisions based on stereotypes or assumptions about the abilities, traits, or performance of individuals of a certain sex, race, age, religion, or ethnic group, or individuals with disabilities; and

- Denying employment opportunities to a person because of marriage to, or association with, an individual of a particular race, religion, national origin, or an individual with a disability. Title VII also prohibits discrimination because of participation in schools or places of worship associated with a particular racial, ethnic, or religious group.

Schools should note that the EEOC also handles charges related to retaliatory actions taken against those employees, a type of claim that has been on the rise over the last few years. As most schools know, having procedures and checks in place to avoid discrimination, harassment, and retaliation is vital to running any business. The EEOC website provides facts and guidance on the major areas of discrimination law, including age, disability, equal pay, national origin, pregnancy, race, retaliation, sex, and sexual harassment.

Fair Labor Standards Act (FLSA)

The DOL, through the Employment Standards Administration, enforces the FLSA at the agency level. The FLSA requires that certain employees are properly paid for the time worked and requires employers to pay these employees overtime pay at one and a half times their normal rate for any hours worked beyond the standard forty-hour work week. The regulations for this particular law were updated in 2005, requiring all employers to revisit their classification of their employees. The Department of Labor spent quite a bit of time creating interactive information on this topic on its website.

Although the FLSA, in the school world, has the most impact on overtime pay and classification of workers as salaried or hourly employees, it also regulates an entity's ability to use child labor. For schools that use students to perform various functions on campus either during or outside the school year, this law is also quite important.

Just as the anti-discrimination laws tend to come up in the context of disgruntled employees, the FLSA is often a main compliance focus from the agencies. It can also come up when an employee is terminated and his or her lawyer argues that the employee should have received overtime payments for the last several years. While compliance with the FLSA can be difficult, it is truly a key area for schools to be in compliance with, particularly in light of the new regulations and the school-related audits that have been done in this area within the last few years.

Family and Medical Leave Act (FMLA)

Schools with over 50 employees during any 20-week period in the previous work year must comply with the FMLA. This law provides time off for employees for the birth and care of the newborn child of the employee; for placement with the employee of a son or daughter for adoption or foster care; to care for an immediate family member (spouse, child, or parent) with a serious health condition; or to take medical leave when the employee is unable to work because of a serious health condition. Schools have slightly different rules than regular employers—rules that take into account the slightly different nature of school work and the need for consistency within the classroom.

In 2008, new rules were proposed for the FMLA, and it was amended to include time off to care for family members who are members of the armed services. The FMLA has fairly technical provisions that are very important for schools to follow when an employee is going to be out for an extended period of time. The Department of Labor has quite a bit of information on this topic, including the new amendment, on its website.

Employment Verification

Given the current political focus on illegal aliens, schools should ensure that their I-9 compliance is up to speed. This form asks for a variety of documents to assure the employer that the new employee is actually allowed to work in the U.S. The form has recently been revised and all employers should take the implementation of the new form as a good time to ensure that the old forms are present and accounted for in the appropriate files.*

Editor's Note: I-9s should be kept in their own file, not within individual employee personnel files.

Benefits Compliance

Compliance with the various benefits laws is one of the most important areas of regulatory law. The many requirements here include those related to cafeteria plans, health and dental benefits, life insurance, and retirement plans. Most of these laws are overseen in one way or another by either the DOL or the IRS, or both.

STUDENT-RELATED LAWS

Schools are often surprised to learn how little federal regulation there is in regard to the actual student component of schools. While there are some regulations that do apply, many only apply upon the receipt of federal financial assistance, a discussion too lengthy for this chapter, but described briefly below.

NONDISCRIMINATION

Many of the same nondiscrimination issues that arise within the employment realm arise for students. Again, most are triggered by receipt of federal financial assistance. The following are the most likely areas in which a family might make a claim against a school.

AMERICANS WITH DISABILITIES ACT (ADA)

The ADA applies to independent schools as places of public accommodations. This law requires that schools accept otherwise qualified students into their schools and make reasonable accommodations for the students within the school program. Schools are not required to accept students that would not otherwise be qualified and they are not required to make accommodations that fundamentally alter the program of the school or unduly burden the school in providing the accommodation. As anyone is likely to guess, many of these terms have become terms of art. Again, the entirety of the ADA is beyond the scope of this chapter, but schools should understand that they do have obligations to students that have disabilities that rise to the level of substantially limiting a student in a major life activity. Schools generally see this most in areas of learning disabilities.

Other areas of the ADA include making accommodations for those visiting the campus, such as providing sign language interpreters for parents during school productions or using particular hearing devices. The ADA also influences decisions made during building or renovating processes.

It is unclear at this time what agency would follow up on an ADA-related complaint with regard to an independent school. As far as we know, the Office of Civil Rights within the Department of Education has never exercised its potential authority in this area, although it would seem a likely candidate for doing so. The Department of Justice, Civil Rights Division, is another potential candidate for regulation in this area. We may find out the answer to this question sooner rather than later as, at the time of the writing of this chapter, there are proposed amendments both to the ADA itself and its regulations. Invariably, when such amendments are made the actual application of the law becomes less sure and litigation and agency action are bound

to ensue.

SECTION 1981 CLAIMS

The second major nondiscrimination issue that comes up in this area is 42 USC 1981, often known as a Section 1981 claim. This law forbids discrimination on the basis of race in the making of contracts. Because the relationship between schools and their students is based in contract, this nondiscrimination is seen as broadly applying to racial nondiscrimination principles across the spectrum of student-related school activity. However, this law is unlikely to come under agency purview as the claims are generally brought by individuals within courts of law as opposed to by agencies for enforcement proceedings.

REVENUE PROCEDURE 75-50

Around the time of the desegregation of the public schools, many cases were brought to court questioning the ability of nonprofit organizations to discriminate on the basis of race while enjoying tax-exempt status granted by the very government that was requiring desegregation. In response, the IRS issued *Revenue Procedure 75-50* to delineate guidelines and record-keeping requirements for private schools regarding racially nondiscriminatory policies and practices. This procedure requires that "the school admits the students of any race to all the rights, privileges, programs, and activities generally accorded or made available to students at that school and that the school does not discriminate on the basis of race in administration of its educational policies, admissions policies, scholarship and loan programs, and athletic and other school-administered programs." Along these lines, the procedure requires the following steps from schools:

Organizational Requirements

A school must include a statement in its charter, bylaws, or other governing instrument, or in a resolution of its governing body, that it has a racially nondiscriminatory policy regarding students and therefore does not discriminate against applicants and students on the basis of race, color, national origin, or ethnic origin.

Statement of Policy

Every school must include a statement of its racially nondiscriminatory policy regarding students in all printed material dealing with student admission, programs, and scholarships.

Written Advertisement References

Further, every school must include a reference to its racially nondiscriminatory policy in other written advertising that it uses as a means of informing prospective students of its programs. The IRS has provided the following language as sample language that schools may use: "The M school admits students of any race, color, and national or ethnic origin."

Publicity

The school must make its racially nondiscriminatory policy known to all segments of the general community served by the school. In doing so, the IRS has specified that the school must use one of the following two methods to satisfy this requirement:

- *Newspaper Publication*
  The school may publish a notice of its racially nondiscriminatory policy in a newspaper of general circulation that serves all racial segments of the community. This notice must be repeated at least once annually during the school's main marketing period or, if there is no obvious marketing period, during the school's registration period.

- *Broadcast Media Publication*
  The school may also choose to use broadcast media to publicize its racially nondiscriminatory policy if this use makes such nondiscriminatory policy known to all segments of the general community the school serves.

As with many of the regulations related to the IRS, there are nuances within this procedure that provide certain exceptions and alternate approaches. Schools should thoroughly review this area and be aware that statements related to it are part of Form 990, which nonprofits must file every year. Interestingly, this procedure does not provide a private right of action for an individual, but failure to follow it may result in the loss of the school's nonprofit status.

IMMIGRATION

Although schools might run into immigration-related issues with both students and staff, the vast majority of schools only face immigration issues with students. Students from other countries may be in our schools with student visas (F-1), student exchange visas (J-1), or dependent visas (when a parent is here on any number of visas and the student has a visa related to that parent visa). Most schools do not ask students for documents showing that they are legal residents, although schools that have student visa programs often provide that information to students. The J-1 visa requires the school and family to work with a separate sponsor organization, except in the very rare event that a school itself sponsors J-1 visas. Beyond that, the F-1 visa takes up most of the immigration stage.

To enable students to come to the U.S. on F-1 visas, schools must be approved through the Student and Exchange Visitor Information System (SEVIS). Your school must go online and file a petition with the U.S. Immigration and Customs Enforcement Agency (ICE) through SEVIS. This is a relatively new tool that has put all visa processing for international students online. It is designed to closely track which schools are authorized to sponsor students coming into the United States, as well as to track individual students coming from abroad.

Initially, SEVIS required all schools to become recertified to sponsor international visas. The new process requires school visits for every applicant school as well as the collection of a larger scope of information. If your school needs to begin this process, it is best to do so early. The processing rate depends on the location of the school, but the process can take anywhere from three to six months before a school is authorized to issue an I-20 form that provides students with the requisite documentation to apply for a visa from the consulate. In order to be certified as a sponsoring school, the school must prove that it is an established, bona fide school, that is has the necessary facilities, personnel, and finances to provide instruction in recognized courses, and that it provides such courses to the students. The school must also delegate select employees within the school's administration to be "designated school officials" ("DSOs") who will have a variety of responsibilities related to international students. Additionally, the school must present a statement from its accrediting body as well as a certification from a state public official acknowledging the school's compliance with state requirements.

Beyond these basic requirements, once a school is approved it must work within the SEVIS system to fill out the variety of forms that students need to enter the country, work with the students and families to get the appropriate interviews done and forms provided, then closely track the student within the country and within SEVIS. There are a myriad of rules relating to updating student profiles, student transfers, how long students may stay, etc. It is vital for schools that want to sponsor F-1 students to maintain their SEVIS accounts properly and comply with the system requirements.

SCHOOL MANAGEMENT COMPLIANCE ISSUES

Tax Compliance Issues

Federal tax compliance is one of the areas to which schools need to pay particular attention. Independent schools must remember their nonprofit status as they wind their way through the maze of tax regulations that apply to all businesses in general and nonprofits in particular. Brief descriptions of the biggest issues are below. Many, if not all, of these topics are thoroughly covered on the IRS website, and further resources may be found through NAIS and NBOA.

Compensation

Often one of the more intricate areas of tax law within schools, compensation can be quite complicated in light of the benefits offered to staff. On-campus or school-provided housing, tuition remission or reduction for staff, financial aid awards, and other benefits all give pause when considering the appropriate taxation on benefits.

Intermediate Sanctions

Closely related to the overall category of compensation, the IRS imposes intermediate sanctions when it feels that certain disqualified people (such as heads of school, business officers, board members, or major donors) receive compensation or payment beyond the reasonable value of the services or property provided. This area has been growing in importance to the entire nonprofit community and the IRS's interest in this area is unlikely to lessen.

Unrelated Business Income Tax

Although schools and other nonprofits may bring in funds from a variety of services related to their missions, money earned outside the school's mission is subject to tax under the Unrelated Business Income Tax rules. This area changes regularly and schools would be wise to keep an eye on it. Recent issues include the taxability of sponsorships of arenas and other parts of campus, income derived from snack machines, summer camps, and community rentals. While triggering tax in and of itself does not threaten a nonprofit's existence, if the taxable activities begin to overtake those activities consistent with the nonprofit's mission, the nonprofit's status may be in jeopardy.

Donations

As with all nonprofits, it is vital to ensure that donations are handled properly both in expenditure and documentation.

Noncash donations such as stocks, art, vehicles, and other objects have special rules that must be followed. Activities such as school auctions and raffles trigger additional compliance issues. NAIS's publication *Auctions and Raffles* is a good resource in this area.

Form Compliance

The federal tax world requires a broad array of forms, the most common of which are listed below. These are outside the usual array that all employers must have, such as W-2s, W-4s, 1099s, and similar employment-related filings.

- **Form 990** – General information tax return filed by nonreligious 501(c)3 organizations. This form, as well as its schedules and instructions, have been recently updated. Careful attention should be paid to the nuances of this form. This form must be made available to the public upon request, either in copy or online.

- **Form 990-T** – Tax return filed by nonprofits to report unrelated business income tax. This form is now also required to be produced to the public except under very limited circumstances.

- **Form 8283** – Donation form required from the donor to file with his or her taxes for donation of noncash property. (The amount of the donation that can be taken is over $500.) This form must also be signed by the donee in the appropriate section.

- **Form 8282** – Form filed with the IRS by the donee when certain noncash donations are sold, exchanged, or otherwise disposed of within three years of donation.

- **Quid Pro Quo Disclosure** – In those situations where an item valued over $75 is purchased for more than its fair market value, the school is required to provide a quid pro quo disclosure statement. In the case of an auction, the statement must be provided at the time of purchase or receipt of the auction item.

- **Form W-9** – Taxpayer identification number and certification form often obtained from individuals when the school has reason to file an information return to report income paid to an individual. Schools may find a need for this form during fundraising gaming events.

- **Form W2-G** – A form used to report gambling winnings. The school would provide this form to an individual when the individual receives:

  - $600 or more in gambling winnings and the payout is at least 300 times the amount of the wager (except winnings from bingo, keno, and slot machines);

  - $1,200 or more in gambling winnings from bingo or slot machines;

  - $1,500 or more in proceeds (the amount of winnings less the amount of the wager) from keno; or

  - any gambling winnings subject to federal income tax withholding

- **Form 1096** – This form is used to summarize a variety of information returns that are sent to the IRS.

LABOR COMPLIANCE ISSUES

There are a variety of record-keeping requirements that fall under the labor compliance area; the Department of Labor has a number of online resources to help schools comply. However, one of the main areas that schools must be on top of is related to retirement plans, namely 403(b), 401(k), 457(f), and 457(b) plans. The DOL and the IRS have both been very interested in ensuring that these plans follow their respective regulations. Even schools that work with an outside plan administrator must ensure that the mandatory procedures are followed.

ENVIRONMENTAL ISSUES

The EPA, perhaps needless to say, is the regulatory body that provides audits, often unannounced, and enforces the law in environmental compliance areas. According to the EPA, there are four main bodies of compliance about which schools need to be truly aware. At the same time, if a spill or other environmental incident occurs and damages property or causes harm in some other way, these and other environmental laws and regulations also create liability.

Resource Conservation and Recovery Act (RCRA)

This act amends the Solid Waste Disposal Act of 1965. It requires the appropriate disposal of any number of items that schools routinely have on campus, particularly items found in art studios and chemical labs. It also handles the regulation of underground storage tanks. The states tend to be involved with how the overall state waste disposal structure handles waste under this law, so all schools need to know what state procedures have been put into place to ensure compliance.

Toxic Substances Control Act (TSCA)

This act covers a wide range of areas, including asbestos and lead-based paints.

Comprehensive Environmental Response, Compensation, and Liability Act (CERCLA)

This act is most well-known for its application in the event of spills, particularly oil spills.

Emergency Planning and Community Right to Know Act

Similar to CERCLA, this law concerns hazardous materials and chemicals that could impact the community in the event of a spill or other release into the environment. Although many schools don't believe this law may apply, schools that have pools, ice hockey rinks, or other reasons to have large stores of some common chemicals (such as ammonia) may find themselves inadvertently within these laws.

The EPA has begun working more closely with independent schools to consider the application of these laws and how best to communicate training in these areas. In the meantime, the best resources for educational institutions are through the work the EPA has done with higher education.

TRANSPORTATION ISSUES

Schools that have their own school bus fleet should be aware of the variety of laws that come into play with commercial drivers licenses as well as school bus regulation. Transportation regulations overlap significantly with state law and can cause confusion in the field. Because so many schools have moved away from maintaining their own fleets, a brief mention in this area seems sufficient. The Department of Transportation, particularly its National Highway Traffic Safety Administration, is largely in charge of this area.

RECEIPT OF FEDERAL FINANCIAL ASSISTANCE OR FUNDS

No regulatory compliance conversation would be complete without a brief word about the impact of receipt of federal financial assistance and the ties such assistance brings. A more complete conversation about what constitutes the ties of federal financial assistance and the ins and outs of the regulations such assistance triggers may be found through NAIS, and its two publications in this area *(That's a Lot of Money! Should I Take It or Leave It? Federal Financial Assistance and Independent Schools,* as well as *Top Six Federal Programs: Are They Triggering Obligations for Your School?).* However, all schools should understand that many of the top programs that independent schools tend to participate in, such as the school lunch and school milk programs administered by the Department of Agriculture, may be seen as receipt of federal financial assistance. Receipt of assistance may trigger any of the following laws, and then some:

- **Age Discrimination Act of 1975** – The Age Discrimination Act and its implementing regulations prohibit discrimination on the basis of age in programs or activities receiving federal financial assistance.
- **Section 504 of the Rehabilitation Act of 1973** – Section 504 and its implementing regulations generally prohibit discrimination on the basis of disability in programs or activities receiving federal financial assistance. Schools should be aware that the Americans with Disabilities Act, which applies to almost all independent schools, contains many similar obligations. However, Section 504 requires certain kinds of plans and other steps that

the ADA does not require.

- **Title VI of the Civil Rights Act of 1964** – Title VI, as amended, and its implementing regulations generally prohibit discrimination on the basis of race, color, or national origin in programs or activities receiving federal financial assistance. While this law is similar to other nondiscrimination laws that generally apply to independent schools, in some cases the standards of liability being applied are slightly different.

- **Title IX of the Education Amendments of 1972** – Title IX and its implementing regulations generally prohibit discrimination on the basis of sex in education programs or activities receiving federal financial assistance.

- **Drug-Free Workplace Act of 1988** – The Drug-Free Workplace Act and its implementing regulations generally require federal grantees and contractors to maintain drug-free workplaces.

- **Family Educational Rights and Privacy Act** – The Family Educational Rights and Privacy Act and its implementing regulations generally require schools to comply with certain policies regarding student education records and personally identifiable information contained in such records. The Act also allows for review and appeals of grades, among other things.

- **Military Recruiting** – 10 U.S.C. § 503 – The Military Recruiter laws provide military recruiters with access to students and contact information unless certain board actions are taken.

STATE AREAS OF COMPLIANCE

As noted earlier in this chapter, many of the areas most important to school regulatory compliance exist at the state level. Indeed, much federal compliance is administered by the state in some capacity. Many of the most important regulatory issues will occur in these kinds of agencies:

ATTORNEY GENERAL'S OFFICE

Prosecution of cases including:

- Student abuse or neglect
- Financial crimes
- Nonprofit-related issues

CHILD AND FAMILY SERVICES

- For specific calls related to suspected abuse
- Occasionally will come to schools to talk with a child

LAW ENFORCEMENT

- May perform background checks
- May receive reports on abuse
- Involved with school security
- A part of criminal enforcement

STATE DEPARTMENT OF EDUCATION

- Licensing requirements
- Accreditation requirements
- Basic rules and enforcement in areas of records retention, transcripts, attendance, etc.
- State civil rights issues

STATE ATHLETIC ASSOCIATION

- Regional athletic rules, including recruitment, transfers, and eligibility

STATE DEPARTMENT OF REVENUE / DEPARTMENT OF TREASURY

- State tax exemption, particularly in areas of exemption from state property tax

STATE DEPARTMENT OF TRANSPORTATION

- Transportation of students
- Buses
- Vans

STATE DEPARTMENT OF LABOR

- Employment discrimination
- Unemployment insurance / claims
- Workers compensation
- Other regulatory issues that may overlap with federal laws

SELF-REGULATION

Finally, although not an agency, schools often find themselves in legal hot water because of their own self-imposed compliance issues. Schools often forget that in an industry that is largely unregulated in many parts of the country, their own self-regulation can be their undoing in some instances. Because the school relationship with families and employees is tied to a contractual relationship, the promises made in school handbooks, policies, bylaws, and other sources often creates an expectation in other parties. When schools fail to follow their own regulations, they undermine the promises made in these policies that the other party reasonably expects to be fulfilled. This is one area over which schools have significant control, as they can review and revise their own policies at will, providing that they are in compliance with the law.

Regulatory compliance represents the labyrinth that is today's business world. This labyrinth is made only more complicated by the subject of our industry: students that are not yet adults. While this chapter provides much daunting food for thought when taken as a whole (especially with the realization that much of this only scratches the surface), schools should bear in mind that reasonable compliance is not created overnight. It is only attainable by building systems within the school for each regulatory area, systems that are unlikely to fall into place simultaneously. Business officers often take the lead, but should remember that it helps to have the vested interest and input from other divisions and offices within the school. A thoughtful and holistic approach over time will bring schools and staff into compliance—hopefully before an audit!

NBOA

Important Websites

Comprehensive Environmental Response Compensation and Liability Act (CERCLA): *www.epa.gov/superfund/policy/cercla.htm*

Department of Agriculture (USDA): *www.usda.gov*

Department of Education (DOE): *www.ed.gov*

Department of Homeland Security (DHS): *www.dhs.gov*

Department of Labor (DOL): *www.dol.gov*

Department of Treasury: *www.ustreas.gov*

Emergency Planning and Community Right to Know Act: *www.epa.gov/oem/content/epcra/index.htm*

Employee Retirement Income Security Act (ERISA): *www.dol.gov/dol/topic/health-plans/erisa.htm*

Environmental Protection Agency (EPA): *www.epa.gov*

EPA and Higher Education: *www.campuserc.org*

EPA Link for Schools: *cfpub.epa.gov/schools/index.cfm*

Equal Employment Opportunity Commission (EEOC): *www.eeoc.gov*

Fair Labor Standards Act (FLSA): *www.dol.gov/esa/whd/flsa*

Family and Medical Leave Act (FMLA): *www.dol.gov/esa/whd/fmla*

Federal Emergency Management Agency (FEMA): *www.fema.gov*

FLSA Classification of Employees: *www.dol.gov/compliance/laws/comp-flsa.htm*

Healthy Schools Initiative: *teamnutrition.usda.gov/healthy-schools.html*

I-9 Form (revised): *www.uscis.gov/files/form/i-9.pdf*

Internal Revenue Service (IRS): *www.irs.gov*

IRS Subsite for Charities and NonProfits: *www.irs.gov/charities/index.html*

National Highway Traffic Safety Administration: *www.nhtsa.dot.gov*

Occupational Safety and Health Administration (OSHA): *www.osha.gov*

Office of Civil Rights (OCR): *www.ed.gov/ocr*

Office of Non-Public Education (ONPE): *www.ed.gov/about/offices/list/oii/nonpublic/index.html*

Resource Conservation and Recovery Act (RCRA): *www.epa.gov/rcraonline*

Student and Exchange Visitor Information System (SEVIS): *www.ice.gov/sevis*

U.S. Citizenship and Immigration Services (USCIS): *www.uscis.gov*

U.S. Immigration and Customs Enforcement (ICE): *www.ice.gov*

Chapter Seven

RISK MANAGEMENT
Setting Up Your Safety Net

IN THIS CHAPTER:

- The most efficient way to identify risk

- Paving the road to mitigation with sound school policies

- How to avoid reinventing the wheel

- When to transfer, when to share

- Calculating risk's total cost

by Janice M. Abraham

Janice M. Abraham
President and CEO, United Educators Insurance

Janice M. Abraham joined United Educators Insurance as President and CEO in January 1998, and also serves as President and CEO of United Educators Management Company. Janice has over 15 years of experience in serving the higher education community through her work at Whitman College as Chief Financial Officer/ Treasurer, in various senior positions at Cornell University, and at the National Association of College and University Business Officers (NACUBO), where she served as staff associate. Prior to her work in education, Janice was an international banker for J. P. Morgan. *Business Insurance* named Janice as one of the "100 Top Leading Women" in the field of insurance in 2000. She was also named the "2004 Insurance Woman of the Year" by the Association of Professional Insurance Women, and received NACUBO's Professional Development Award in 2005. In 2006, she was named a *Business Insurance* "Woman to Watch" for her leadership in the industry.

RISK MANAGEMENT

Setting Up Your Safety Net

Risk management can be overwhelming for independent schools. Multi-national corporations have a Chief Risk Officer; large universities have a risk management department, internal auditors, and a general counsel's office; and mid-sized colleges may have a risk manager, a health and safety officer, and a security force. Independent schools typically have none of these. The duties and responsibilities for risk management fall on the business officer, faculty, division heads, head, and ultimately, the trustees. This chapter is intended to lay out the foundations of risk management for independent schools and to chart a course for developing a risk management program. The ultimate goals of a risk management program are to keep the community safe and the school on track to accomplish its mission.

The list of things that can go wrong at a school is too extensive to enumerate. A strong risk management program will identify the risks that could be the most damaging to the school and will develop plans comprehensive and flexible enough to respond to a broad array of risk, some of which may be outside the original plans. This chapter will also address Enterprise Risk Management, an emerging concept in the field.

Getting Started

Risk management has four steps. Following these steps will not make risk disappear, but will help the school be prepared to help individuals and the community recover and continue serving students:

1. IDENTIFICATION

2. MITIGATION

3. TRANSFER AND SHARING

4. MEASURING AND COMMUNICATING

STEP 1: RISK IDENTIFICATION

The first and most important step in risk management is risk identification. A risk management committee (often known as a safety committee) is the most efficient way to identify risks. The committee should have representatives from each division of the school (i.e. upper, middle, lower), athletics, business office, human resources, facilities, residential life, infirmary, etc. Each of the members of the risk management committee should be charged with working with their respective departments on risk identification. The committee, on an annual basis, should answer these questions:

What could happen that would prevent us from accomplishing our mission?

What keeps us up at night?

Where have things gone wrong in the past?

Have we experienced accidents or claims in specific areas?

Examination of loss run provided by insurance companies will help guide this analysis.

Have our peer institutions experienced accidents that could happen at our school?

Are there new trends or new activities that may bring new risks?

A standing committee is the most desirable route to risk identification, and some states mandate the existence of a safety committee. An alternative is to have the business officer or a designee conduct interviews and inspections with individuals and departments who would otherwise comprise the committee, and develop an assessment for presentation to the administrative team and board. Obtaining buy-in and commitment to the process is a substantial part of risk identification, so this second option is recommended only as a last resort to initiate the process.

The following risk categories are a guide (but not an exhaustive list) to stimulate discussion around the questions listed above:

STUDENT ACTIVITIES IN AND OUT OF THE CLASSROOM

- Athletics

- Field trips and travel outside the school, including international travel

- Science laboratories, art studios

- Theater

- Residence halls

- Social activities

- Technology use

- Boundary training for staff and volunteers

- Teaching during an extended closure of the school building

- Student mental health issues

BUSINESS/HUMAN RESOURCES

- Internal controls and cash handling

- Training for faculty and staff on harassment and discrimination

- Hiring practices, performance reviews, and promotions

- Business continuity plans

- Crisis response plan

FACILITIES/TRANSPORTATION

- Use of facilities by outside groups

- Review of interior and exterior surfaces for hazards

- Use of school vehicles, transportation of students

- Theater, lab, and art studio use

- Age and maintenance of buildings and vehicles

- Information technology security

GOVERNANCE

- Conflict of interest policies

- Executive recruitment and

compensation policies and practices

- Investment guidelines and adherence to policy

REPUTATION

- If an event occurs in one of the areas listed above, what damage could be done to the school's reputation (admissions and fundraising)? How will the school respond?

To do: Following this broad-based risk identification process, the next step is to decide what items deserve immediate attention. Using the grid below, categorize the events or experiences discussed along the axes of severity and frequency.

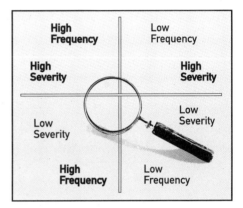

Events that have a high frequency and high severity potential (mission-critical events) move to the top of the list for the next steps in risk management, followed by high severity/lower frequency, then high frequency/low severity, and finally, a group of events that may never occur, low frequency/low severity events.

After completing the risk assessment, it is critically important to immediately address areas that present safety hazards. Knowing of a dangerous condition and failing to take appropriate corrective action as soon as possible can add significant liability to a school if an event occurs after the assessment.

STEP 2: MITIGATION

The risk identification process described above produces a list of priorities to aid in the development of policies, procedures, and practices to mitigate risk. The definition of mitigation is to reduce severity of the event, not to eliminate it altogether. Although eliminating all risks is a lofty goal, a more practical goal for risk management is to reduce the severity and frequency of incidents.

Well-written, understood, and practiced policies and procedures are the foundation for risk mitigation. It is not necessary to reinvent the wheel and draft all policies from scratch. There are many sources for policies that can be the starting point for the school's own policies. Outside legal counsel with independent school expertise should be involved in the review of policies to ensure adherence to local laws.

The school's policies should articulate how decisions will be made for exceptions to policies so that fairness and consistency are built into the process. The inclination for many schools is to find a way to say yes to new activities. This proclivity should be balanced against taking on risks that are not acceptable to the school or its insurance company. A conversation with the underwriter at the insurance company will help frame the risk, articulate a cost-benefit for undertaking the new activity

and decide whether the school (and its insurance company) are willing to share in the new risk.

Policies and procedures are the foundation of the effort, but risk management falls apart if the school does not consistently offer training to educate the community and reinforce the policies.

To do: As an initial step, develop training programs that address the highest priorities identified at the school. The following areas often rise to the top for independent school training needs:

- HARASSMENT AND DISCRIMINATION PREVENTION
- BOUNDARY TRAINING FOR TEACHERS, STAFF, AND VOLUNTEERS
- DRIVER TRAINING IF STUDENTS ARE TRANSPORTED
- PRACTICE FOR CRISIS RESPONSE, INCLUDING COMMUNICATION DURING A CRISIS

STEP 3: TRANSFERRING & SHARING

Financing

After potential risks to the school have been identified and ranked by priority of concern, and plans have been developed to try to reduce or limit the risk, what remains is to finance those identified risks.

As a school evaluates the different forms of transfer of risk and sharing of risk, it has several options to consider:

1. Through contracts with outside groups, transfer the risks through "hold harmless" agreements, indemnification, and other contract language.

2. Join a Risk Retention Group (a captive insurance company owned by policyholders), risk pool, or risk-sharing consortium to acquire insurance.

3. Purchase insurance from a commercial company.

Contracts

Schools should use legal contracts to transfer risks that it cannot control. Construction, contracted food service, contracted security, and use of school facilities by outside groups are a few of the areas that should include a contractual transfer of risk. Sometimes the outside party refuses to agree to a contract that transfers risk. In these cases, the school must decide if it wants to proceed with the agreement or find another party to perform the work.

Contracts come in many forms, and can be oral or written. Proper contracting policies are an important part of a risk management program and should specify required provisions for transferring risk, who must review the contract prior to agreement, and who is authorized to approve a contract. Too often independent schools rely on oral or "handshake" agreements in lieu of written contracts. These informal agreements can lead to confusion, misunderstandings, and perhaps the school assuming responsibility for losses that should be the responsibility of the other party. A written agreement does not have to be a lengthy document, but it should clearly state who is responsible in the case of a negative and unanticipated event. Using written agreements can save money, and potentially an important relationship, in the event of an accident.

The school's attorney should be involved in reviewing contracts and including language that appropriately transfers risk. Risk can be transferred in a contract through "hold harmless" agreements and indemnification, and by requiring that the school be added to the contracting parties' insurance policies as an additional insured. It is also important to pay attention to the limits of insurance carried by the contracting party, the coverage provided by the insurance policy, and the financial strength of the insurance company.

As an example, United Educators managed a claim in which a school thought the company it had hired to provide security was liable for any claims associated with the conduct of its employees. Unfortunately, after a sexual molestation claim was filed against a security company employee, the school discovered that the contract language shifted such risks back to the school. Other common pitfalls include exclusion of sexual molestation coverage from the contracting party's insurance and a $1 million limit on the contracting party's insurance. One million dollars might have been an appropriate amount ten years ago, but it is inadequate for catastrophic losses in the twenty-first century. The settlement value of a serious injury or death has risen significantly over the past 10 years, and insurance coverages by the school and outside parties should reflect these increased exposures.

To do: Develop a policy identifying who has authority to sign contracts. Train staff and teachers to follow the policy. Use a local attorney to review and write contract language that protects the school and transfers risk where possible. Insist on written rather than oral or handshake agreements for all work done by contractors or for use of facilities by outside groups.

In some cases, schools may allow their facilities to be used by outside groups who are not able to provide insurance, hold the school harmless, or indemnify the school in the event of an accident. To cover these situations, NBOA offers the Tenant-User Liability Insurance Policy program (TULIP) to provide access to insurance for such groups. If the school allows a group to use its facilities without appropriate protection, such as a written contract including indemnification, a hold harmless agreement, and insurance, the school should do so only with full knowledge and understanding of the risks in the event of a major loss.

Insurance

The following types of risks are commonly transferred and shared through insurance policies.

- **Property.** Provides protection in the event of fire, flood, wind, earthquake, or other peril. Most property policies cover all physical damage risks, but special attention should be paid to the proposed coverages and exclusions to ensure that appropriate limits and necessary coverages are obtained. Business interruption coverage is included in property insurance policies. If an event covered by a property insurance policy occurs, business interruption coverage would compensate for lost tuition if a school must shut down for an extended period, and the cost of temporarily relocating to another facility. Schools should take the time to understand what extra expenses they might incur and analyze a wide variety of events that could force a closure for an extended period, causing a significant loss of income. This analysis can be part of a business continuity plan.

- **Liability or casualty.** Coverage that pays for legal and indemnity expenses in the event someone (student, employee, parent, or visitor) accuses the school of causing harm. Liability/casualty policies (often called third-party policies because they cover damages to others, not the school) should be maintained in the school's permanent records. These policies should never be discarded, in case a claim is filed years later. Types of liability coverage are described below.

EDUCATORS' LEGAL LIABILITY, DESIGNED FOR SCHOOLS, INCLUDES:

- **Employment practices liability**, including discrimination and harassment allegations from faculty or staff

- **Directors and officers coverage** protecting trustees and officers against allegations of wrongdoing

- **Failure to educate** (also known as Errors and Omissions), to cover such instances as allegations that the school has not followed its policies and procedures for student discipline

General Liability

Provides coverage if students, visitors, or parents (not including employees in the course of their job) are harmed on school property or at school events. This coverage ranges from the most common claim of slips and falls to sexual molestation, athletic injuries, and field trip accidents. There are usually two limits for general liability policies, the amount that will be paid for any one claim and the total amount (aggregate) that will be paid in a given policy year. Traditionally these limits are $1 million and $3 million respectively.

Auto Liability

Provides coverage for school-owned cars, vans, and buses. When employees and parents drive their personal cars on school business, normally their personal auto insurance is the primary coverage and the school's auto liability coverage is supplementary after the personal auto policy is exhausted. It is vital to communicate this to staff and volunteers, since many people assume the school's insurance will cover them in these instances. Physical damage coverage can also be purchased for school vehicles.

Umbrella/Excess Liability

Provides coverage above the primary general liability and auto liability policies. Schools generally buy $10 to $25 million in excess coverage.

Workers' Compensation

Laws exist in all states to require insurance that covers medical costs and lost wages if an employee is injured on the job. Most states do not allow employees to bring a suit against an employer in the event of an on-the-job injury. However, some states allow injured employees of outside contractors to bring suit against the school. Special attention should be paid to contracts with food service, construction, and other outside contractors to ensure adequate workers' compensation coverage and transfer of risk. See the section above on contracts.

If a school does not take action to transfer risk, it is essentially self-insuring by acknowledging a risk exists and accepting financial responsibility for it. For risks that are rated high severity, this option should be undertaken only with the full knowledge and support of the board of trustees. For a business officer to do otherwise would be a potentially career-ending decision, as well as a financial and/or public relations disaster for the school.

PURCHASING AN INSURANCE POLICY

Independent schools without extensive professional staff may rely on insurance company professionals for guidance on driver training, ergonomic training, student activities, travel, etc. Working with a company, Risk Retention Group (RRG), or risk consortium with a long track record of specialization in independent schools will extend the limited resources of the business office staff. Other aspects to consider when buying an insurance policy:

- Financial strength of the insurance company

- Breadth of coverage (are the risks that must be covered included, or are additional policies needed?)

- References from other independent schools on claims-handling practices

- Risk management resources available:

  1. Are there engineers available to consult during building construction or renovation?

2. Will they offer training programs for worker safety?

3. Will they review policies on student activities?

After selecting a commercial company, RRG, or risk pool, the next step is deciding on appropriate deductibles and limits.

Deductibles

The first consideration is how much of the risk the school is willing to absorb before insurance begins. An analysis of the frequency of losses may help to shed light on the appropriate deductible level. Where the school has a history of frequent low-level losses, an insurance underwriter will price these into the policy if the school wants a low deductible. This can translate into paying too much for a policy that covers low-level, frequently occurring incidents. In general, insurance works best when protecting against catastrophic losses, not ordinary business activities. Maintaining an appropriate deductible while emphasizing strong risk management will be a better use of the school's resources than paying a premium for a low deductible to cover all levels of losses.

To do: Review the history of claims and dollars spent over the past three to five years, and determine how much of those initial losses the school would be willing to pay. If losses have been focused in one area, i.e., athletics or maintenance, is it possible to take a slightly higher deductible and charge the offending department for losses they incur, thereby creating an incentive for improved risk mitigation and practices? Or you might

create a central fund to pay for losses within the deductible level, sharing any funds remaining after a two- to three-year period among departments, creating an incentive for improved risk practices.

Limits

How much insurance to purchase depends on a variety of factors. The location of a school is important, since the value of claims can vary greatly depending on the judicial jurisdiction. Some areas are infamous for high legal costs and settlement values, while others benefit from a more moderate legal climate. The perception of the school in the community, the size of the endowment, and other resources will also have a bearing on the potential exposure a school might face in a catastrophic claim.

To do: Ask a broker, insurance company, RRG, or risk pool for benchmarks on limits purchased by peer institutions, factoring in size, location, and resource differences. Sharing this information with the board (and others on a need-to-know basis) is essential. Schools that decide to save modest amounts of money by reducing the amount of insurance purchased without the knowledge of the board place the school in jeopardy. Purchasing higher limits of coverage can be sound financial management, as the incremental cost is typically modest for liability coverage above $10-15 million.

Similarly, securing property insurance that provides full replacement costs, including any changes needed to meet new building codes, will support a total rebuilding in the event of a catastrophic loss. After the floods and winds of Hurricane Katrina in 2005, schools began to pay more attention to business interruption insurance purchased as part of property insurance. They reviewed the length, scope, and terms of their coverage in the event of an extended shutdown of the school. A thorough review of the school's location on flood plain maps and procurement of appropriate flood insurance is also essential, whether the school is on a coast or close to a lake, stream, or river.

TOTAL COST OF RISK AND RISK TRANSFER

Deciding to purchase an insurance policy for property, workers' compensation, liability, or automobile exposures is only the tip of the iceberg in the decision to transfer identified risks. The idea of including all aspects of risk in the cost calculation, moving beyond the price of an insurance policy to include tangible and intangible risk costs, is increasingly popular with trustees. The total cost of risk includes:

- Any deductible or self-insured retention an institution maintains

- Other tangible and intangible costs and disruptions an institution faces when an accident, lawsuit, or other risk occurs

Examples include:

1. Enrollment drops after negative publicity from a teacher's behavior with students.

2. Parents demand a series of meetings and rally around a teacher who is not promoted but who is popular with students.

3. The head of school cancels a fundraising trip to give a deposition or attend a trial.

- Costs of the risk management committee and supporting its (and outside counsel's) work in risk identification and risk mitigation, including policy development and training

- Costs of litigation or payment to a claimant that are not paid by insurance, either because the claim is not covered by the policy or there is a dispute with the insurance company

- The cost of the insurance policy

The final accounting of the total cost of risk should include the credit to the school for a reduction of losses and expenses based on a well-developed and practiced risk management program. Treating risk management as an investment rather than cost, balancing the tangible and intangible costs against the savings in reputation, money, and time for the claim that never occurs, is the ultimate goal of a total cost of risk calculation.

OUTSIDE ASSISTANCE: INSURANCE AGENTS AND BROKERS

Most independent schools use an insurance agent or broker to evaluate risk transfer needs and purchase insurance. Agents are appointed by and work for the insurance company, while brokers are independent and represent the school. Some firms act as an agent for some lines of insurance (for instance, property), while acting as a broker on other lines. It is important to understand the relationship the agent or broker has with the insurance company, RRG, or risk pool. Brokers can be paid either by commission (generally 10 to 15 percent of a premium) or by fee. Compensation by commission rather than fee raises a host of issues and can put the broker and school at odds while negotiating premiums. Following a series of high-profile investigations by state attorney generals, it is becoming standard practice for brokers and agents to provide full disclosure of the total compensation they receive for placing business.

Independent schools have a tendency to use local brokers with some tie to the school. A potential drawback of this arrangement is that local brokers may lack the broader expertise on risks that are unique to schools, such as sexual molestation, athletics, and faculty contracts. In addition, brokers with ties to schools, whether as parent, donor, or trustee, present a potential conflict-of-interest challenge for the school.

There is a growing number of brokers with a strong regional presence who have developed expertise on independent schools while also maintaining close ties to the communities they serve. A list of brokers with education expertise can be found on United Educators' website, **www.ue.org**. Brokers with special expertise in independent schools will have identified the best insurance companies for independent schools, bringing these additional resources to the relationship.

If a broker is independent, experienced with independent schools, and willing to be compensated by an annually negotiated fee rather than commission, no potential conflict exists. The broker can serve as advisor and consultant as well as provide insurance placement. This can be a cost-effective means to bring expertise to the school, and negates the need to hire an additional consultant for review of insurance policies and risk management practices.

Questions to ask a potential broker:

1. Which other independent schools do you serve?

2. What are the emerging risk trends independent schools face?

3. Are you willing to be paid by fee rather than commission?

4. Have you completed a risk assessment for an independent school?

STEP 4: MONITORING AND COMMUNICATING

Though they are frequently forgotten or treated as unimportant, monitoring and sharing the results of risk management initiatives are vital steps in a successful program. An annual report to the board should include the results of the first three steps in the risk management program:

1. Results of the risk identification exercise
   • The Risk Assessment Grid or the resulting priorities of risks are helpful ways to illustrate the breadth of risks the school faces.

Note: A summary of claims may illustrate the inherent risks but may also invite trustee-level claims management, which is not desirable.

2. New and changing risk mitigation initiatives
   - Include a list of new training programs and the number of faculty, staff, volunteers, and students receiving training.
   - Include a list of the policies and procedures created and/or reviewed

3. List of insurance policies
   - Include limits, deductibles, and name and quality of companies, RRGs, and/or risk pools used by the school.

Additional reports to the risk management committee and others involved in the risk identification and mitigation activities will help to maintain interest and motivation for continued involvement in what should be an annual process of risk management.

ENTERPRISE RISK MANAGEMENT

Enterprise risk management (ERM) is an evolving management concept used in businesses and nonprofits. ERM is a holistic or comprehensive approach to risk and can help a school think and plan for potential risks across functions or divisions. ERM proposes a range of questions to ask, from the esoteric,

"What could happen to prevent us from achieving our mission?"

to the mundane,

"What keeps us up at night?"

Asking these questions of all constituents will begin to set the stage for an effective ERM program.

The risk categories listed above are a starting point for asking the difficult ERM questions and developing a strong ERM program, ranging from investment strategies to ethics concerns to recruiting and retaining the highest quality students. ERM moves beyond the business officer's traditional scope of buying insurance and basic risk mitigation to include external economic trends that may hamper recruiting of students, demographic shifts in a community, and competition from new schools (independent, public, or charter) in the region.

ERM takes the basic concepts of risk management and extends them to cover all aspects of the school. The framework for developing an effective ERM program, addressing the most important risks and opportunities the school faces, is simply an extension of the four basic steps for tackling any risk management project. As a starting point, before embarking on a school-wide ERM initiative, this process can begin in specific areas of the school, expanding to encompass more of the school's mission at a later date.

RESOURCES

There are additional resources available on a wide variety of risk management topics including contracting, risk identification, and risk mitigation:

- Available to members of the University Risk Management Insurance Association: *www.urmia.org*
- Available to members of United Educators Insurance, a Reciprocal Risk Retention Group: *www.ue.org*

- Available to members of the National Association of College and University Attorneys: ***www.nacua.org***

- Available to members of the National Association of College and University Business Officers: ***www. nacubo.org***

NBOA

Chapter Eight

ADMISSION AND ADVANCEMENT

Your Partners in a World of Uncertainty

part one:
The Admission Office

part two:
The Advancement Office

IN THIS CHAPTER:

- Where your two worlds meet

- Balancing the bottom line with the human stories

- Financial projections: getting on the same page

- The four sectors of fundraising

- The phases of a capital campaign

part one by **James Irwin Mitchell**

and part two by **Gwinn H. Scott**

James Irwin Mitchell

Director of Admissions, Alexander Dawson School

Jim Mitchell moved to Boulder from New York City in 1971 to start JMA, Inc., a national research and communications firm, where he served as president until leaving the company in 1997. Prior to his position at Alexander Dawson School in Lafayette, Colorado, he taught in the School of Journalism at the University of Colorado, founded American Wilderness Experience, and was co-chair of the United Nations Association Afghan-Ed Project, working to restore education to the rural areas of Afghanistan. Jim is a former co-chair of the Association of Colorado Independent Schools admission group, a regular presenter at national admission conferences, on the faculty of the Admission Training Institute of the Secondary School Admission Test Board, and has a seat on the board of directors of the Association of Independent School Admission Professionals.

THE ADMISSION OFFICE

Your School's Gateway

T he world of the admission officer is an ever-changing universe of expectation, uncertainty, resilience, patience, satisfaction, dissatisfaction, long hours, and plain hard work. It is an office that deals daily with the unpredictability of human nature. Parents, grandparents, teachers, psychologists, coaches, neighbors, rival schools, siblings, and children (sometimes as young as 3 years old!) may determine whether or not your school will get a coveted candidate to attend.

Were you to ask an admission officer to list all the tasks that fall under his or her job description, an entire novel might be recited back to you. There are so many different types of jobs they do, from conducting and analyzing marketing research, demographic trends, and psychographic studies, to meetings on what kind of coffee roast to serve at a neighborhood recruiting party, to delicately asking a family to explain an apparent irregularity in their financial aid application, to working on a script for a new school video, and so forth and so on. Good admission people have eclectic interests and abilities, love people, are good communicators, can work both collaboratively and independently, know when to put their oar in, and when to back off.

"But wait," you say, "this jack-of-all-trades thing sounds familiar…." You are right! Yours is also a world in which you do "everything," wear many hats, and have to be nimble, proactive, and reactive—ready to lead. You both also share the need to get specific results, both have significant financial responsibilities, both work in a school-wide sphere, and both have crucial access to your head of school.

However, your day-to-day lives are, of course, significantly different from each other, and you two frequently have different personality "types." There is a tendency (perhaps reinforced by a stereotype) to come at a problem from different ways of thinking: the admission officer from a more non-linear, person-focused point of view, and the business officer from a more linear, bottom-line-focused point of view. However, admission officers also constantly deal with number problems and business officers constantly deal with people problems. Working together, and working to understand each other's perspectives, will create a powerful degree of harmony that can help the school be the best it can be.

To get to know your admission colleague well, try to go beyond meetings by sitting together at lunch or at a school sports event. The trust that can develop from social or even quasi-social occasions can help immeasurably in building solid working relationships. Be patient when you cannot get a yes-or-no response. Try to avoid, "What do you mean you don't know how many 7th graders we'll have six months from now?" Or, "I need to know by tomorrow how many families will receive financial aid next year!" Odds are good that your colleague is not trying to be evasive, and not trying to deprive you of information—it's just that sometimes your colleague doesn't have the answer…yet.

> *Understanding the uncertainty the admission officer lives in will help you figure out when to push for more detail and when to accept an answer at face value.*

WHERE YOUR WORLDS OVERLAP

In schools, the business and admission offices come together, at times, from different perspectives (and even priorities) to help give substance and direction to school planning, procedures, and policy. The areas in which they overlap are typically budgeting, financial aid, and strategic planning.

Office Budgeting

It would be pure folly for a business officer to present a budget to the head or board without significant input from the admission office. After all, in tuition-driven schools, admission is responsible for 85%-95% of a school's operating income. In business, a VP of Manufacturing would never think of budgeting for a capital expansion of a factory or adding another shift of workers without sitting down first for a serious chat with the VP of Sales. Those who do, do so at their own peril.

Mind you, you do not always have to agree. In fact, knowing if your admission office is generally bullish or bearish is important (check the last several years' enrollment projections against actual enrollment to get some insight). Always tap into the office's knowledge base before plunging ahead with a budget based on what might be no more than the head or board's wishful thinking. If you do not find the basis for an enrollment forecast reliable, you may suggest outside market research to help clarify the picture, thus avoiding an internal conflict by relying, at least to some degree, on an external expert opinion.

Financial Aid

Typically, the financial aid committee includes the head of school and representatives from the admission and business offices. There are many different models for handling financial aid, but most schools include a financial officer as a key player in decision-making. The financial officer can be relied on to analyze a 1040 federal income tax return and other financial statements, and should not be afraid to ask for additional documents such as loan papers or mortgages if it will help clarify a case. Remember that a school is under no obligation to give money to a family, and that any resistance to providing documentation may in itself be a red flag. The financial officer provides a valuable perspective in determining a family's ability to pay, and is in a good position to evaluate the recommendations of, for example, the SSS (School and Student Service for Financial Aid) *Parents' Financial Statement*. However, the forms and the calculations done by the service company are guidelines, and are not meant to replace the judgment of those on the financial aid committee. All they do is crunch the numbers supplied by the family. It is the committee's job to look into the accuracy of the numbers and the story behind them.

The admission officer will typically know more about the human side of a financial aid request. There might be extenuating circumstances that are not expressed by the numbers. For example, do grandparents live with the family? What is the value of the student to the school? Will the student add diversity? Is it a legacy student? Do the parents drive Fords or Ferraris? Does the family have a second home? Is Mom or Dad active in the parent organization? Where do they vacation? Does a divorced parent have single or joint custody? Is there a family trust available for tuition? How young is the student and how many years of commitment is the school prepared to make? Is the student from a key feeder school? The list could go on and on. What is key is that both financial and "human" viewpoints be taken into consideration in deciding whether a family qualifies, and if so, how much of an award to give.

Planning

Schools with foresight and the will to succeed well into the 21st century are creating administrative teams that include finance and admission directors as strategic partners with the head in the planning process. Enlightened schools ask

125

finance and admission to work together to prepare an enrollment forecast and school-wide budget. Here again, knowing your counterpart in admission is vital. Is your colleague optimistic or pessimistic? Future-oriented or present-moment oriented? Familiar with strategic thinking or new to it? Strategic planning should not be done in a vacuum, and the nexus of the worlds of the business officer and admission officer is where economics and marketing meet. It is an exciting place that has room for the measurable and the imaginable, a perfect point from which to plan for the future.

Advising Each Other

Since the jobs are so different, finance and admission people can usually be very good sounding boards for each other. Try out a proposal for the head on your admission colleague first. It can help clarify your own ideas and strengthen your presentation. Greater understanding often leads to an alliance that can help push an idea through, since it has the backing of both finance and admission. Many admission people were once teachers, although an ever-increasing number are being recruited for their marketing expertise. Typically, in neither case will there be extensive experience in finance, so by offering to advise them any time they need financial assistance, you will be sure that what you ultimately are responsible for is credible.

A YEAR IN THE LIFE OF AN ADMISSION OFFICER

Not every admission officer does everything on the following chart, and some undoubtedly do more, but it will give you a pretty good idea of the breadth of your colleague's work. The admission work year has four basic parts:

Marketing Plan

This outlines what the current market situation is for the school, what enrollment goals the school is setting for the near and long term, what the school should actively do to achieve those goals, and how the results will be measured.

Implementation

The activities that admission will create and engage in throughout the year to reach the goals of the marketing plan.

Checking

Evaluation of the marketing plan's progress: one or more checkpoints during the year to see if a mid-course correction is needed.

Assessment

A more formal evaluation of the admission season of the just-ended year. What worked? What didn't? How cost-effective was it? Were resources over-used or under-used? What should be repeated, eliminated, or tweaked? All these questions need to be answered before starting the cycle over again with the marketing plan for the next year.

A Year in the Life of an Admission Officer

TOPIC	ASSESS	PLAN	IMPLEMENT	CHECK
Advertising Purchased media: radio, TV, magazines, newspapers, internet, billboards, transit	June	July	August	January
Applicant Assessment The admission funnel: inquiry, visit, application, assessment, shadow, acceptance, enrollment	June	July	All Year	February
Budgeting Financial resources to execute the plan	June	November	July	Monthly
Branding Creating a unique identity	June	July	August	January
Departmental Staffing Maximizing interactive efficiency, minimizing redundancy	June	November	January	June
Developing a Specific Strategic Advantage Things your school has that families want and can't find elsewhere	June	July	August	January
Diversity Recruitment Ethnic, racial, socioeconomic	June	July	September-May	January
Enrollment Management Balancing class sizes, genders, and academic, athletic, and artistic excellence	August	August	September-May	January
Event Management From open houses to school fairs, retention meetings to new family picnics	June	July	August-May	January
Expanding the Admission Role Enlisting appropriate participation from faculty, staff, parents, students, administration, board, and alumni	June	July	August-May	January
Facilities Utilization Selecting different venues for specific functions	June	July	August-May	

Chart is continued on next page.

A Year in the Life
of an Admission Officer

TOPIC	ASSESS	PLAN	IMPLEMENT	CHECK
International Student Recruiting Brokers, agents, direct recruiting, travel	June	July	September-July	March
Local/Regional Independent School Groups Joint, collegial research, professional development, and marketing	April	May	September-May	March
Marketing *EVERYTHING!*	June	July	August	January
Measuring Results Keeping a finger on the pulse of how everything is working	June	July	September-August	Monthly
New Family Welcome Program Helping new families integrate into the school community	August	September	May-August	July
Parent Council Filling a key pipeline with information	June	July	September-August	January
Publications Marketing materials such as viewbook, inserts, postcards, newsletters, etc.	June	July	August-May	January
Public Relations: **Internal Communications** Keeping everyone in the school community connected	April	June	August-May	January
Public Relations: **External Communications** Working with the media to cover the school	June	July	August-May	January
Real Estate Brokers/HR Directors Directing relocating families to the school	June	July	October, April	May, November
Research and Needs Assessment Getting information needed for good decision-making	June	July	August-May	Monthly

Chart is continued on next page.

A Year in the Life
of an Admission Officer

TOPIC	ASSESS	PLAN	IMPLEMENT	CHECK
Statistics Knowing all about families, funnel trends, interviews, why people did and did not choose the school	June	July	September-August	Monthly
Summer Camps/Programs Research, marketing, recruitment	August	January	February, June, July	May
Website Manage online identity of the school	June	July	August-May	Daily

These are "simply" the predictable, recurring tasks of the office, because, as in your life, each day is also filled with the unpredictable needs of the school. The most important one is meeting with prospective families (and speaking to them on the phone). Then there are the special reports for the head and board, which are necessary but time-consuming. It is also important for admission people to have a pulse on the life and culture of the school. Contact with students through coaching, substitute teaching, clubs, chaperoning a dance, or going on a class trip are all worthwhile activities.

WORKING TOGETHER

Time is probably the most precious commodity in a school, with everyone wishing there were more of it to do not only what has to be done, but to be able to reflect upon what could be done to move the school forward with new ideas and programs.

Because of this, everyone feels that their time is very valuable, so when you have a meeting with your admission colleagues, make sure that you are well prepared, and expect the same from them. Be clear about the subject of the meeting so they will know how to get ready, and tell them in advance how long you expect the meeting to last. Try to avoid the jargon trap, or your colleagues may misinterpret what you are saying. As with all good meetings, summarize it before you break up, and follow it up with a list of action items (noting whose responsibility it is to complete each one) and a timeline. These simple steps can save many good ideas from descending into the black hole of forgotten initiatives.

Since admission people live largely in a world of uncertainty and negotiable outcomes, you are more likely to get the outcomes you are looking for if you engage them early in the process of problem-solving. They should reciprocate, and consult with you before promising anything that would impact the budget, fiscal policy, or financial protocols. By keeping communication lines open and honest, you can nip potential problems in the bud.

To run a good office, your admission colleagues need to know how to build a zero-based budget, how to make projections, how to manage their budget, and how to make cuts if they are asked to. Your willing participation upfront to help them understand these tasks will make life better and easier throughout the year. Remember, too, that in most cases they are your peers. They do not work for you, and you do not work for them. Working as colleagues who keep the big picture in mind, who never forget that even the most mundane tasks serve those larger ideals, you and your admission officer can be great partners, supporting each other through challenges, and sharing the joys of each others' successes.

NB⦿A

Gwinn H. Scott
Senior Consultant, Marts & Lundy, Inc.

Gwinn H. Scott joined Marts & Lundy, Inc., a national fundraising consulting firm based in New Jersey, after 18 years at The Baldwin School in Bryn Mawr, Pennsylvania, an independent school for girls. While at Baldwin, she served as the alumnae director and as the director of development. As senior consultant at Marts & Lundy, Inc., Gwinn has served numerous independent schools, including National Cathedral School, William Penn Charter School, The Lawrenceville School, Holton-Arms School, and Madeira School. She has also worked with many colleges and universities on a variety of fundraising issues, including Barnard, Carnegie Mellon University, Middlebury College, Mount Holyoke College, and Tulane University. Gwinn has served on the board of directors of Marts & Lundy, Inc., and as a trustee of the Baldwin School. She is a graduate of the Baldwin School, and attended Salem College and the University of Pennsylvania.

THE ADVANCEMENT OFFICE

Fundraising: Behind the Scenes

The institutional advancement officer is often caught between the donor and the business office, and must skillfully satisfy both: responding flexibly to donor needs while adhering to sound donation procedures. The intent of this chapter is to give the reader a sense of what it feels like to be in these shoes, and to offer suggestions for how the business officer can anticipate the needs of the institutional advancement officer ("IAO") so that the two can work in harmony.

There are four sectors of institutional advancement ("IA") as defined by CASE (the Council for Advancement and Support of Education), a membership organization that supports IA in independent schools, colleges, and universities— nationally and internationally. These areas are constituent relations, fundraising, communications, and advancement services.

CONSTITUENT RELATIONS

These are the relationships a school has with its alumni, its current parents, parents of graduates, grandparents of students, friends and faculty, and foundations and corporations. Some schools employ directors of alumni relations who manage programs designed to involve alumni in the school. Such programs might include annual reunions, book clubs, regional gatherings, alumni awards, young alumni programs, student internship programs, etc. Generally, a school will have an alumni board of key volunteers who implement these programs.

Schools also have current parent associations comprised of parent volunteers who implement programs like benefits, dinner dances, book fairs, pumpkin sales, etc. Usually these two groups (alumni and parents) are managed by a paid professional in the IA office. The purpose of these organizations is to connect (or reconnect) their constituents with the school to ultimately instill a desire to give voluntary financial support.

Corporate and foundation relations are usually under the purview of the IAO with some help from key volunteers who have relationships with these organizations. In most cases, proposals for financial support are generated in the IA office and reinforced by the volunteer. Generally, corporate support is limited for independent schools (except through corporate matching gift programs). Foundation support, however, can be quite significant, depending on the relationships between volunteers and foundation boards.

Fundraising

This sector refers to annual giving support, capital and endowment support, and deferred or planned giving support from constituents of the school. The IA office oversees all aspects of the fundraising program. In most IA offices there is a director of annual giving who implements the solicitation of alumni, current and past parents, grandparents, friends, faculty, corporations, and foundations.

- **ANNUAL FUNDS**
  An annual gift is typically repeated yearly and contributed for current operating support of the school, though some donors make annual fund gifts for designated purposes. The annual fund director orchestrates a program of direct mail (2-6 solicitations per year), telephone, email, and personal face-to-face visits for the requesting of gifts, and relies on a vast number of key volunteers to make the program successful. In larger schools with significant resources, there can be a number of assistants to the director, some of whom carry 100 to 200 prospective donors each. In most schools, annual fund goals are set based on capacity, history, demographic change, and the needs of the school budget.

- **CAPITAL FUNDS**
  Campaigns for capital and endowment support can operate at the same time as the annual campaign. Many schools seek capital support as an ongoing operation, others as a special 5-7 year program. These campaigns often request significant financial support for new structures, renovations, fields, tennis and squash courts, pools, or performing arts facilities; they may also raise funds for

endowing programs for faculty salaries, sabbaticals, financial aid for students, etc. The IAO directs this aspect of the fundraising program. Some schools are able to hire one or more major gift officers to assist in the solicitation of major donor prospects. In capital initiatives, donors have the option to pay their gifts over a period of 3-5 years, hopefully providing them a way to make a truly large gift to the school. In many cases, donors give appreciated securities for these purposes. Some donors can also contribute gifts of closely held stock, which the school may have to hold for a certain period of time. Other donors give gifts of highly valued personal property such as artwork, antiques, real estate, etc., which must be evaluated by an independent appraiser.

- **PLANNED/DEFERRED GIFTS**
The area of planned or deferred gifts gives the prospective donor an opportunity to contribute to a special purpose while living or after death. These gifts are generally a source of support for endowments and major capital initiatives. Some schools have IA officers with special expertise in this area. Others hire a planned giving officer or use outside resources, such as fundraising consultants or the school's counsel. These gifts can be executed through bequests, pooled income funds, annuities, income-producing properties, or charitable trusts, and usually involve the donor, a lawyer, and the IAO and/or school head.

COMMUNICATIONS

The communications sector of IA includes interfacing with all forms of media (from print to internet). Some schools also include writing, editing, and managing admission materials and curriculum copy in the communications officer's job description. Depending on the size and resources of the school, there could be one to three communications professionals on staff; other schools may use outside sources for publication design or writing. Communicating the spirit and essence of the school is crucial to developing the school's image in the community. Some school communications officers have expertise in public relations, which can be invaluable in times of crisis. Today, there is significant exposure of the negative aspects of incidents in school life, which takes the best planning to counter.

A crucial area of overlap between the communications director/IAO and the business officer is the new 2008 Form 990 (to be filed for fiscal years ending January 1, 2009, and later). The revised form requires a detailed summary of a school's mission and programs. It is advisable to have the communications director or IAO complete this section (rather than the business officer), so that the language is compelling and in line with the school's other branding. This form is publicly available to prospective parents; with the right touch, it can become an excellent marketing tool.

ADVANCEMENT SERVICES

This is the area where IA staff are responsible for general record-keeping and reports: prospect research, data entry, acknowledgments of gifts, biographical information on constituents, etc. Sometimes referred to as the "back room," this sector supports all the work done in the IA office. Without it, the programs could not run. All names, addresses, phone numbers, and email addresses for donors and prospective donors are included in these "back room" computer files, along with past giving histories. Biographical information, including colleges attended, occupational history, volunteer activities, and number of children are all added to the record and to individual profiles prepared by staff to help develop a strategy for cultivation and solicitation. Weekly and monthly reports on gifts are generated to keep volunteers and staff apprised of progress toward annual and capital goals. Formal gift acknowledgments and personal letters of thanks are generated in the IA office. Occasionally, in anticipation of a capital effort, the IAO will contract with an outside vendor to screen the constituency for indicators of wealth. A multi-pronged effort goes into securing funds to ensure the future of the school.

One of the responsibilities of the board of trustees is to ensure the financial stability of the school. Most schools have an institutional advancement committee, which helps plan campaigns and initiatives, which are then recommended to the full board for approval. It is well-known that trustees must lead the way in all fundraising programs with their own personal commitments and then engage others to follow. In years past, trustees looked at cost-per-dollar-raised to evaluate the effectiveness of the IA program, hoping to spend as little as possible. There has recently been a shift in this thinking to an expanded sense of fundraising staff dollars achieving greater ROI (return on investment).

WHERE DOES THE BUSINESS OFFICER FIT IN?

The answer? Everywhere. The business officer understands the vagaries of the operating budget—what tuition must be, what faculty salaries can be, and what role voluntary contributions play in the balance. Typically, when 80% of the budget comes in through tuition and 80% is paid out in salaries and benefits, there is little left for other expenses. And so the greatest attribute of the business officer should be a willingness to communicate and collaborate with the IAO on the issues surrounding the operating budget and the need for balance. This relationship is a key factor in the success of the school's fundraising program.

IA officers are constantly pushing the envelope, so to speak, in engaging and involving potential donors. They get their prospects passionate about programs and projects. They spend countless hours (and even years) developing relationships with prospective donors in order to ask for a significant gift. Often viewed as "party animals," IAOs are continually engaging prospects in the life of the school, recounting interesting anecdotes about students or faculty, reviewing the purposes of a campaign, and persuading prospective donors of the impact their gifts can have on the school.

The business officer has a great deal of information that can be critical to the IA operation, and which can help the IAO in networking or strategizing. The business officer should meet with the IAO early on to work on a variety of projects such as the setting of the operating budget. What will the annual giving number be? Some schools use the line item number in the budget for their annual giving public goal. How is that number calculated? Is it a percentage above last year's actual receipt? Or is it a much greater number based on budgetary deficit? What is attainable? What does the prospect pool look like and will there be a new initiative implemented in the annual giving program? These are topics that provide a rich conversation between the IAO and the business officer.

STRATEGIC PLANNING

Many schools are involved in long-range planning for the future. This requires plotting tuition increases, financial aid allocations, faculty salary and benefit increases as well as annual giving support, endowment income support, and all the other resources available for the next five or so years. It means that the two officers must work together to discuss these specific aspects of the planning process. It seems reasonable for the IAO to have a seat on the finance committee of the school and the business officer to have a seat on the IA committee. This adds to the understanding of the checks and balances of each operation and ensures optimum results.

CAPITAL CAMPAIGNS

Quite often, after a long-range planning process has been accomplished, a capital campaign is approved by the trustees. A typical campaign schedule involves a two-year quiet phase and a five-year public phase. Sometimes the campaign is preceded by an internal

audit to determine if the school's IA office and administration is ready to conduct a campaign. In many cases, schools will conduct feasibility studies and/or consultation gatherings to ascertain whether the very top prospective donors understand and approve of the objectives and potential goals of a campaign. Feedback from the testing phase (feasibility study and consultation gatherings) is important in calculating how much the school might raise. Wealth screening of the constituency will also add to these calculations. The IAO will then draft a case for support to be shared with potential donors: a compelling document that identifies the needs of the school, communicates why these needs are essential for the future, and explains what the costs of these needs are.

In most schools, the campaign budget is created outside of the operating budget. The IAO will prepare a campaign budget with line items including travel costs, publications, consulting, additional staffing and benefits, entertainment, kick-off events, meetings, donor recognition, audio-visual equipment, and information systems. The business officer should review this budget before it is sent on to the IA or finance committee. A campaign budget could be as much as 10-20% of the campaign goal.

The first two years of a campaign are sometimes called the "quiet leadership phase." This phase almost always involves a lead gift (which may determine in large part what can be raised, and can be as much as 12-20% of the overall goal). Next, the board will be called upon to make significant contributions. The combined gifts of the trustees are critical for success. If the board is perceived as making stretch gifts, the constituency will follow. Results from the quiet leadership phase of the campaign will also assist in determining a final goal. A campaign may also be kicked off by an advance from the endowment, to be paid back with interest.

The business officer and IAO will need to work on the gift policies and procedures for the campaign. Decisions on the following issues should be resolved before the campaign gets underway: named gift opportunities for brick and mortar and endowment objectives, gift guidelines (including what types of gifts will be included in the campaign total and which will be excluded), use of written pledges, the counting of verbal pledges, donor requests for uses of gifts, use of matching gifts, gifts in kind, realized bequests, bequest intentions, life income gifts, charitable trusts, gifts of life insurance, and gift annuities. Once decisions are made about gift policies the trustees should approve the procedures.

Business officers need to understand the intricacies of gift-giving—since donations are tricky and often unpredictable. If the trustees approve a capital goal of some magnitude, it does not follow that the gifts will accrue immediately. More than likely, the gifts will follow behind the expenditures for a campaign effort. If the campaign involves bricks and mortar, the gifts will not necessarily come in when bills must be paid. The IAO and the business officer should collaborate on these points. Many schools invest in an issue of bonds to cover the cost of new or renovated

buildings. This bond issue means that the IAO will be asking donors for unrestricted gifts to the school, as the bond will go toward the new building.

USING CONSULTANTS

Many schools have times in their lives when outside expertise is important, in particular during a capital campaign, when aspirations for the school may be great, yet IA staffing is new, young, or under-trained. Often, business office consulting is necessary to plan for the increased activity, particularly when planned gifts are involved. Outside help can also be employed for a host of other issues, including public relations, institutional branding, marketing, strategic planning, deferred maintenance, technology, and investing. This expertise comes with costs, but can be of tremendous benefit to the school.

CONCLUSION

Philanthropy is about giving people who care deeply about the school an opportunity to make a difference…to advance the cause of that school and ensure its future. It's about endorsing people's belief in the mission of the school through the support of its leadership, programs, students, and faculty. While you, as the business officer, are not out "selling" the school the way the IAO is, you are still intricately involved in the process. When you and the IAO work in harmony, your partnership can produce optimum results for your treasured institution.

NBOA

Chapter Nine

TECHNOLOGY
Bits & Bytes, Dollars & Cents

IN THIS CHAPTER:

- How to budget for an unknowable future

- Who should run the show?

- Creating a fiscally responsible technology plan

- TCO & ROI: the unique case of education

- Acceptable use policies & other approaches to internet safety

by Terry Decker

Terry Decker
Director of Technology, The Westminster Schools

As Director of Technology for the Westminster Schools in Atlanta, Georgia, Terry Decker is responsible for the institution's academic and administrative technology teams, technology budgeting, and technology vision and strategic planning. Under Terry's direction, the school has engaged in many exciting technology initiatives highlighting student achievement and innovation in academics and sports. Terry has worked with numerous educational institutions, both public and private, for over 14 years, collaborating with district administrators, technology coordinators, and teachers to help institutions design and implement comprehensive technology plans. Terry's experience has given him a fundamental and unique background with which to help schools reach their technology goals while simultaneously reducing costs. Recently, Terry authored an article for the Technology Issue of *Net Assets* entitled "Budgeting for Technology in Education: The Business Officer Confronts the New ROI."

TECHNOLOGY

Bits & Bytes, Dollars & Cents

Technology: what once started as a vocational program has been transformed into one of the most vital components in the educational world. This change has not only affected the way students learn, but also the way institutions operate. Some of the many challenges that business officers face in schools include how to:

- ACCURATELY FORECAST TECHNOLOGY EXPENSES OUT ONE, TWO, OR FIVE YEARS
- DETERMINE THE VALUE OF ADDING TECHNOLOGY
- FIND THE RIGHT LEVEL OF STAFFING TO SUPPORT IT

Developing an all-inclusive technology plan enables schools to anticipate future expenses and integrate new technology in an organized and fiscally responsible way. An effective technology plan will address foreseen initiatives and detail procedures for tackling new ideas and technologies as they become available. The technology plan should be viewed as a road map. there is no one right path, but it should lead in an organized and responsible direction. The plan should address the following areas of budgeting:

- analysis of total cost of ownership (TCO) and return on investment (ROI)
- staffing and organizational structure
- policy and procedures

CREATING A TECHNOLOGY PLAN

Developing a viable plan requires input and buy-in from all members of the school community (not just the technology department). First, form a Technology Planning Group (TPG), which should include board members, administrators, teachers, technology staff, students, and parents, if possible. It's important to survey these different groups to hear their thoughts on the current state of technology within the school and their desired enhancements, as they will ultimately be its users. Establish your school's technology goals (discussed in more detail below), and make sure other members of the school community have the opportunity to vet them.

From this initial survey, you will be able to evaluate the school's current position and its most pressing needs. Work with your TPG to compile a list of improvements, prioritized according to available funding and relevance to the school's technology goals. Every school is different, but the general rule is to select those projects that affect the largest number of users or meet a critical need.

The next step is to work within the team to determine where the school wants to be—or is required to be—in terms of technology. Sometimes this is determined by state and federal regulations. Most states have specific requirements for technology planning and these should be evaluated before fully developing a plan. Even if your school is not required to follow the state or federal regulations, it is still a good idea to at least become familiar with the laws. This will give the team a good idea of the goals of other schools within the state.

Once a master technology plan is determined, each individual department of the school should establish its own technology plan. These departmental plans should include expectations for incorporating technology, establish minimum technology proficiency for departmental staff, and establish procedures on managing the use of new technology.

Once requirements and priorities are determined, the TPG should focus on budgets, professional development, TCO/ROI analysis, policy and procedures, and staffing. Once these are complete, the TPG can present the plan to the school board or senior administration for approval, then share the approved plan with the entire school community.

BUDGETING

Creating an accurate technology budget can seem daunting to even the most seasoned business officer. Since technology is integrated into all aspects of education, it can be difficult to try to lump it into one or two areas. You should be able to accurately build a technology plan to cover the next three years. You can extend it to cover five years but due to the fast pace of change in this field, the fourth and fifth years of the budget should be considered general guidelines only.

This budget should include salary and benefits for those faculty and staff allocated to technology. The following chart gives a suggested breakdown:

Salary and Benefits	20%
Operations[1]	15%
Professional Development	5%
Capital Improvements[2]	15%
Software	10%
Hardware	35%

1. Funds used by the technology group for internal purposes. 2. Technology that lasts longer than 5 years or is used for infrastructure.

Essentials. The first step in creating the budget is to include items essential to the school's operations. These can include telecommunications (internet and phone service), annual software licenses, and hardware maintenance agreements. These required pieces of the budget should be accounted for before anything else is considered. The amounts may change from year to year but they should be treated like utilities in terms of their importance. Also essential are items that the technology department members use throughout the year, such as consultant/contractor fees, software and hardware used by the technology team, furniture and office equipment, and training.

Salaries. The next step is to add faculty and staff salaries. This number should include both the academic technology group and the administrative technology team. Only allocate the portion of the salary that is related to teaching or supporting technology. This will give you a more accurate picture as to the total amount spent on staffing.

Professional development. It is important that enough funds be allocated for teacher training, especially when introducing a new technology initiative, such as a new piece of hardware or software. These funds can be used to cover the costs of hiring a training specialist, or paying salaries for those who attend training outside the normal workday.

66

Technology is one of the largest line items in a school's budget, and the need seems to increase every year. Typically, technology spending should average between 6-8% of the total operating budget.

99

Many different educational technology conferences are held every year, some on a national or state level, and others local. The largest is the National Educational Computing Conference (NECC), sponsored by the International Society for Technology in Education (*www.iste.org*). This yearly conference is a great place to learn how to better utilize your existing technology and evaluate new trends in the field. The NECC conference is a terrific environment in which to network with other schools from around the world on the use of technology in the classroom. The professional development budget should try to allocate enough funds to allow the school's key technology staff and administrators to attend these conferences.

Capital improvements. This section of the budget pertains to items that are considered infrastructure, or which have a long life expectancy (greater than five years). These include cabling, network switching and routers, video distribution, and telecommunications equipment. In general, the equipment cost for this area is significantly higher than other areas due to the high volume of data it is designed to support. This is especially true if a school is looking to update outdated technology equipment. Outside of major upgrades, the capital improvements budget is designed to cover the replacement or addition of small numbers of equipment.

In most cases, equipment spent on capital improvements can be depreciated over a longer period of time. The following table gives an example of a depreciation system that is generally used for property placed in service after 1986:

In Wall / Ground Copper Cabling	25 years
Fiber-Optic Cabling	30 years
Network Switching & Routing	10 years
Wireless Access Points	7 years
Lightning Protection	25 years
Video Distribution Equipment	15 years
Digital Telephones	15 years

Software. This line item encompasses software used throughout the school,

including the following applications: desktop (Office, etc.), antivirus, classroom management, image editing, and email. Also include any software used at the classroom level in this list.

The current trend by the major software vendors is to encourage schools to purchase annual licensing contracts. Some have even removed the option to purchase an upgrade of a product if you have not paid for annual subscriptions. This can greatly increase the cost of the school's software budget. In most cases, unless the school plans on upgrading the software before three years, they are better off not purchasing annual software subscriptions. The obvious exception to this would be antivirus and security software, but some companies do not charge for updates and only charge if a school needs to add more licenses or wants to upgrade to the latest version.

Open source software is also starting to take hold due to the increasing cost of commercial software. Open source software allows an individual or organization to use or even modify a program for its own use. Most are free while others charge a nominal fee. The quality and functionality of this software can rival that of commercial counterparts. The one thing to consider when using open source software is that there is no one to call in the event of a problem, though most open source software applications have an online service area where people can ask questions, propose enhancements, or report problems. Some of the more popular open source software used in schools include:

- **OPENOFFICE**

Consists of a word processor, spreadsheet program, presentation software, drawing tools, and a database program. This program can read to and write from Microsoft Office® applications.

- **GIMP**

Image-editing tool similar to Adobe Photoshop®

- **SCRIBUS**

Desktop publishing similar to Adobe PageMaker®

- **MYSQL**

Database software similar to Microsoft SQL Server®

Hardware. The final section of a technology budget is hardware. This includes desktops, laptops, printers, network servers, and other devices used within the school. Hardware is the largest section of a technology budget, but the actual percentage of the total budget dedicated to hardware will vary from year to year depending on the school's "refresh rate" (the rate at which a specific piece of hardware is due to be replaced). Most schools operate on a four-year refresh rate. This works well if the hardware is used for standard applications such as internet browsing, office applications, or email. The downside is that in most cases the final year will not include a vendor warranty, unless it was purchased with the equipment.

Any time a new piece of equipment is added, it must be determined whether the purchase is a one-time purchase or will be added to the refresh list. All equipment should be placed in one of these two categories.

Which type of computer hardware to purchase has been an area of debate for many years in the education field. Some schools are mostly Macintosh-based while others are PC, but most are a combination of both. There is no clear advantage to either platform; it all depends on which direction the school wants to take. In general, a Macintosh system can cost between 10-15% more than the comparable PC-based system, but the Macintosh does have an easier user interface that can reduce the amount of training required.

TOTAL COST OF OWNERSHIP (TCO) AND RETURN ON INVESTMENT (ROI)

TCO and ROI are used throughout the business world to look at the costs associated with a specific capital expenditure and evaluate its benefit to the organization. Due to the popularity of these methods in business, many school systems have adopted their own form of TCO and ROI strategies to examine the overall costs of specific initiatives. Developing a TCO and ROI plan for an educational environment requires changes to the typical TCO formula.

TCO analysis was first introduced by the Gartner Group in 1987. It focuses not only on the direct cost of the expenditure (i.e., the initial purchase), but all other costs associated with that purchase. An automobile would be a good example. A TCO analysis on an automobile would not only look at the initial price paid for the vehicle but also the routine maintenance, repairs, and fuel required to operate it. Typically, a TCO review establishes an anticipated life expectancy for the purchase to help determine the overall financial impact over a specific period of time.

ROI, on the other hand, tries to determine the value of a specific acquisition to the organization. Using the automobile example above, you can determine ROI by gauging the overall impact of the purchase. If you needed to use the vehicle to get to work and there were no other alternatives, the ROI would be positive: you would eventually make more money than the initial purchase price. If, on the other hand, you could have taken public transportation for less, the ROI would be negative. Financial costs are not the only things to consider when looking at ROI, but this tends to be the area that most people focus on.

In general, to create a TCO you need to first establish the anticipated life expectancy of the purchase. Then add in all the other costs associated with it (maintenance, staffing, support, training, utilities, etc.), divide that total by the life expectancy, and arrive at the TCO for the purchase. While this is a simplified method of calculating TCO, it does give the user a good idea of the true costs associated with acquiring a certain asset. Many educational institutions overlook the ancillary costs associated with a purchase.

A great resource for conducting TCO and ROI analysis is the website provided by the Consortium for School Networking (CoSN), a national organization serving the K-12 market that focuses on technology to improve learning. CoSN's web site for TCO can be located at **www.classroomtco.org**, and their ROI at **www.edtechvoi.org**. (CoSN refers to ROI as VOI, or Value Of Investment.)

STAFFING AND ORGANIZATIONAL STRUCTURE

Staffing and structuring correctly are vital steps in creating a positive technology environment for a school. An adequate number of staff dedicated to supporting technology can increase productivity within the school community and foster a better learning environment. The better people are prepared to use technology the more willing they will be to use it. A sufficient staffing level also helps to reduce the amount of downtime experienced by users.

Staffing a technology department for a school varies greatly from the standard business model used for companies. Staffing is typically determined by estimating the user-to-staff ratio. This can vary depending on the type of business and the corporate philosophy, but in general the number is 50 to one: for every 50 users in a company there is one technology support person needed. The average in the educational field is 140 to one. While this may sound inadequate, in most cases this is acceptable because the average educational user does not require the same level of support as a corporate counterpart. However, the older the student, the greater the support required. Older students are more reliant on technology and use it to a higher degree than those in the lower grades.

The amount of technology within a school can also help determine the amount of staff required to support it (not including academic support, those who support classroom instruction and teacher training). The following formula details the number of support staff required based on the number of computers within a school:

$$S = (C / R)$$

S = SUPPORT STAFF
C = NUMBER OF COMPUTERS
R = LEVEL OF RISK (100, 140, 200)

What is risk? It can be defined as the potential negative impact of a future event. Risk can be assigned to taking an action as well as to not taking the action. If a school does not have an adequate number of staff positions to support its technology, the inherent risks include longer periods of downtime, loss of productivity, and a reluctance to use technology. On the other hand, having too many people can cause higher salary and benefit costs, lack of motivation on the part of technology staff, and inefficient use of resources.

Choosing a lower level of risk in one area can allow you to accept a higher level in another. For example, if a school has a risk level of 50 for academic support positions, this may allow for a higher level of risk in the support staff. In most cases the academic support positions can help to reduce the amount of work required by the support staff, reducing the total number of staff required.

If a school has 500 computers (this can include laptops, desktops, servers, etc.) and assumes a risk level of 150, the amount of support personnel required would be four. If a school changed its risk level to 100, the number would be five, 200 would mean three, etc.

Determining the number of academic support personnel can also be determined by a formula, but it is based on the number of faculty they must support rather than the number of computers. The risk numbers are considerably lower due to the nature of the work. Academic support personnel work directly with faculty and students and this interaction requires a greater amount of time to be effective. The formula for academic support is:

$$AS = (T / R)$$

AS = ACADEMIC SUPPORT
T = NUMBER OF FACULTY
R = LEVEL OF RISK (50, 70, 100)

If a school has 300 teachers, and has a risk level of 70, then using the above formula the number of academic support staff required would be four. A risk level of 50 would require six, and at a risk level of 100 would require three.

The organizational structure of the technology staff is also an important part of the technology plan. A centralized technology department that provides both administrative and academic support personnel can help reduce overlap in duties, reduce support cost, and improve communication.

Larger schools tend to separate the administrative and academic technology groups. Each has its own budget and reports to its own supervisor. In most cases this is rooted in history. when technology first arrived in schools, it was primarily used for administrative support, such as business office functions, attendance, and grading systems. The technology support personnel were hired to support these functions and they often reported to the business officer.

Once technology started to take hold in the classroom, most schools used existing faculty to support it. They had a good understanding of the classroom environment and were in most cases less expensive than dedicated technology support personnel. These technology support faculty would report to a principal or an assistant superintendent. There would be limited collaboration between the two groups and each tended to go in its own direction, regardless of what the other was doing.

With technology use increasing throughout every school, and budgets straining to keep pace, it makes sense to merge the two groups. A unified departmental structure has several advantages:

IMPROVED COMMUNICATION
The new group will collaborate together on projects that will enable them to better understand what is happening within the school.

IMPROVED TEAMWORK
The group will not see one another as outsiders vying for the same budgetary resources, space, or time.

REDUCED COSTS
By combining the two groups, a school can increase productivity and establish a certain level of cross-training, requiring less staffing.

CENTRALIZED MANAGEMENT
Establishing a single management team will ensure that the entire technology team is working efficiently and following a single plan.

A technology department requires a technology director responsible for overall planning and operations. Smaller schools may assign multiple roles to a single position, e.g., the technology director might also be in charge of the school network. This person is responsible for supporting the mission of the school system as well as helping to design and implement the technology plan. Departmental composition determines the director's superior. For schools that elect to separate academic and administrative departments, the administrative group should fall under the chief financial officer of the school, while the academic group should report to the chief academic officer. A unified department should report to an assistant superintendent or chief academic officer, because a unified department affects all areas of the school and has direct contact with the classroom environment. But each school is different; the administration must evaluate the strength of the technology director as well as the structure of the school.

In selecting a technology director, care should be taken to ensure that he or she is able to apply standard business practices in an educational environment. The director should have experience working with students, teachers, and school administrators, as well as an understanding of the school's operational guidelines. The director needs to be a good communicator, and be able to understand broad technology terminology. If the director has limited or no experience in an educational environment but is a good fit in all other aspects of the job, then the director should be assigned a faculty or administrative mentor.

All technology staff should have experience working in a classroom environment, if only for a few days during the school year. This will enable the staff member to see what is happening in the classroom and better understand the use of the technology. This understanding can help to reduce user frustration and help foster better communication between the technology staff and the school community.

Some schools contract with outside vendors for administrative support in an effort to reduce costs. While it may be less expensive to hire an outside vendor there are also risks to consider:

LITTLE OR NO CROSS-TRAINING
Companies that provide technical staffing solutions typically employ personnel from the business world. The contractors soon learn that working in an educational environment is different from the business world. What makes sense in one area does not necessarily hold true in the other. Cross-training of employees allows for a faster response to issues that arise within a classroom. A contractor may be able to fix a problem, but may not be able to explain to a teacher the benefits of using that device within the classroom. The faculty member is then required to place another

call to academic support personnel to have questions answered.

LITTLE CONTROL OF THE QUANTITY OR QUALITY OF THE SUPPORT PERSONNEL
Contract employees have limited loyalty to the school and may not possess the patience and clear communication skills required for work in education.

The advantages of hiring an outside vendor are greater for smaller institutions that have a limited budget for staff, while larger institutions are better served with in-house personnel.

POLICIES AND PROCEDURES

Every school should have certain policies and procedures in place for acquiring and using technology. Schools should maintain:

- A PURCHASE POLICY
- AN INVENTORY CONTROL POLICY
- AN INTERNET SAFETY POLICY
- AN ACCEPTABLE USE POLICY

A purchasing policy is used to set controls on the acquisition of new technology. The policy is used to ensure that the purchase:

- is obtained at the best possible price
- can be supported by the technology team
- is in line with technology plan goals
- is inventoried

All technology purchases should be approved by a designated purchasing staff member within the technology team (regardless of the origin of funding). This person is responsible for ensuring that all costs are considered for the purchase, that the purchase follows all licensing laws, and that the price is within limits.

A centralized purchasing system also allows for a more accurate school inventory. Once a product arrives, it is immediately entered into a central inventory management system, tagged, and distributed to the user. The technology team can then enter all the relevant information (date purchased, price paid, location of equipment, etc.). An accurate inventory has many uses including creating an accurate budget, ensuring proper licensing for software, allowing generation of depreciation schedules, and providing helpful information in case of loss.

With the wide use of the internet in education, care needs to be taken to ensure that it is used responsibly and that users understand the consequences of their actions. While there is a lot of equipment that can limit inappropriate material, no system can prevent it all. All school systems need to take reasonable steps to ensure the privacy of their users. This includes having a properly installed firewall, internet filter, and email spam filter. All security systems should be reviewed yearly to ensure they are functioning properly and updated with the latest security settings.

There is debate among educational technology leaders about the use of internet filters and whether their benefits outweigh the costs. Some schools do not use filters at all, and monitor inappropriate internet behavior in other ways. However,

the U.S. Department of Education stipulates that any educational institution that receives e-rate funding must have an internet filter in place. While non e-rate schools are not bound by these regulations, it is still something to be considered, as it can prevent users from viewing inappropriate material, ensure that a school's limited bandwidth is used primarily for educational purposes, and provide an easy method of tracking usage.

Yearly internet safety training is important for all users of the school's network. Training for students should be classroom-based to allow the students to ask questions and focus on the material without distractions. The faculty and staff training can be text-based. A great resource for both schools and parents is GetNetWise (*www.getnetwise.org*). This site details the risks associated with various internet communication tools and provides suggestions for reducing risk.

The acceptable use policy (AUP) is an important document that helps keep users informed of what behavior is and is not allowed, and what level of privacy should be expected on the school's systems. Many recommend separate AUPs for students and faculty, as faculty are typically given a greater amount of freedom than students. Some schools require parental consent before a student is allowed to access the school's systems. This is to ensure that if issues arise parents have been informed of the school's expectations. All AUPs should contain the following information:

- What is allowed & not allowed on the school's systems

- The level of privacy (if any) that can be expected

- User responsibilities & expectations

- The school's policies on copyright laws

- Consequences for violating the AUP

The AUP is an important document for both the school and the users to help establish the primary rules and regulations when using school equipment. The AUP should be posted in all computer labs and libraries to ensure that the users are able to use it as a reference when needed.

CONCLUSION: "DIGITAL NATIVES"

Today's students have been surrounded by technology nearly from birth. Many have spent their entire lives surrounded by and using computers, videogames, ipods, cell phones, and videocameras, and they text in a strange language which seems to have lost all its vowels. They are considered "digital natives," while most teachers and administrators are "digital immigrants." It can be daunting to try to navigate their unfamiliar universe, but ignoring it ensures that the students will not have the best guidance they need to confront the world they will be living in (and creating): that of the 21st century.

NBOA

Chapter Ten

ENDOWMENT MANAGEMENT

Saving Today, Preserving Tomorrow

IN THIS CHAPTER:

- Effective investment committees:
  a reality, not a dream

- Managing risk in your portfolio

- Restricted, unrestricted, or quasi-endowment?

- Asset allocation: strategy & prudence

- Getting your spending policy right

by John S. Griswold

John S. Griswold
Senior Vice President, Marketing Services and External Relations, Commonfund Group

As head of Commonfund Institute, John Griswold directs Commonfund's educational, market research, and professional development activities. John initiated the annual Commonfund Benchmarks Studies to chart the performance of educational endowments, foundations, operating charities, and healthcare institutions, which collectively survey the investment performance and practices of over 1400 nonprofit institutions. He supervises and speaks at Commonfund's annual Endowment Institute, Commonfund Forum, monthly Trustee Roundtables, and nonprofit investment conferences in the U.S., Europe, and Canada. Prior to Commonfund, John spent seven years as a partner in an investment management firm. He is a member of numerous nonprofit boards including The Boys and Girls Clubs of America and Pomfret School. He attended Yale University and Columbia Business School, is an Accredited Investment Fiduciary (AIF) and holds a certificate from the Endowment Institute at Harvard University. He authored this chapter with William F. Jarvis, also of Commonfund Institute.

ENDOWMENT MANAGEMENT

Saving Today, Preserving Tomorrow

Endowments of one kind or another have existed for centuries at colleges, universities, and independent schools. While some institutions benefit from substantial endowments and others have modest funds, the purpose is the same: to support the mission of the institution over the long term. In fulfilling this apparently simple purpose, a host of issues and tasks must be considered. It is the purpose of this chapter to outline those issues and tasks for the benefit of school trustees, investment committee members, and staff.

Unlike other investment pools—for example, pension funds—the nature of endowments is not to provide assets that can be set against future defined liabilities. The support the endowment gives to the institution is strategic rather than tactical. In the words of Nobel laureate James Tobin, "The trustees of endowed institutions are the guardians of the future against the claims of the present. Their task is to preserve equity among generations."[1] This concept of intergenerational equity—the idea that, as Tobin said, "The existing endowment can continue to support the same set of activities that it is now supporting"[2]—lies at the heart of contemporary endowment management practice. Trustees have a moral and ethical obligation, as well as a legal one, as fiduciaries, to maintain the purchasing power of the endowment in perpetuity.

long-term principles of intergenerational equity set forth by Tobin, with a goal of enabling them to maintain their real value after inflation and expenses over time. Viewed in this light, these "quasi-endowment" assets can be combined with true, unrestricted endowment for the purposes of their management and investment.

RESTRICTED VS. UNRESTRICTED FUNDS

Donations to independent schools take many forms, from cash and marketable securities to less liquid investments such as private capital and real estate. The intent of the donors with regard to the uses to which these gifts may be put is equally varied, and can range from very specific to very general.

The importance of these considerations for the management of the endowment is that while funds dedicated to a particular purpose are conventionally lumped together with unrestricted funds and thought of as endowment, in fact it is unrestricted funds that can by their nature provide the strategic support that meets the definition set forth by Tobin. This is because the future will undoubtedly pose challenges that even a farsighted donor may not be able to foresee.

It is nonetheless true that funds dedicated, for example, to scholarships or for the endowment of professorships or even for the maintenance of buildings, while they are by their nature restricted, can be managed according to the same

BOARD ROLE AS FIDUCIARY

An independent school's board of trustees has many responsibilities, only some of which are financial. With respect to all its functions, however, the board as an entity and the trustees as individuals bear both common-law and statutory responsibilities, chief among which are their duties as fiduciaries.

In the law, a *fiduciary* is one who is entrusted with the property of another, and who is charged with a high degree of responsibility in carrying out that trust. Classic common-law formulations of the duties of fiduciaries focus principally on two: (1) a duty of *loyalty,* which is the duty to act in the best interests of the beneficiary (in this case, the institution), and to avoid conflicts of interest; and (2) a duty of *care,* which is the duty to pay attention and to exercise reasonable prudence.[3]

Although the duty of loyalty is critical in the context of investment oversight, modern fiduciary law has focused mostly on the duty of care. It has been reformulated into a broad concept that

---

1 Tobin, James. 1974. "What Is Permanent Endowment Income?" *American Economic Review,* 64:2, pp. 427-32. 2 Ibid. 3 Some courts and commentators have also analyzed a duty of "good faith" or of "responsibility," but this discussion generally does not appear to create responsibilities that are not already part of the duty of care.

is often called the "Prudent Investor Rule." Critical components of the modern Prudent Investor Rule include:

Standard of care

The fiduciary should exercise ordinary business care and prudence under the facts and circumstances prevailing at the time of action or decision. In general, the question of whether fiduciaries have met this standard will not be judged with the benefit of hindsight.

Total return investing

Fiduciaries are permitted to consider expected total return, including capital gains as well as income.

No requirement to consider investments in isolation

Fiduciaries can consider investments in the context of the portfolio as a whole (thereby encouraging diversification and taking into account the impact of inflation), and may also consider the institution's mission and its short-term and long-term spending needs.

Delegation

Fiduciaries may delegate the making of investment decisions, or other investment-related functions, to others, provided they use reasonable care and skill in selecting and overseeing the outside advisor.

The Prudent Investor Rule has been incorporated into various widely adopted statutes, including the Uniform Management of Institutional Funds Act (UMIFA), applicable to most endowment funds, and the Uniform Prudent Investor Act (UPIA), applicable generally to trusts. The new Uniform Prudent Management of Institutional Funds Act (UPMIFA), which has passed in many states and is proposed in several more, unites UMIFA and UPIA, and incorporates a broad, clear,

and flexible formulation of the Prudent Investor Rule.

In addition to these fundamental duties, fiduciaries may be subject to specific responsibilities imposed by federal and state statutory law. In addition to UMIFA and UPMIFA, state laws increasingly relate specifically to nonprofit governance. These are based on the federal Sarbanes-Oxley model (such as California's Nonprofit Integrity Act of 2004), as well as specific rules with respect to excess benefits and similar topics under the Internal Revenue Code. In each case, it is the duty of trustees to familiarize themselves with the relevant statutory responsibilities that apply to them and their roles on the board or board committees.

Because of these multiple responsibilities, it is essential that an endowment have a clear organizational structure for decision-making and oversight. Responsibilities should be spelled out in an "investment program responsibilities" section of the school's investment policy. It is important to evaluate the strengths and weaknesses of the entire organization objectively and to develop a clear understanding of the resources required.

INVESTMENT COMMITTEE ROLE AND COMPOSITION

Committees of the board, such as the investment committee, are fiduciaries to the extent that they accept the responsibilities delegated to them by the board. This is true whether or not the members are themselves trustees of the institution. It is therefore very important that investment committee members understand the responsibilities they are undertaking.

The role of the investment committee is to act as fiduciary with respect to the endowment. The investment committee's goal for the endowment should be to maintain the intergenerational equity to which Tobin refers. While the board should approve the investment policy statement and its principal components, matters such as portfolio construction and the retention or termination of specific portfolio managers are better left to the specialists on the investment committee or its staff. The steps in achieving this goal are to:

- Determine the institution's return objective and risk tolerance.
- Craft an investment policy statement and model investment portfolio that reflect this risk tolerance.
- Determine the appropriate management model (i.e., internal vs. external managers).
- Evaluate, retain, and supervise investment managers, outside consultants, and other professionals to implement the investment policy.
- Assess current spending policy and future spending needs.
- Craft a spending formula that optimizes the endowment's contribution to the institution's future spending needs while maintaining its real value over time.

These steps appear simple when stated, but they are challenging to achieve in practice.

For this reason, it is important that the investment committee's membership be drawn primarily (though not exclusively) from individuals who are experienced in investment management. In particular, it is desirable that the committee include people with experience not only in traditional stock and bond investments, but also in less liquid alternative investments (e.g., marketable alternative strategies such as hedge funds and absolute return strategies, venture capital, private equity, natural resources, and distressed investing). These strategies have provided a source of additional risk-adjusted return to perpetual investment pools such as endowments. In this regard, a balance of special expertise and generalist perspective is healthy.

Investment committee meetings should typically occur no more than four to six times per year. They should be formally conducted, with an agenda and minutes to record the discussions and conclusions of the group. When decisions are made, the chair should report these to the board.

While it is important to conduct the meetings in such a manner that there is a free and frank exchange of views, it is equally important that issues be conclusively resolved without impasses, delays, or compromises that can impede the effectiveness of the committee. In this regard, the committee chair plays a key role in setting the agenda and guiding the committee's deliberations.

Experience suggests a few guidelines for an effective investment committee:

- The committee should be small enough to allow for discussion by all members.

- When a decision seems too difficult to reach, it may be helpful to refer it to a subcommittee or consult an outside expert.

- The committee should seek knowledge from the endowment's investment managers & other outside experts.

- The committee should control costs and fees in the management of the fund.

- It should strive to maintain continuity of membership, attitudes, & philosophies.

- The chair should keep the board informed.

INVESTMENT POLICY AND ASSET ALLOCATION

The investment policy statement is the tangible result of the investment committee's work. It should be a written document, prepared by the investment committee and adopted by the board, and ideally should be reviewed by an attorney who is familiar with the laws governing endowment investments in the institution's jurisdiction. It should contain the following items:

- **Definition and function of the investment policy statement.** This section states that the policy is being adopted in partial fulfillment of the board's fiduciary responsibilities.

- **Statement of purpose.** This section makes it clear that the purpose of the endowment is to support the institution's mission and long-term goals by ensuring intergenerational equity.

- **Objectives of the endowment.** This section specifies the respective performance goals and benchmarks for the endowment, both absolute and relative, and specifies which benchmarks are to be used for each asset class or type of investment.

- **Target asset allocation.** This section describes the "policy portfolio," which specifies the percentage target weightings for the portfolio and the ranges around those targets.

- **Investment policies, guidelines, and restrictions.** This section specifies which types of investments are authorized in each asset class and sets forth restrictions to be imposed on investment managers and other service providers.

- **Manager selection and evaluation.** This section describes how due diligence shall be conducted on managers, and outlines the roles and responsibilities of the staff, investment committee, and the board.

- **Risk management.** This section describes the risk parameters that should be followed by the endowment and its managers. Risks should be measured and assessed in light of the board's risk tolerance and return objectives, bearing in mind that all investing involves some level of risk.

- **Cost parameters.** This section describes how expenses should be measured, controlled by negotiation, and compared to industry norms and practices at peer institutions.

- **Roles and responsibilities.** This section describes the responsibilities of the board, the investment committee, the staff, outside consultants, and volunteers.

- **Communications.** This section describes required reports by investment managers and summarizes the institution's spending policy and its policy for rebalancing the portfolio at periodic intervals. It should also specify the requirements for reports by the committee to the full board.

Of these items, the investment committee should spend the greatest amount of time on the asset allocation section. Studies have consistently shown that more than 90% of the variation in investment returns is derived from asset allocation, rather than from security selection or market timing,[4] so it is very important to determine an allocation appropriate for the institution. The asset allocation is also the embodiment of the committee's attitude toward investment risk, and as such it should represent a strategic rather than an opportunistic view of the investment direction of the endowment.

Since maximization of risk-adjusted returns is the goal, it is important that the portfolio be diversified so that returns of the various asset classes chosen are not highly correlated with each other. In this regard, as discussed above, it is relevant to note that the proposed UPMIFA legislation requires that investment decisions be carried out in the same manner a "prudent investor" would use for his or her own investments. The investment committee should review the investment policy document at least annually to reflect upon changing circumstances and make revisions as necessary.

ROLE OF THE POLICY PORTFOLIO

The target asset allocation categories, considered as an investment portfolio, form the "model" or "policy" portfolio for the institution. The role of the policy portfolio is to serve as the practical expression of the investment strategy. The asset classes may include domestic equity, domestic fixed income, international equity, international fixed income, real estate, venture capital, private equity, hedge funds, commodities, and cash. The purpose of allocating among asset classes is to ensure the proper level of diversification within the endowment. It is the returns on this portfolio that are measured against the benchmarks specified in the investment policy statement.

As time passes, certain asset classes will have higher returns than others and the portfolio will need to be rebalanced in order to restore it to the target levels. This is accomplished by proportionally selling those assets that have increased in value and using the proceeds to purchase those that have lagged or decreased—a practice which may seem counterintuitive until it is realized that buying low and selling high is the goal of every good investor.

Within the policy portfolio's target asset allocation categories, the investment policy statement may indicate percentage ranges above or below which the endowment may vary from the target. These represent opportunities to express a more tactical view on particular investment opportunities without

---

4 Brinson, Gary P., L. Randolph Hood, and Gilbert L. Beebower. 1986. "Determinants of Portfolio Performance," *Financial Analyst Journal, July/August, Vol. 42, No. 4: 39-44.* See also, Brinson, Singe and Beebower. 1991. "Determinants of Portfolio Performance II: An Update," *Financial Analyst Journal May/June, Vol. 47, No. 3: 40-48.*

departing from the overall allocation scheme.

MANAGER SELECTION AND EVALUATION

Most investment committees probably spend too little time on investment policy and too much on manager selection. Selecting and evaluating managers can be fun and even profitable, and with the assistance of consultants it is all too easy to spend a great deal of time analyzing the metrics of managers in various (perhaps too many) investment styles. Care must nevertheless be exercised in evaluating, retaining, and monitoring managers.

The primary criteria for a manager should be:

- **Long-term track record.** A manager should have a record of superior performance, on both an absolute and peer-comparison basis.

- **Diversification.** A manager should contribute to the appropriate diversification of the portfolio so it is diversified not only by asset class, but also by the styles and strategies of the various managers.

- **Integrity and competence.** A manager should be able to demonstrate success based upon the claims it makes for its investment philosophy and process, over multiple market cycles. Management and staff should be stable and of high quality.

- **Size and growth rate relative to the strategy.** Ideally, a manager should be small enough to take advantage of the opportunities presented by its strategy while having sufficient scale to

be credible and to operate efficiently.

- **Costs.** Management, trading, and custody costs should be reasonable in light of the returns received and the risks being taken.

Due diligence in manager selection can be assisted by a competent consultant or manager of managers, but fiduciary responsibility for manager choice lies ultimately with the investment committee and the board. For this reason, it is important to document the manager selection process and to ensure that the hiring of managers, when recommended by the investment committee, is approved by the full board.

Once a manager is hired, its performance should be monitored on an ongoing basis. This should include the following:

- **Performance analysis.** A manager's results should be monitored individually and then combined to assess its contribution to overall portfolio return. Performance should be stated against an appropriate benchmark as well as against a universe of peer managers.

- **Controls and risk management.** The endowment must have appropriate controls and risk management procedures. These should include periodic reviews of all internal policies and practices, as well as ongoing oversight of external investment managers to assure compliance with written guidelines.

- **Operations.** Internal and external resources must be in place for custody and pricing of the securities in the portfolio. The institution may choose to open a custodial account at a brokerage or a bank to achieve these means, or the investment manager may provide the account.

It is also crucial to focus on costs. Cost control involves three types of activity:

• Diligent investigation of alternative service providers and industry norms

• A firm approach to negotiating fees

• Efficient management of the firms managing the endowment's funds including avoidance of unnecessary portfolio turnover and wasteful practices.

Obviously, different investment strategies carry with them different cost profiles. The costs of a traditional long-only equity manager will be different from those associated with a hedge fund manager. Ultimately, the goal is to maximize total portfolio return, net of all costs.

PORTFOLIO RISK MANAGEMENT

Traditionally defined, "risk" means "the possibility of harm or loss." In investment management, risk generally refers to the effects of market volatility and the possibility that an investor may have to sell at a disadvantageous time.

For an independent school, however, risk has a deeper meaning: that of potentially being unable to fulfill its mission, educate its students, support its facilities, or pay its staff. For this reason, risk management professionals refer to a "galaxy of risks," beginning with market risk and proceeding through a list of risks encompassing liquidity, operational,

legal, and other matters. While a complete discussion of risk management is outside the scope of this publication, a matrix approach may help to promote the discipline that is needed among the board, investment committee, staff, and outside consultants. In such an approach, the investment process is divided into specific steps and each is given a line on the matrix. For each step, the possible risks are identified and evaluated for degree of probability and seriousness of consequences. Alternatives, controls, and defenses are considered, put into place, and regularly monitored. Some of the key questions that might arise in such a risk management exercise are:

• In whose name are the assets in our portfolio held?

• Where are the securities held?

• Is the valuation (pricing) of our investments accurate?

• Are we applying all the resources needed to manage the portfolio effectively?

• What are the laws and regulations with which we need to be in compliance?

• Who is responsible for this compliance?

• Have we conducted adequate due diligence on our investment managers and other providers, and do we continue to monitor their compliance against our standards?

SPENDING POLICY

Spending policy is perhaps the most difficult part of the investment policy to get right, since each institution's financial needs are different and each has current demands that call upon the endowment. In this sense, spending policy is both a part of and a mirror of investment policy. As with investment policy, the goal of intergenerational equity should be paramount.

Before considering the spending rate, it is important to ask: to what does the rate apply? In the last thirty years, the advent of modern portfolio theory has led to a definition of investment return, both in law and among investment practitioners, that includes not only such items as dividends from stocks and interest from bonds, but also unrealized appreciation in the value of investments.

History teaches that it has been difficult to achieve intergenerational equity over time with spending rates much in excess of 5% of the endowment's total return per annum. Average spending rates for independent schools in the 2007 Commonfund Benchmarks Study® are currently at 4.2%. They have averaged 4.5% since 2000, a period which included a jump in spending rates as endowment values declined during the first three years of the decade. To the extent that a school is able to maintain a lower spending rate— say, less than 4%— it is, in effect, banking its return for the future. Why would an institution seek to do that?

One reason might be a desire to increase the proportion of operating expenses supported by the unrestricted portion of the endowment. Some notable institutions, such as Yale University, have gone through periods in which they lowered or froze spending levels in order to enable the endowment to catch up with spending needs and contribute more to the institution's budget going forward.

As important as the spending rate is the manner in which it is applied. It is disruptive to the institution's mission if spending exhibits volatility in real dollar terms from year to year; therefore, various smoothing techniques have been adopted. In recent decades the use of a three-year moving average, calculated over months or quarters, has been the prevalent method. Some larger endowments have adopted the so-called Yale or Stanford method, in which spending is calculated by taking into consideration both the previous year's spending (to maintain consistency) and inflation (to provide for real growth). However it is calculated, the spending formula should ideally be optimized to enable the endowment to deliver a consistent and growing stream of income to support the institution over the long term, while also guarding against erosion of the endowment's principal.

ROLE OF GIFTS AND GIFTING POLICY

Although investment policy is of great importance in helping the endowment fulfill its mission over time, it is very difficult for an institution to maintain the real value of its endowment while spending 5% or more per year. In addition, most institutions want not just to stay in the same place but to grow, adding new programs and expanding existing ones. For this reason, it is very important that an institution understand the importance of gifts to its endowment.

A sound investment program demonstrates good stewardship to potential donors. As noted above, gifts that are designated for a particular purpose are helpful but do not carry the same strategic advantage for the institution as unrestricted gifts, which can be applied in the future to support the institution's mission as it evolves. It is therefore desirable, other things being equal, for the institution to maximize unrestricted gifts to endowment. In positioning itself to receive gifts of all types, it is also desirable for the institution to have a written gift acceptance policy, in which it states its practices with respect to gifts. Such a policy should address the following issues:

- **Standards of ethical practice.** This section confirms the policy of the institution to be fair and honest in its dealings with donors. It prohibits the provision of legal and tax advice and the acceptance of gifts that might jeopardize the organization's tax-exempt status.

- **Guidelines for acceptance of outright gifts.** This section sets forth the endowment's policies and practices for each type of asset. While marketable securities are relatively straightforward, specific policies are stated for the various categories of nonmarketable and alternative assets, including standards that enable the endowment to refuse gifts that are too difficult to value or are otherwise deemed not to be in the best interest of the institution.

- **Authority to negotiate, accept, decline, or disclaim gifts.** This section enables the institution to avoid undesirable or inappropriate gifts and to negotiate changes where appropriate and acceptable to the donor.

- **Recognition of donors.** This section provides the rules under which donors will or will not be recognized.

It can be useful in helping the institution maintain a consistent approach to this sensitive area.

- **Gift restrictions and limitations of use.** This section sets forth the circumstances under which the institution will honor a donor's specific restrictions. It also sets forth the procedures required for approval of unusual donor conditions.

- **Endowment and gift limitation agreements.** This section requires that all limitations be documented and states that unrestricted gifts will be subject to the institution's investment and spending policies.

- **Accounting and investment standards.** This section states that the endowment will operate in compliance with applicable accounting policies.

- **Guidelines for acceptance of planned gifts**. This section provides for treatment of bequests, charitable remainder trusts, and other types of planned gifts.

It can be seen that while gifts are important in themselves, it is equally important to plan for how to receive them, and how to refuse well-intentioned but inappropriate gifts.

CONCLUSION

A brief document such as this cannot, by its nature, provide a comprehensive guide to all the issues that an endowment manager or investment committee will face. (A list of helpful publications is provided in the Endowment Management Toolkit at *www.nboa.net*.) It is also essential that the board and investment committee be able to consult with outside experts and counsel to ensure that the relevant issues are being identified and the appropriate steps taken.

Chapter Eleven

FOOD SERVICE
The Myriad Aspects of Mealtime

IN THIS CHAPTER:

- Your options: cash cafeterias to all-inclusive board plans

- P & L vs. management fee structure

- Why a nonmandatory food program can fizzle

- The deal with scoreboard deals

- Your in-house catering enterprise

by Tina Rodriguez

Tina Rodriguez
Chief Financial Officer and General Counsel, SAGE Dining Services, Inc.

Tina Rodriguez co-founded SAGE Dining Services, Inc., the nation's leading provider of dining services for independent schools, in 1990, and currently serves as its CFO and General Counsel. SAGE blends Tina's passion for culinary excellence and financial integrity with her commitment to education. Previously, Tina served as Adjunct Faculty member at the Johns Hopkins School of Professional Studies in Business and Education, where she taught a variety of courses on strategic planning and management to MBA candidates. She received the school's Excellence in Teaching award in 1996. Tina has been active for years in addressing numerous organizations on the topic of food service management and nutrition. Prior to her work at SAGE, Tina was a Manager at Bain & Company, an international strategy consulting firm. She is a summa cum laude graduate of the Wharton School of Finance and a cum laude graduate of Harvard Law School.

FOOD SERVICE

The Myriad Aspects of Mealtime

Food service plays a pivotal role in building and bolstering the sense of community that is unique to independent schools. Anthropologists and sociologists increasingly note that sharing meals can strengthen social ties. During your career, you and other senior administrators at your school will make choices about food service that will have a direct impact on the feeling of fellowship on your campus and the sense of communal connection to the institution. Those choices—program structure, operational procedures, relevance to the mission, and cost—all deserve careful consideration.

FOOD SERVICE OPTIONS

Schools opting to provide on-site food service face a broad range of dining alternatives, ranging from running a cash cafeteria to implementing a mandatory board plan. Each choice, described in detail below, has implications for nutrition, food quality, operational efficiency, and finances.

A school may also choose to avoid food service altogether, often because its smaller scale makes on-site food service prohibitively expensive, or because it lacks kitchen facilities. In these situations, the school may contract with local fast-food or catering establishments to transport pre-made meals on-site daily, or students may simply bring lunch from home.

Option #1: Cash Cafeteria

In a cash cafeteria, students are in charge! Each day, each student decides whether or not to patronize the cafeteria, which food to select, and how much to spend. A parent may give a student five dollars to spend for lunch, but once that money is in the student's hands, parents and administrators have little control over how it is spent. The student decides whether to spend some or all of it on a healthy lunch at the cafeteria, or on a soda and a magazine.

By necessity, cash cafeterias cater to the tastes of their young patrons. Yet from a nutrition standpoint, cash operations provide challenges. These cafeterias tend to specialize in "kid-friendly" foods: burgers, fries, pizza, soda, and sweets. Few, if any, vegetables are served. Vegetables have no perceived economic value: they "appear" on the dinner plate at home, but they are not on menus of fast-food establishments frequented by students.

Economically, a cash cafeteria operates as a profit-and-loss-focused business. The goal is to break even or make a profit. Every school day is a new challenge to coax money from students' pockets to cover fixed costs. These costs fall into two categories: those required to prepare and serve the food, as well as "gatekeepers," expensive, pre-portioned containers and single-serving packages, which require an investment in hardware and wiring for cash registers and scanners, as well as additional personnel to prevent theft. These "hidden costs" do not directly enhance the dining experience but are critical to the efficient financial management of the cafeteria.

From a social standpoint, since each person makes an individual decision whether to participate in the program, cash cafeterias do not promote community inclusiveness on campus. Indeed, they may prove to be divisive, contributing to a sense of "haves" and "have-nots" among the student body.

Cash cafeterias contribute to a reasonable level of discontent among parents as well. Parents of students with food allergies worry that their child may be exposed to potential allergens brought to school by fellow students. Depending on the severity of the health condition, administrators may need to create "allergen-free" zones in the dining area or restrict the types of food permitted on campus.

Option #2: Declining Balance Operations

Declining balance operations are similar to cash cafeterias, but with one critical distinction: parents deposit funds into a debit account, guaranteeing that all funds will be spent on school-provided food (which pleases parents). This option also makes parents happy because it permits them to add money to their child's account via the internet, which is far more convenient and timely than writing checks. Another advantage to this model is that many systems provide parents with a printout of their child's purchases. A parent can then analyze the child's spending habits and counsel the child on nutritional choices. In both of these important ways, adults gain a modicum of control over children's decisions.

Eliminating currency has advantages for schools as well. First, use of debit cards or pin pads speeds customers through the line so that more patrons can be served in less time during the same lunch period. Students also tend to spend more, since the money is "invisible." A declining balance plan also simplifies record-keeping, eliminates the need for daily trips to the bank, and reduces the risk of theft by cashiers.

Option #3: Nonmandatory Board Plans

The nonmandatory board plan allows a school to provide a full and complete meal to those students who choose to participate. Unlike cash and declining balance operations, board plans are per meal, not per item ("à la carte"). For a fixed price, students are permitted to choose anything offered in the cafeteria.

There are many variations of nonmandatory board plans. Some schools place strict limits on the quantity of food selected—for example, a student may be entitled to only one serving of an entree, starch, vegetable, and beverage. Others allow their students to go through the cafeteria or servery once per meal period, and select anything they wish. Other schools permit their students to return to the servery for "unlimited seconds."

Unlike à la carte plans, board programs strive to create a range of choices to please broad audiences. Typically, a nonmandatory board program offers a selection of entrees, vegetables, starches, sandwiches or deli bar, salads or a salad bar, and a variety of beverages and desserts. The offerings are intended to appeal to the entire school community, including students, faculty, and administrators. Because of the variety of foods served, board programs can be nutritionally sound and encourage healthful eating habits.

Financially, nonmandatory board operations are very difficult to operate successfully over the long term. Schools must achieve a high level of participation for a nonmandatory program to be financially viable: ideally, 75% or greater. Generally, a community is initially highly satisfied when a cash or declining balance operation is transformed into a nonmandatory board plan, but in subsequent years, the novelty of the program wears off and participation levels off or begins to decline. Customers are no longer awed by the wide variety of offerings; the variety becomes standard. They begin requesting "improvements" like organic products, expensive entrees and the like, which are difficult to fund. The high fixed cost of running the kitchen must be spread over a high proportion of participants to allow the school to break even while offering reasonable meal plan costs to parents, so the school begins to work harder and harder to increase participation in the program, or is forced to raise the cost of the plan. What typically happens next is that meal plan configurations begin to multiply. Schools that allowed students to "opt in" only at the beginning of each semester start creating monthly, weekly, and even daily meal plans to improve participation. With every new configuration comes additional administrative cost, and participation seldom improves dramatically.

Meanwhile, students in a nonmandatory plan behave as though their food is "free"—they paid the cost of the plan, and feel entitled to as much food as they wish. It is common to observe students helping themselves to far more product than they can consume, and liberally "sharing" the food with their friends who are not on the meal plan. This puts schools in a difficult position: policing their cafeterias for illicit "sharing," or facing the financial consequences of these acts. This problem does not exist in cash or declining balance operations, because students pay for each item à la carte.

While a nonmandatory board program does improve the quality and quantity of food offerings, it still divides the community into "participants" and "nonparticipants." Concerns also remain about students bringing food allergens into the cafeteria.

Many schools select this model, however, because they want to provide parents a choice. They do not want to require every family to contribute to the program, fearing the political backlash of such a decision.

Option #4: All-Inclusive or Mandatory Board Plans

The all-inclusive board plan is the gold standard of food service. Students pay a flat fee as part of tuition, which entitles them to full participation in the program. Typically, such plans offer a variety of entrees, starches, vegetables, beverages, fruits, and desserts. Students are served an appropriate portion of food, then are welcome to return for "unlimited seconds."

Since this is an all-inclusive program, schools no longer need "gatekeepers" to restrict access and prevent theft; cashiers and cafeteria monitors are not necessary. The cost of expensive packaging and single-serving containers is eliminated. Food can be provided not only in the servery, but also in salad bars, deli bars, beverage stations, and specialty stations scattered throughout the dining hall. This reduces crowding, shortens lines, and increases customer satisfaction.

In an all-inclusive board plan, adults are in charge. While students can choose from a broad spectrum of foods, administrators and parents help determine the types of foods that are served, which typically end up being more nutritionally balanced than cash or declining balance systems.

On a per-student basis, the all-inclusive board plan is the most cost-effective food service option. Schools can amortize the high fixed cost of the dining service over the entire student body. Nonproductive costs are eliminated, and money can be devoted solely to providing food service for the community.

Some schools, however, are reluctant to increase tuition to fund an all-inclusive board plan. They worry about the perceived competitive disadvantage of charging higher tuition than neighboring schools, and are concerned about affordability for students receiving financial aid. Ironically, the all-inclusive board plan is the most economical way of serving healthful meals to students. Properly managed, it will represent a savings for families, who already pay retail prices to feed their children. The real issue is not the cost but the timing of the transactions; families do not notice the money they spend on lunches weekly, but they do notice the onetime charge on the tuition bill.

Some schools are also wary of adopting all-inclusive board plans because they are concerned about restricting parent choice. This raises the broader question of each school's mission and philosophy, and how schools view food service in that light. Tuition payments already reflect the cost of providing the entire range of services to the community: athletics, foreign languages, chorus, drama, etc. Parents' tuition supports these departments, whether their child participates or not. If a school decides that food service is mission-critical, food service can be viewed in that same light.

The mandatory board plan can dramatically strengthen the sense of community at a school. Students, faculty, and administrators gather daily to share a meal and reaffirm their connection to the institution and to one another. Because of the breadth of this type of program, schools should be able to accommodate most dietary and health preferences, allowing all students to share meals together in the same setting.

The all-inclusive board plan is a receptive environment in which to further the school mission. Schools committed to sustainability can engage the community in recycling, composting, and minimizing use of processed foods. The higher cost of eco-friendly products becomes more affordable when spread across the entire school community.

Further, since all students participate in the dining experience, the all-inclusive board plan can provide educators with an "extended classroom" in which they can continue their educational mission and even involve the community in the cooking process. The dining service can coordinate with faculty to stage international theme meals, introduce students to unusual foods, and perform cooking demonstrations.

Before adopting a community-inclusive board plan, a school must assess whether its current facility can produce the volume of food needed. Among issues to consider are the adequacy of stovetop and oven space, warming ovens, refrigerators and freezers, and dry storage.

WHO PROVIDES THE SERVICE?

Schools have three options for providing food service on campus: contracting for daily meal delivery with a local caterer, operating food service in-house, or signing a long-term contract with an outside vendor. The chart below illustrates preferences for each choice, based on proprietary survey statistics compiled in 2007.

Option #1: Daily Meal Delivery from Local Restaurant or Caterer

As mentioned above, operating an on-campus dining facility is not feasible for all schools. They may lack adequate kitchen facilities or may have a small student body, which makes on-site food service prohibitively expensive.

Food Service Providers

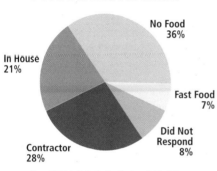

Source: SAGE Dining Services, Inc. Proprietary Survey Statistics, 2007

For these schools, local fast-food establishments or catering companies provide a solution. These firms will take orders daily and deliver the product to the door. Schools can choose to offer pizza one day, tacos another day, and deli sandwiches the next. Typically, parents help coordinate the process, collect the funds, and assist in the distribution of food to the students.

This system has two obvious advantages. First, it offers busy parents an alternative to packing daily lunches for their children. It is a no-stress, totally voluntary program. Second, there is no financial risk for the school. Parents pay in advance, and there is no long-term commitment to the catering companies.

There are also two disadvantages. The first is poor nutrition; the second is food safety. Products delivered to the school at the appropriate hot or cold temperature may sit in hallways for extended periods of time, waiting to be distributed to students. During this time, food temperatures may creep into the "danger zone"—from 41 to 140 degrees Fahrenheit—allowing harmful bacteria to develop. Students could even develop food poisoning because of the way the food might be handled and distributed by school personnel.

Option #2: Operating Food Service In-House

Many schools choose to operate their dining services as a department of the school. In this model, the school hires all management and support personnel, contracts directly with food vendors, pays all of the costs of the operation (including liability insurance), and acts as the liaison between parents and the dining operation on menu offerings, prices, and other policies.

By making the food service staff directly accountable to the institution, many schools feel they wield maximum control over cafeteria decision-making. They achieve total transparency in purchasing and financial management decisions, and are ensured that the dining hall is managed by a staff steeped in the unique culture of the institution.

The success of this model is predicated on a stable and talented workforce, particularly the food service director. Schools with a talented director and long-tenured staff can remain highly satisfied with their dining program. However, if that director falls ill, resigns, or retires, that stability will be affected.

Financially, a school managing its own food service faces both advantages and disadvantages. In many states, schools are not required to pay state or federal unemployment insurance for the dining service workforce. Contractors' unemployment rates vary by state, and could reach 10% of payroll.

Schools enjoy further advantages in hiring. A school may be able to place certain conditions on its workforce, such as belonging to a particular faith community, which may be critical to the school's mission. Private contractors are not entitled to any exceptions to Title VII of the Civil Rights Act and cannot restrict hiring in this manner.

On the other hand, schools may find it difficult to deal objectively with problem employees because of the close-knit nature of the community. It may be easier to tolerate an individual's underperformance than expend political capital to disengage that person from the community.

In addition, many schools feel obliged to offer a single benefit package to all employees: faculty, administrators, and support staff. Granting food service workers the same insurance and retirement benefits as teachers is very

expensive and not standard in the food service industry.

Schools which purchase their own food are assured that the invoice price is the real cost of the product; the manufacturer did not make hidden payments to any contractor. But schools lack the scale and leverage to negotiate the best prices for the product. While the invoiced price will be real, it will also be high.

In addition, schools are unable to provide the food service team with a peer network or professional development. There is little opportunity for the management team to learn about trends in cuisine or school food service. The dining program may not evolve as quickly as students or parents expect, and may not remain competitive in the local marketplace.

Option #3: Using Outside Contractors

Many schools view outsourcing food service as an opportunity to focus their resources on the school's mission: educating students. Administrators avoid the need to personally involve themselves in menu writing, nutrition management, negotiating with food vendors, managing dining service employees, and overseeing the health and safety aspects of the dining program. These advantages can translate to hard-dollar savings for every school.

However, there are trade-offs. Professional management companies are for-profit businesses that expect to make a profit for their services. This may be a negotiated fixed-dollar number or a number based on a formula. Alternatively, a contractor may agree to "take over" the food service operation with no explicit charge to the school, but in exchange the contractor will keep all proceeds and will have full discretion over decision-making in the cafeteria.

Another concern is financial transparency. Schools operating their own dining service know the actual cost of every aspect of the operation: the real cost of the purchases, the actual fringe and tax costs, and the true cost of insurance. Schools using outside contractors may receive limited financial reports, and even those financial statements may not reflect the actual cost of listed items. For example, some contractors may purchase food from related companies at inflated prices, and pass those charges to clients as "invoiced cost." Schools may lack a true picture of the financial state of the food service operation.

Perhaps the most important advantage to this model is the high level of customer satisfaction the contractor can engender. Food service professionals are capable of providing superior menus, food quality, and customer service. Schools can help ensure that their contractors are responsive to the needs of the community by providing assistance with menu design, signage, health concerns, catering support, and similar issues.

FINANCIAL STRUCTURE

There are two basic ways a school can structure its food service operation: as a "profit and loss" ("P & L") operation, or as a "management fee" operation.

A P & L operation is one that works as a stand-alone business on campus, with the goal of breaking even or making a profit. This model encompasses a range of possibilities: from the daily fast-food delivery paid in advance by parents, to school-run cafeterias budgeted and operated to break even, to contractor-managed facilities where the vendor bears the risk of profit or loss.

The financial advantage of this model is clear: dining services will be budget-neutral, their costs borne by those who patronize the operation. The disadvantage, however, may be in service. Cafeterias save money by lowering food quality, reducing portion sizes, raising prices, paying low wages and benefits to staff, and keeping staffing levels low. The dining service may make such decisions to raise profits, which may reduce perceived quality and lead to dissatisfaction and complaints.

Under the "management fee" model, schools pay the direct costs of the operation, as well as a fixed fee (profit) to the contractor. This model aligns the interests of the school and the contractor to minimize many of the service and quality concerns a P & L may engender. The contractor operates in the same manner as a department head on campus. There is no financial disincentive to providing the "extras" the community may require.

The obvious disadvantage is financial risk. Many administrators fear that contractors operating under a "management fee" model have no incentive to operate within the budget, and the school may face budget shortfalls as a result. Schools entering into this arrangement need to receive detailed financial statements on an ongoing basis, so they are aware of potential cost over-runs and have an opportunity to make changes to minimize those losses.

WHAT IT COSTS

A typical food service statement is divided into five sections: revenue, food cost, labor cost, operating expenses, and contribution. Data should be tallied weekly, monthly, and on a year-to-date basis, with comparisons to budget at each level.

To be truly comparable, the food service statement should be based on the accrual method, reflecting usage, not purchases. The difference between product purchased versus food sold in the period can be found in inventory.

Revenue

The first section of the food service financial statement details sources of revenue. Typical revenue categories include board operations, cafeteria (cash) sales, catering functions, summer program sales, and vending. Each type of sale has different cost implications. It is important to know the revenue breakdown to understand potential operating variances.

Food Cost

Predictably, food cost is a major expense category for a food service operation. Food is further detailed by category: meat, groceries, frozen products, beverages, dairy, bakery, and produce. All food categories except bakery and produce

should have associated inventory as well. Food cost can range from 30% to 50% of the total cost of a standard operation.

Schools may wish to serve organic products because they believe them to be healthier and better for the health of the planet, but these schools will experience dramatically higher food costs than the norm. The price of organic milk, for example, is approximately 50% more than conventional milk. Since milk is a high-volume purchase for most schools, that single organic product can significantly impact the bottom line. Organic produce, in general, can be anywhere from 50% to 200% more expensive than conventional product. As the supply of organic products increases, prices of these products will fall, but in the meantime, a commitment to organic food service is a very expensive proposition. The exhibit below details key product and pricing comparisons as of early 2008.

Cost Difference of Organic vs. Conventional	
MILK: half pint	204%
gallon	56%
EGGS: whole	53%
liquid	82%
CHICKEN: whole	263%
boneless breast	77%
BEEF PATTY	113%
PRODUCE: Carrots	208%
Mixed Greens	41%
Red Delicious Apples	45%
Oranges, CA	123%
Tomatoes, FL	43%
Celery, MI	194%

Source: SAGE Dining Services, Inc. Purchasing Dept. data

Labor Cost

Labor is the second major financial component of a food service operation. The cost of management and hourly paid personnel, payroll taxes, and fringe benefits can represent between 30% and 50% of the total cost of the operation.

Many factors influence labor costs at a school. Hours of operation, types of service, and level of catering are major drivers of cost. Further, a workforce that has been pre-screened for criminal history, drug use, and eligibility to work legally in the United States is more expensive than otherwise. The higher cost of this verified talent is offset by the increased sense of security of the campus community.

Operating Expenses

There are a host of other costs involved in food service operations: paper supplies, cleaning, equipment rental, general insurance, and more. All told, these expenses represent between 8% and 15% of the total food service budget.

Many schools choose to use eco-friendly or sustainable products to help protect the environment. These goods, particularly paper and cleaning supplies, can significantly affect the budget. As illustrated in the exhibit below, the cost of eco-friendly products can be 50% to two times higher than that of conventional product. Schools need to look at these costs when deciding to operate in a more sustainable fashion, and make decisions that are in line with their mission but that also respect budgetary constraints.

Cost Difference of Eco-Friendly vs Conventional Paper & Supply	
Plates: 9 in	267%
6 in	67%
Bowl: 12 oz	100%
5 Compartment Tray	75%
Cups: 16 oz Hot/Cold	200%
8 oz	150%
Cutlery: per piece	67%
Floor Cleaner	29%
Glass Cleaner	56%
All-Purpose Cleaner	29%
De-Greaser	30%

Source: SAGE Dining Services, Inc. Purchasing Dept. data

ADDITIONAL CONSIDERATIONS

Breakfast Programs

Medical research has definitively shown that students who eat a healthful, balanced breakfast perform better in school. Yet breakfast remains an elusive goal for a growing number of time-pressed students and faculty. Many schools offer à la carte breakfast programs to address this need, which can range from very simple ("grab-and-go") to more elaborate (made-to-order omelettes). Even in community-inclusive lunch programs, breakfast is available at an additional charge, and students are expected to pay for their meal at the time of purchase. Since the food service staff typically arrives to work very early in the morning, assigning breakfast preparation duties to existing staff is a simple matter. Further, with proper pricing, breakfast programs can enhance the financial viability of the entire dining program. Breakfast is a profitable, low-food-cost meal. Students benefit, and the school earns incremental returns as well.

Catering

A talented, on-site food service staff is a valuable asset for every school. These individuals can do far more than cook lunch; they can support the dining needs of the entire campus community. This includes providing meals and refreshments for staff meetings, catering private lunches for the head of school, hosting awards dinners for athletic or academic departments, and even serving elegant meals for board or alumni meetings. There are four elements to consider in developing in-house catering capabilities: pricing, billing and collections, equipment, and staffing.

Pricing Policies

A school's ability to influence catering pricing depends on the type of dining program it has in place. In P & L operations, the vendor controls pricing and pockets any profits from catered events. Under management fee arrangements, schools retain pricing discretion for catered events.

Catering functions fall into two categories: internal and external. "Internal" functions are those supporting the staff or administrative departments of the school. Many schools consider student groups and parents' clubs to be internal organizations as well. "External" catered events serve outside organizations. Many schools rent their facilities for meetings, weddings, retreats, and private parties. Although the individuals booking the

event may have a close connection with the school, the event itself is not related to the function or mission of the school. Most schools view these events as a source of incremental profit. Schools price such parties at a substantial mark-up over cost, yet one that is competitive with the outside marketplace. While private catering companies may charge a 50% or higher premium over cost to cater an event, a school may seek a 30% contribution above cost. (This is in addition to room rental, security, cleaning, and other fees routinely assessed under the circumstances.)

Deciding how much to charge for internal catered events is more complex. Schools with community-inclusive board programs often choose to have their internal functions priced at cost. Since the cost of the dining program is already factored into tuition, schools can enjoy low-cost catering as an added benefit, and the cost savings from replacing outside caterers with internal staff can be substantial. However, the "at-cost" pricing strategy may have unintended consequences. For example, departments which previously paid market rates for services may expand their demand for catered parties, instead of leaving budgeted dollars unspent. In other words, budgeted cost savings could be eroded by higher consumption. Many schools add modest surcharges of 10% or more to the cost of catered internal events. Schools operating cash, declining balance, or optional board programs often rely on this revenue to balance their dining service budgets. These programs require the additional contribution from catering to help offset the high fixed cost of the entire food service operation.

Collections Policies

Schools need to develop policies for billing both external and internal catering customers. Most professional catering companies require their customers to pay a large deposit upon placing an order, and to pay the remainder in advance of service. Most schools with external catering functions adopt similar policies as well. For internal catered events, schools need a system by which to charge a department's budget for catering services. Typically, the person booking the function approves the itemized invoice at the time of the event. The signature is the authorization needed to "pay" the invoice. However, when the internal group is a student organization or parent group, collecting payment for functions can become a delicate matter. Some schools require such organizations to pay in advance. Other schools extend credit, but only if the groups act responsibly and pay their bills promptly.

Equipment Needs

Schools requiring on-site catering may need to invest in appropriate serving equipment, china, tableware, and/or suitable tables and chairs. While it is possible to lease such items from rental companies, the cost of a few rentals often equals the purchase price. Schools are better served by accumulating their own catering equipment, and supplementing it each year as needs evolve. The rental cost, or its equivalent, should be charged to each external party using that equipment.

Staffing Levels

Of course, food service staffing levels need to reflect the anticipated burden that catering will place on the operation. While a certain level of internal catering can be accommodated by existing staff, once requests become more elaborate, or the timing of events stretches into weekend and evening hours, there will be additional labor costs. This may be reflected in overtime pay, or the cost of additional staff needed to support the operation. For large events, temporary waitstaff can provide needed coverage. Schools with extensive catering operations may hire a catering manager to supervise events, supplementing the regular management team.

A well-constructed catering program can benefit the school financially, making the dining program economically viable while enhancing the experience of the entire campus community.

Faculty Dining

When designing their dining programs, many schools understandably focus on the students: the foods students like, the foods students will try. Yet it is also important to focus on the adults in the population: the faculty and staff. A high-quality dining program can be an enormous benefit to a school's ability to recruit and retain talent. The availability of freshly prepared meals, geared to adult tastes, eases the pressures faced by already-stressed staff. A well-conceived dining program also builds community by encouraging faculty, staff, and students to share common eating spaces and to get to know one another on a social level.

In community-inclusive board programs, the cost of faculty dining can be calculated into the fixed cost base that is funded via student tuition. In these programs, faculty may be able to eat without charge. In other types of dining plans (cash, declining balance, nonmandatory board plans), the cost of faculty dining must be addressed separately. Schools that earn large profits from their student dining operations may choose to subsidize faculty meals from dining service profits. Otherwise, schools may require faculty to pay for food à la carte, or provide them with a fixed daily allowance with which to purchase a meal.

Summer Programs

Many schools operate summer programs to generate additional income. Food service should be considered as part of the "package" to further enhance the school's revenue.

Ideally, schools can bundle the cost of lunch into the total cost of the program, creating a complete, one-price "package." Schools which subcontract their facilities to outside organizations can require the camp to provide some level of food service through the school's dining program. Summer food service need not be as extensive as what is provided during the school year. Daily offerings can be simple box lunches for campers, or they can include the full array of hot and cold foods. Weekly summer menus can be prepared in advance, with input from summer program coordinators. These can be used to market the lunch program to participants.

Summer food service programs provide schools opportunities to better manage costs. Many food service operations suffer because the hourly paid staff must endure long layoffs during school shutdowns. Inevitably, the best employees find alternate employment and do not return for the following school year. A school's ability to provide year-round employment to food service employees can significantly impact the caliber of persons attracted to these positions, as well as reduce turnover. Summer programs are also a convenient way to use random inventory items that accumulated over the prior school year. Using this inventory helps conserve cash and manage food cost during a slow period.

Vending

Vending sales provide another avenue for schools to meet the community's dining needs, as well as to make money for the school. These sales should be managed as part of the overall dining program, and revenues and costs should be budgeted and reported in the consolidated food service statement. This is particularly true in cash, declining balance, and nonmandatory board programs, because vending sales can cannibalize cafeteria sales. The price of vended products must be consistent with pricing in the manual food service operation.

The question of how to structure the vending program is a classic "make or buy" decision. A school can manage vending in-house or contract with an outside vending company to provide this service.

Schools choosing to manage their own vending program control the types of products sold as well as pricing. Dining service employees can order the product and fill the machines during quiet periods, at no additional cost. The dining services manager can report sales, deposit funds in the bank, and remit appropriate sales tax to the state. If the vending machines are located in or near the dining area, and there is ample storage space for vended products, managing vending internally is a viable option. If vending machines are scattered throughout the campus, however, the decision is less clear. The dining service may need to hire additional staff to perform this task, reducing the profitability of the program. Further, security risks multiply with distance and program complexity. Schools managing vending internally can acquire beverage machines from the major soda companies for free. The caveat is that the school must commit to selling only that vendor's product through that machine. Snack machines must be purchased outright. They can be leased or purchased directly, at a cost of approximately $3,000 to $5,000 per machine.

Alternatively, a school may contract with an outside vending company to provide the machines, restock the product, and remit sales tax to the government. In exchange, the school receives a percentage of reported gross sales. Typically, commissions range from 20% to 35% of sales for beverages, and up to 20% for snacks. Of course, there is no guarantee that the vending contractor is accurately reporting the total proceeds from the machines! Further, the outside vendor is permitted to adjust pricing in order to provide that level of return to the school. The vendor also controls the product offerings.

> Schools need to be wary of any lack of symmetry between vending prices and dining program pricing, to avoid cannibalizing cafeteria sales.

Some schools sign agreements with major soda companies in which the vendor provides the athletic department with a scoreboard in exchange for an exclusive, long-term contract with the school. These "scoreboard deals" may be worth tens of thousands of dollars to the school, but there is a catch: the dining service is forced to purchase all beverage products consumed on campus from that soda company, at grossly inflated prices. More importantly, the soda company dictates when, where, and how its products will be sold on campus, and requires its logo to be prominently displayed at every point of sale.

With growing national concern about childhood health and nutrition, legislators are beginning to focus on beverage contractors and vending programs. Specifically, many jurisdictions are limiting the types of products that may be sold in vending machines, and limiting the hours that students can access the machines so as not to compete with the more nutritious and economical lunchtime offerings. As this legislation evolves, schools will need to take a fresh look at their vending policies and evaluate their choices.

CONCLUSION

Business officers face a wide range of choices in designing and structuring their food service operation. A well-designed program can build and strengthen students' ties to the school and to one another. A thoughtful menu, coupled with a great partnership between the food service team and your faculty, staff, and administration, can enhance the school's mission.

Alternatively, food service can be a source of student and parent complaints. Fielding issues from students as well as food service employees can impinge on administrators' time. A poorly designed menu can lead students to make poor nutritional choices, and may expose children to potentially harmful food allergens.

Making the right choice for the entire community is the challenge the business officer faces. Done well, food service is an area where schools can demonstrate leadership in the community. Every school seeks to educate its students to succeed in the complex world they will inherit, and to instill in all participants—students, parents, faculty, and administrators—a lasting bond to the institution and to one another. Food service can accelerate the achievement of this important goal.

NBOA

Chapter Twelve

SUMMER AND AFTER-SCHOOL PROGRAMS

*The Golden Opportunity
of Your Off-Peak Hours*

IN THIS CHAPTER:

- Reasons to have a summer program

- Meeting parents' needs

- After-school care: a smorgasbord of options

- Scheduling and pricing: the nitty-gritty

- Spotting hidden revenue potential

by Suzanne McCanles

Suzanne McCanles
Head of School, Oakhill Day School

Suzanne McCanles has served as an educator in independent schools for the past 16 years. She is currently in her second year as Head of School at Oakhill Day School in a suburb of Kansas City. Prior to this position, she spent 14 years at The Barstow School, with nine as Director of Auxiliary Services. Her role at Barstow allowed her to build a summer program from 50 students per day in 1998 to 600 students per day in 2007. This program incorporated after-school classes, lessons, and special events. Her sound educational background as a teacher allows her to use that same creativity to build profit centers that are true to the school's mission. Suzanne has presented at numerous independent school association conferences, and privately consults for many summer programs across the country. She recently held her third Summer Director's and Extended Day Director's conference in Kansas City.

SUMMER AND AFTER-SCHOOL PROGRAMS

The Golden Opportunity of Your Off-Peak Hours

To parents, summer programming means quality care, enrichment opportunities, safety, fun, and flexibility. To school administrators, summer programming means marketing potential, revenue, additional employment opportunities, specialized classes, and summer work for faculty. To students, summer programming means friends, fun, freedom, adventures, and downtime. It is up to the summer director to make sure all of these wants and needs come together to create the perfect balance in June, July, and August.

To create a successful summer program, a school should understand the program's unique dynamics and its place within the complex operations of the rest of the school. A summer program that is treated as an extension of the regular school year, with a director who is present to take care of the program year-round, is more likely to succeed. This chapter will outline the value of summer programming and illuminate how you, as the business officer, play a crucial role.

WHERE TO BEGIN

There are many summer program models within the independent school community. Some schools rent their facilities to external groups, others offer coach-led sports camps, and some appoint outside directors to oversee performing arts and academic enrichment courses.

I have researched every model out there, and know the pros and cons of each. I help schools start new summer programs, revise current summer programs, redefine existing programs, and create plans to change summer programs over time. Throughout this chapter, I will focus on the model I recommend—one in which a dedicated summer director oversees the entirety of the school's summer program from pricing to scheduling to marketing. I believe this model produces the greatest profit while meeting all of the school's needs in the most efficient way possible: one director, one program, one campus, one philosophy.

Just as an independent school is driven by its mission, a summer program should be as well. It is important to align the summer program's mission and vision with the school's mission and vision—with a unique summer "flair." This will drive scheduling, class offerings, hiring, and the overall look and feel of the program. It is also important to have conversations about the importance of the summer program with key administrators. The head of school should grasp the big picture—the entrepreneurial nature of the program—in order to set the tone for the entire school community. The admission director and marketing director should work hand in hand with the summer director to engage the program's captive audience of parents and follow up with them when summer turns to fall. Division heads could take advantage of the opportunities that exist within the varied class offerings—academics, arts, sports, etc. The faculty should come to know that the summer program is what naturally occurs in June (not that the summer program is staging a coup in June and taking over the school). The facilities coordinator should be made aware of the key role his or her position plays in making the transitions from spring to summer and back to fall as smooth as possible. Finally, the business office should work hand in hand with the summer office to track all expenses and revenue and to stay in communication with the summer office on all other overlapping areas. Good communication between all departments is vital.

> *If your school has an existing summer program, before you look to change it, I recommend evaluating it from top to bottom.*

Does the program reflect the school's mission? Does the program have a vision? Does the program encompass all that your school expects from it? Does your director have the time and freedom to create a successful program? Once these questions are answered, it is time to look at the most important reasons to have a successful program—the benefits a summer program bring to your school.

REASONS TO HAVE A SUMMER PROGRAM

- To use the facility in a profitable way
- To use the program as a teacher feeding ground
- To provide year-round salaries to academic-year faculty and staff
- To get prospective students on the campus and into the building
- To give parents the year-round care they expect and need
- To allow students to grow in academics or enrichment areas
- To provide an opportunity for alumni and current students to seek summer employment
- To make a name for the school in the community
- To provide cash flow and profit

USING THE FACILITY IN A PROFITABLE WAY

Although there are many ways to find a monetary return during the summer, it is important that summer programming maintain the school's image and reputation. If a school rents its facility to outside groups, the school ultimately has no control over the program's image, quality, class size, and hiring. Further, as you consider creating a program for your school, it is important to look at your facilities with an objective eye. Rooms and spaces may be utilized in different ways and for different audiences than typically used during the regular school year. For instance, a middle school classroom may be turned into a dance studio; an upper school classroom may become a camp room for first graders. It is important for key administrators to discuss room usage

with the faculty, assuring them that their rooms will be secure, but letting them know that some supplies and equipment may be used by summer teachers. For example, it is not cost-effective for the summer program to purchase 50 staplers to use for the summer, then store the staplers for 10 months to reuse the next summer. A simpler alternative would be for the summer teachers to use the classroom staplers, replacing any lost or damaged staplers at the end of the summer through the summer program budget.

Smooth logistics are the most important part of a successful program. It is crucial for the summer director to begin meeting with the facilities coordinator, business officer, and head during the fall to anticipate any challenges (including, especially, construction) foreseen for the coming summer, and to hammer out the various procedures that will need to exist during the summer (arrival, dismissal, field use, gym use, dining hall use, etc.). Continued meetings should occur on a monthly basis to review progress and new issues. Working together as a team in the early stages of planning will ensure that everyone is on the same page. Finding out in April that the gym will be unavailable for three weeks in June puts the summer director in a bind and potentially harms the integrity of the basketball camp.

School maintenance and renewal typically occur in late summer. If the business officer, facilities coordinator, and summer director are proactive, they can schedule work in a manner that benefits all parties. The summer director may be able to assign rooms in such a manner that they can be painted or repaired during the summer without disrupting programming. I have witnessed summer programs run with minimal disruption during major construction, due to clear communication, constant updating, and an atmosphere of teamwork.

TEACHER FEEDING GROUND

Most schools are continually searching for excellent, innovative teachers. The summer program can help in two ways: 1) by providing a pool of potential teachers who are already acclimated to the school and students, and 2) by providing a student base for the applicant to teach. This is a great opportunity to observe and evaluate a teacher's style, interaction with students and parents, overall discipline procedures, attitude, effectiveness, and flexibility.

SUMMER WORK FOR FACULTY AND STAFF

Most teachers and staff are contracted and compensated for 10 months out of the year; many teachers and staff want opportunities to earn additional money when school is out. The summer program fills that need. Staff can serve as teachers, coaches, field trip leaders, office assistants to the director, or extended care supervisors. Not only can staff increase their salaries, but they may also be afforded the opportunity to grow professionally by taking on additional responsibilities. Other staff such as food service workers, custodians, maintenance crew workers, receptionists, and nurses may also earn additional pay due to

summer program needs.

ADMISSION OPPORTUNITIES

A campus that sits idle during the summer months is a missed opportunity to attract prospective families. A successful summer program not only maximizes traffic, but also creates many opportunities for the admission office to reach out to prospective families. Families may be hesitant to call or ask questions of the admission office during the regular school year, fearful of the potential commitment level that brings, but when those same families are on campus participating in summer classes, they may be more willing to engage in a conversation about the school and may be more receptive to admission materials.

PARENTAL NEEDS AND WANTS

With more dual-working parent households, as well as increased parental demand for specialty courses, summer programs are in demand. If possible, I recommend that summer programs offer everything parents and students could possibly desire—sports, performing arts, fine arts, enrichment classes, field trips, swimming, etc.—rather than carving out a "niche." Independent schools are known for educating the whole child; summer programs should be no different. Summer programs should also be as convenient and flexible as possible. Weeklong, half-day classes which can be linked together to fulfill an entire summer are much more appealing than two four-week sessions. Parents want flexibility, including the ability to select vacation times without being penalized. Many parents pick and choose courses from a myriad of various summer programs throughout their area. Enabling them to come to you as seldom or as often as they like is a plus.

Safety is another important factor with all parents. Staffing your program with certified teachers, well-trained staff, nurses on campus, and multiple adults per field trip will attract parents to your summer program.

CLASS OFFERINGS

A successful summer program offers a wide variety of courses, and might include the following: academics (both remedial and advanced), early childhood classes, extended care, sports, adventure offerings, field trips, tutoring, themed enrichment classes, performing arts and fine arts studies, technology classes, and upper school courses. A successful program tracks the "cash cows" and offers those classes three to four times throughout the summer, whereas normal courses are only offered twice. Enrollment procedures should allow summer directors to easily identify when class is becoming popular. If there is a strong demand for a particular class, I recommend allowing overenrollment or adding another section and another teacher rather than turning away enrollment.

Summer programs may run from one week to 12 weeks, depending on your school's calendar and the climate of your immediate community. I think it's best when 90% of the classes offered are half-day, one-week options. A typical schedule might be 9am-3:30pm or 8:30am-3:30pm, with extended day options before and after these hours. This allows a parent to select many class offerings throughout the summer, regardless of job schedules or previous commitments, creating a unique experience for the child. Forcing parents to sign up for 2-week or 4-week blocks does not give them the flexibility they need during summer vacation. Academic classes should be 4-6 week half-day classes to allow parents to see student progress. Enrichment courses such as sewing classes or field trips may be one-week full-day classes to allow time to properly finish the chosen activity. Early childhood classes should offer even more flexibility to allow parents to utilize the program based on their comfort level.

> A successful program tracks the "cash cows" and offers those classes three to four times throughout the summer, whereas normal courses are only offered twice.

Bus usage is a must for summer programs. Schools may choose to contract buses and drivers or to lease a bus or two for the summer. Depending on the number of trips you offer off-site, leasing a bus may be the most cost-effective route. If you lease a bus, you will need summer staff that can obtain a Commercial Driver's License (CDL), so they can supervise the trip and drive the bus. Lead teachers are often willing to obtain a CDL, because they know where they are going, how long it takes to get there, and like the flexibility to change plans if need be.

The business officer should discuss all insurance issues related to field trips with the school's insurance provider.

As you consider the summer program offerings, don't forget that the school's own coaches may want to run summer sports camps. It's a good idea to have written policies addressing such camps. Although these sports camps may be important to the community, it is imperative that they enhance rather than compete with the summer program. Such clinics might be offered before or after the main summer program.

EMPLOYMENT OPPORTUNITIES FOR THE COMMUNITY

In addition to school-year teachers, the summer program can provide employment to upper school students and alumni. High school students or college-aged alumni may come back to the program year after year to enjoy their summer work as teaching assistants and field trip counselors. This interaction between the young students and older students can be a joy to see. As with all summer program positions, the school should have a salary scale for these positions, with first-year teaching assistants earning around minimum wage. The school might give teaching assistants a \$.50 raise for their second year and a \$1 raise for their third year. Teaching assistants might make anywhere from minimum wage to \$11 per hour, depending on length of service in the program. Similarly, teachers newly graduated from college might start at around \$14 per hour, and others at around \$17-\$18 per hour depending on

experience. Teachers might receive a \$1 per year raise, up to \$20 per hour. After that, they might receive a \$1 raise every 3 years. This system encourages longevity, yet keeps teachers from making \$40 per hour after 20 years of teaching in the summer program. The summer director should also have office assistants—one for a smaller program and two to three for a larger program. The director will need assistance starting in February, when enrollment begins: the paperwork can be overwhelming for one person.

MARKETING AND ADVERTISING

The summer program exists for many reasons, yet one of the main goals is to make a name for the school in the community. Students who attend a program in the summer create a bigger pool of potential applicants for the school year. Summer advertising typically runs from November through May, while regular school advertising tends to be year-round. To conserve both budgets and to show cohesiveness, schools can create dual advertisements. Marketing materials should be designed to reflect the regular school year but have a fun summer flair, and should include direct mail pieces and well-designed, thorough website copy.

PROFIT CENTER

For many schools, the number one reason to have a summer program is to increase auxiliary revenue to help support operations. This makes the business officer an important partner with the summer director in steering the program in the right direction at all times.

Pricing

When it comes to setting prices for each course offering, the summer director should research the area market. It is important to research YMCA camps, town parks and recreation camps, other independent school camps, and any other camps in the area. To attract enrollment in your summer program, prices should be comparable to others in your area. You can utilize "lab" fees or "class" fees to increase the cost of the class. For instance, tennis might cost $80 for a one-week, half-day clinic, but will include a $10 lab fee. This makes the total price $90, but the parent sees that all classes have a base cost of $80, which is the number they will use in comparing your camp with others.

Projection of Profit Per Class

It is helpful to calculate a projected profit for each and every class, based on the expected enrollment per class and all known or estimated expenses, including cost of teacher, cost of teaching assistant(s), cost of materials per student, and any admission fees, bus fees, etc. Once you have determined all expenses per class, you can set the price for the class, based on your school's desired net profit from the summer program.

Canceling of Classes

If possible, the school should avoid canceling summer courses. If there is a class in which only a few students are enrolled, examine ways to make it profitable, such as not having a teaching assistant in the classroom, cutting down on materials, etc. If you must cancel a class, try to do this only once or twice per summer. The school does not want a reputation for canceling summer classes.

Summer Budget

The business officer and summer program director should create a budget with line items that need to be tracked, such as marketing materials, buses, teachers, assistants, payroll taxes, etc. In addition to the direct costs associated with the summer program, there are a number of indirect costs related to the operation of the summer program that should be considered. These include cost of compensation and benefits for the maintenance staff, allocation of compensation and benefits for business office staff and any other administrative support that is not directly charged to the program, an allocation for general overhead such as insurance, copiers, and the like, and an allocation of utility costs (gas, electric, water, etc.) for the facilities used by the program. These are important costs to consider when evaluating the overall profitability of the program. There can be a perception of profitability, which may not be the reality if all of the indirect costs are not factored into the analysis. Both the summer director and business officer should monitor the budget throughout the year. The summer director will become better at managing the budget if he or she is involved with it from the beginning.

Other (Optional) Fees

• *Registration or Application Fee*: It is common to charge a fee of $20 to $50 per enrollment or registration form.

• *Credit Card Fee*: If you accept credit cards, you may want to charge a convenience fee of 3-5% to offset the cost to the school, if the school's state allows such a fee.

- *Cancellation or Change Fee*: This may be charged if a parent calls after registration to change or cancel a class. Such a fee might be $10 for any change; canceling an 8-week program would cost the parent $80.

- *Refunds*: The school should set a date and time after which point no refunds will be allowed. Typically, this is three weeks prior to the first day of the program. The policy should be in writing in several places—in the catalog, on the website, and in any paperwork associated with the program.

- *Miscellaneous*: During the summer, parents may want to buy photos taken during the program, DVDs of performances, t-shirts, etc. The school may charge for such extras.

AFTER-SCHOOL PROGRAMS

After-school programming encompasses much more than simply 3:30-6pm. When the school day ends, a whole new world begins, full of classes, activities, and fun. After-school programming can be made up of extended day programs, after-school classes and clubs, and year-round options. These programs not only enrich the lives of students and give parents flexibility, they give the school another profit center. As always, it is important to make sure the after-school programs align with the mission of the school. It is also important to receive parent and student input on how to make the programs worthwhile and attractive. The business officer should play a major role in supporting these programs.

EXTENDED DAY PROGRAMS

Attendees: Extended day can be offered to your youngest students through your middle-school-aged students. Some schools opt to have 8th graders get used to non-supervision; others include them in the after-care program.

Schedule: Before-school care is typically from 7am until the start of school; after-school care usually runs from the end of school until 6pm.

Environment: An ideal setting separates the early childhood-4th graders from the 5th-7th graders. It is important to hold extended day in a comfortable setting with storage cabinets for blocks, toys, craft supplies, and games. The younger students need a place where they can play on the floor, play board games on tables, color, create arts and crafts, and utilize a nearby playground. The older students simply need a comfortable place to hang out—perhaps a classroom, library, or lounge area where there is plenty of seating, a few board games or card games, computer access, and an outdoor play area nearby. It is nice to have a dedicated space for these programs if possible.

Philosophy: The students have probably been in a very structured environment all day long. When school ends, they still need boundaries, but they also need choice and freedom. Students should be allowed to move freely from one area or activity to another.

Activities: For the younger group of students (early childhood through 4th or 5th graders), the extended day director should create weekly plans. These plans might include two arts and crafts activities per day. These projects do not need to be costly, rather, they can utilize typical supplies such as construction paper, glue, glitter, craft sticks, and the like.

Staffing: Running a robust program may require three or four staff members; one to oversee arts and crafts, one to monitor other indoor activities, and one or two to supervise outside activities. The number of students will begin to diminish after 4:45pm, requiring only two staff persons from 4:45-6pm, when the outside option would be closed.

Pricing: There are many ways to achieve profit, but flexibility and convenience are important to parents. One possible model gives parents three options. They can sign up for a yearly fee in August, which gives them a bit of a price break. The second option lets them pay monthly for as many months as they choose. The third option allows them to sign up by day (paying one price if they sign up a week in advance and paying another price for signing up with less notice). Within the daily prices, the school might offer one price for pickup by 4:30pm and another cost for pickup after 5:30pm.

Expenses: The bulk of expenses for extended day are in staffing. Aside from replenishing old games and materials at the beginning of the school year, expenses for materials should be minimal.

ADDITIONAL EXTENDED DAY OFFERINGS

Other revenue-producing options that might be offered include full-day programs for holidays and professional development days, winter and spring breaks, add-ons, family nights, and special events. These are all programs that the extended day director and business officer should monitor to evaluate revenue, expenses, profit, and additional potential.

Full-Day Programs: There are many days throughout the school year in which regular school is closed due to parent/teacher conferences, holidays, or staff development days. However, parents and faculty still need care options on these days. An excellent solution is a full-day care program, from 7am-6pm, staffed by dynamic and energetic staff members. A typical price for such a program might run between $35-$50 per day. A school may also choose to offer other price options, such as hourly or half-day usage.

Winter and Spring Break Programs: Most independent schools have approximately two weeks off for both winter and spring breaks. Many parents continue to want or need child care during these extended breaks. This is a perfect opportunity to name the breaks something exciting such as "Winter Blast" or "Spring Splash" and offer lots of fun activities. During spring break, the extended day program could offer 10 days of full-day fun with six of those days including off-site field trips. The field trips could be offered from 12-3:30pm, allowing parents to sign up for a full-day price or a field-trip-only price. The field-trip-only price would need to reflect the costs of additional staffing, admission to sites, and bus transportation.

Example: A Trip to the Zoo

- 15 students x $78 per student = $1170 revenue for a field-trip day

- 2 staff x $10 per staff from 7am-12pm and from 3:30-6pm = $150

- 2 additional staff x $10 per staff from 12-3:30pm = $70

- Materials = $3 per child = $45

- Bus = $40 per hour x 4 hours = $160

- Admission = $8 per child x 15 = $120

- Profit = $625 for the day

Add-Ons: Extended day is typically made up of the same core of students each night. Parents who do not need the care may feel guilty sending their child to extended care. Offering what I call add-ons gives these reluctant parents a reason to allow their child to attend the extended care program. A typical add-on could begin at 3:45pm and end around 5pm An extended day program might want to try one add-on per month or one per quarter. Ideas for possible add-ons include inflatables in the gym, a movie with a concession stand, a magic show, a balloon artist, an interactive variety show, etc. Pricing for the add-ons can be a flat fee charge of $15 per child per night. Students who normally attend the program would simply be paying the normal pre-registered charge for late pickup. Utilizing add-ons will increase participation in the extended day program, while enriching the lives of the students, and parents will see the add-on as an extra benefit of independent education.

Family Nights: If you are looking for additional ways to get the family involved in the extended day program, this may be the answer. You might want to offer two family nights per year. Family nights might include a movie night at a local theater, a scavenger hunt at the school, swimming at an indoor water park, a scuba experience at a nearby dive shop, or an evening at a fun field trip locale in town. Pricing for these events depends on location and activity. Events could start around 5:30 or 6pm and parents would drive their own children.

Special Events: There may be a need for extended day care throughout the school year depending on your school's event calendar. One opportunity might be child care for the evening of your annual auction. Another opportunity to make money and offer a service is New Year's Eve. A New Year's Eve event might begin at 6pm and have two optional endings: one at 1am and another at 7am. This special event would be a New Year's Eve for children, complete with the creation of a "ball" to be dropped, music, a balloon drop at midnight, food, drinks, entertainment, karaoke machines, flashlight scavenger hunts, fun competitions, party favors, movies, etc. The goal is to give the children a fun night to remember. Pricing for this event might be $100 per child from 6pm-1am, with a possible additional charge of $75 to stay until 7am.

AFTER-SCHOOL CLASSES AND CLUBS

After-school classes and clubs help to round out the after-school experience during the regular school year. Children are involved in all kinds of after-school activities, from music lessons to karate to art class. An independent school can offer as many activities as feasible to allow parents to find all they need or want in one place. These activities might be semester-long commitments, one-time commitments, or seasonal commitments, depending on the nature of the class or club. The extended day and after-school programs can go hand in hand, which can make them more convenient (and thus attractive) to parents. Parents can send their children to extended day until an after-school class begins; the after-school class teacher can pick students up from extended day and drop them back off after class.

Attendees: Most offerings can be geared toward preschool-through-5th-grade students, although a club such as chess may be offered through 8th grade. I have found that preschool and kindergarten students are your biggest market, followed by 1st-3rd grade. Students in 4th and up often have sports activities after school, making these classes more difficult to fill.

Schedule: Typically, after-school classes and clubs are conveniently offered right after school, around 3:30 or 3:45pm. Most classes last an hour, and might run for one week, four weeks, six weeks, or a semester at a time.

Space: Classes are typically taught in classrooms or spaces that are readily available. For instance, the gym will be hard to come by after school due to sports practices; therefore, karate might be offered in a large classroom where desks and chairs can easily be moved.

Philosophy: This particular program is a service to parents and students first, and a way to make profit second. Parents expect a unique experience from an independent school, and these offerings help to provide that uniqueness. After-school classes should enhance, not detract from, the regular school day curriculum. For instance, if a kindergarten class is studying Hawaii as a part of its social studies curriculum, an enriching after-school class might be "cooking on the Hawaiian Islands," taking the learning experience even further.

Offerings: After-school classes can include origami, science, watercolor painting, holiday snacks, mural painting, karate, drama, movement, music lessons (piano, violin, drums, guitar, voice, etc.), magic tricks, and calligraphy, to name a few. After-school club ideas include chess, great books, robotics, etc. I believe it is wise to ask parents and students what *they* would like to see offered. They will undoubtedly come up with great ideas reflecting current interests. I also suggest offering fall courses and spring courses.

Staffing: One person needs to oversee the after-school classes and clubs; this person is typically the extended day director. Faculty must also be hired to teach the classes. The school might pay each teacher $40 per hour, and pay for supplies. It is important to discuss supply needs with the teacher prior to setting the cost for the course. Avoid using outside vendors for after-school classes—not only does this cut into your profit, but it is also difficult to monitor the quality and image of the class. For instance, if you hire an outside drama group to come in to teach a 6-week class, you really do not know their style of discipline, how they interact with children, how they handle parental issues or comments, etc. It is best to stay with your own faculty if at all possible.

Pricing: Prices vary depending on length of course. The first step is to find a great teacher and discuss materials needed to make the course a success. Next, determine all expenses and decide what kind of profit the school wants to make based on 5 students per course (you may have more per class, but you don't want to cancel classes due to low enrollment).

Example: 4-week (4-hour) Origami Course

- Teacher = $40 x 4 hours = $160
- Materials = $5 per child x 5 students = $25
- Price = $50 x 5 students = $250 and a $65 profit
- Price 2 = $65 x 5 students = $325 and a $140 profit
- If 12 students sign up at $65 each, this would yield a $560 profit

EXTENDED PROGRAMMING OPTIONS

Because parents' work schedules do not follow the school's calendar year, many parents are looking for year-round child care that includes enrichment opportunities. Most summer programs do not begin immediately following the end of regular school, nor do they continue until regular school begins in August. An independent school can solve this problem by offering full-day care and field trips. Therefore, it is important to offer this extended programming from the time your regular school year ends until the time your summer program begins (typically about two weeks). It is also important to offer this extended programming from the time your summer program ends until the time your regular school year begins (also about two weeks).

Attendees: This program can be offered to early childhood students through students about 12 years of age. The biggest market tends to be early childhood through 3rd grade.

Schedule: An extended program follows the normal full-day schedule of 7am-6pm. Field trips should be set up to occur at the same time each day, e.g., 12-3:30pm.

Space: Although summer program is usually setting up when the initial extended programming is happening, and the regular school year is preparing when the final extended programming is happening, there is always a way to make space for about 20 students, utilizing the multi-purpose room, the library, a large classroom, or the dining hall. As long as the administration sees the need for this program, there is always a way

to make it work.

Offerings: This program is similar to a regular winter or spring break, but offers even more flexibility. There can be three options to choose from: full-day care, full-day care plus a field trip option, or a field trip option alone. This allows parents to pick and choose what works for them. Each day is themed and designed to keep the students interested and engaged, continually offering freedom and choice.

Pricing: Three options means three prices:

- Full-day fun, 7am-6pm = $35-$50 per day, depending on the going rate in your area

- Full-day fun + field trip option = $75-100 per day

- Field trip option = 12-3:30pm = around $40 for the field trip alone

CONCLUSION

Any successful program at an independent school takes teamwork. When key administrators work together to support each other's programs in service of the mission of the school, success is within reach. Summer and after-school programs can add enormously to the strength of your campus when their aims are communicated clearly to the school community. I encourage you to dive in (or spend some time enhancing your existing program) today!

NB⊙A

Chapter Thirteen

AUXILIARY SERVICES

Extra Initiatives to Enhance Your Campus

part one:
School Stores

part two:
Facility Rental

part three:
Transportation

IN THIS CHAPTER:

- Outsourcing vs. in-house textbook sales

- Merchandise: basics to bells-and-whistles

- Alcohol, tobacco, wear & tear:
  determining liability

- The road to great routes & schedules

- Emergency communication planning

part one by **Quincy H. Waidelich,**
part two by **Pamela Scanlon,** *and part three by* **Kelly H. Sanderson**

Quincy H. Waidelich
Campus Store Manager, The Lovett School

Quincy Waidelich has been Campus Store Manager at The Lovett School in Atlanta, Georgia, since July of 2007. In this capacity, she has been responsible for all students' textbooks and uniforms, teacher and student supplies, as well as spirit wear and merchandise. She also facilitates new product development, maintains a gift store for the faculty/staff and students' families, and oversees all aspects of the mailroom. Prior to her work at Lovett, Quincy was with Neiman Marcus in both Atlanta and Dallas for seven years, serving in such capacities as Sportshop Department Manager, Intimate Apparel Department Manager, and Assistant Buyer of the Silver Buying Office. At Neiman Marcus, she ultimately managed a $5.5 million business and 11 employees, while developing merchandise assortment strategies with buyers and vendors. Quincy is a cum laude graduate of Auburn University with a bachelor's degree in both apparel merchandising and French.

SCHOOL STORES

What It Takes to Go Retail

School stores can support the entire network of a school, providing services to students, faculty, staff, administrators, parents, and alumni in one place. This chapter gives you a clearer idea of what to expect from this unique retail operation on your campus.

MAKING THE DECISION

A school store provides a central place for students and parents to go to purchase their books, buy their uniforms, and find all of their school supplies for a given school year. Faculty use them to facilitate book ordering and obtain the supplies they need for their daily lesson plans. Many stores provide uniforms and practice equipment for physical education, athletic teams, and spirit items for alumni as well. Being able to offer all of these benefits to a variety of the constituents on your campus can streamline operations and create unity.

But first ask—is there a centralized student center that has the proper access, space, and storage to house this dream store? Is it easily accessible to parents as well as faculty and staff? If not, can future new building and renovation plans include space for a school store?

If your school is located in a remote area, having a store may be even wiser than for more centrally located campuses. Consider that students, faculty, and staff living on a remote campus can utilize a store for regular cleaning supplies and other common necessities, in addition to books, supplies, uniforms, spirit items, etc. If your school is in a more built-up area, be sure to evaluate your proximity to other stores when deciding whether or not to open your own (and choosing which items to carry).

STAFFING

Assuming a school store has been given the green light, your next decision is whether to manage the operation internally with school staff, or to contract with a third-party vendor. There are several organizations that specialize in school store operation (though their focus tends to be at the university and college level), yet the rewards of third-party contracting can be modest. By managing stores internally, schools can retain the profits generated, control pricing, and maintain direct control over the service provided to their school community. Another option, good for small stores with minimal products and inventory, is to have the store operate as a fundraising operation, staffed by either a student or parent group.

OPERATIONS & ACCOUNTING

Independent school stores are typically operated separately from the business office, and use their own retail software to run sales reports and manage inventory, yet the business office needs to be able to integrate the financial information maintained in these accounts into its own system. Many software vendors offer software options that integrate the store's accounting software with the business office's accounting software. Clear communication needs to exist between the store manager and the business officer so that all parties have the information they need. The business office should receive daily reports generated by the store and have access to the store's database to stay abreast of sales and account billing information.

Setting an annual budget to project the net surplus to be generated by the store will guide the amount of inventory it should purchase, as well as the desired margin it should use for sales. It is recommended that actual revenues and expenses be compared to the annual budget on a monthly basis.

Sales tax must be managed properly, and payment method practices should be established for cash, checks, credit cards, debit cards, internal school (bursar) accounts, etc. A successful school store is a business entity on its own (with all the complexities and challenges any small business entails), yet is inseparable from the overall financial health of the school, which is the primary responsibility of the business officer. It could be difficult for a parent council or student group to take on this role in a larger store.

Typically, an annual inventory is performed at the end of each school year, and can either be performed by a third-party vendor or by the store's staff. The annual inventory is critical to determine actual cost of goods sold, loss or theft of product, organization, which items sell well, and the like.

OVERSIGHT

The business officer at an independent school typically oversees school store operations, and will be involved with all aspects of the school store on some level. A full- or part-time store manager will report to the business officer. Consistent communication between the two is needed to ensure that bills are paid on time, that employees receive accurate paychecks and benefits, and that equipment, utilities, and inventory are managed wisely.

PRODUCTS & SERVICES

Product categories and merchandise lines can be added or deleted based on the current demands and forecasted desires of those who utilize the store. Some schools expand product lines to increase profitability within the store, by offering merchandise that yields a higher margin than the competitive market of textbooks. The revenue generated by such a store can support the school's bottom line, which can, in turn, help to manage tuition increases. Other schools choose only to cater to the basic needs of the school: textbooks, uniforms, and supplies. These schools may choose not to be a profit

center, opting only to cover their costs and break even.

Textbooks

The growth of online retailing has had an enormous impact on textbook sales for independent school stores. Several online book vendors have surfaced in recent years to take over the role that many schools once had as the primary source for textbooks. Many schools have outsourced their textbook purchasing function to these companies to facilitate easy purchasing and direct shipments to families, which can be helpful to a school that is not able to staff full-time employees to oversee the large task of coordinating, ordering, and selling books. If you choose to use an online book service and keep a school bookstore, your store manager will likely coordinate book ordering between the faculty and the online vendor. In order for this to work smoothly, your store manager needs to communicate consistently with the online vendor.

However, many independent schools continue to be the sole provider of textbooks to their students. These schools are able to control the prices parents pay, earn a profit on book sales, and more easily avoid ordering incorrect editions of textbooks. Internal book sales also help ensure that all students will come prepared with a book in hand on the first day of school. (Some schools take this to the next level and package all of the books required for each student for all of his or her classes.)

Spirit Wear

As schools have grown, so have the

stores within them. Many schools have taken their traditional "bookstores" a step further, and now include large spirit wear departments. Many have spirit merchandise available online, through dynamic website pages that offer memorabilia geared toward alumni, parents, and grandparents. Everything from t-shirts to car flags are marketed in an attempt to appeal to those who live outside of the school's area or who can't easily visit the school's physical store. The store may also work with the athletic program for every sport played at the school to make sure the store carries the items that athletes and their supporters will need for their games.

At most schools, customers can only purchase their spirit merchandise from the school store. Thus, the store should be kept open during sporting and special events, to serve fans and visitors.

Mini Gift Shops

Within many stores, schools are able to create mini "gift shops" for their clientele, which can include a wide variety of items such as gift books, jewelry, lotions, greeting cards, and home décor. These stores may also offer complimentary gift-wrapping and shipping services for their customers.

Cafés

Cafés are often established within, or next to, a school store. These may sell not only beverages and snacks, but also breakfast and lunch for students who choose not to eat in the cafeteria. A bookstore-plus-café can form the nucleus of a campus community center and serve as an important focus for daily social interaction. In addition to accepting cash, checks, and credit cards as forms of payment, student, departmental, and faculty/staff accounts can be established to allow customers ease of purchasing within the store.

Food

Food sales at school stores can be a challenge. Parents may ask that certain food items (soda, candy, and snacks) be excluded from a school store, yet these are often the exact items that students want to buy. The business officer and senior administrators need to weigh the value of certain food sales against health concerns, taking into account the availability of food from other sources. Vending machines are another area of concern and control. Large beverage companies offer very attractive incentives to schools to install vending machines with their products. A school can take advantage of these offers, or purchase its own vending machines and maintain them with private local vending machine operators. Food sales may be completely restricted at boarding schools with concerns about food in dorm rooms.

CONCLUSION

A school store can add a great deal of value to your school, but requires significant resources to maintain. The right answer for your school is somewhere between cost and benefit. We hope this chapter has provided you with a foundation from which to make the decision to begin or change your campus retail operation.

Pamela Scanlon

Business Manager for Finance and Facilities,
Albuquerque Academy

Pamela Scanlon is a financial management professional with diversified experience in budget administration, investments, institutional risk management, financial analysis, fund/cash flow management, and accounting. She has been with Albuquerque Academy, a coed day school of 1085 students, for 20 years. She is responsible for the management of various fiscal and operational aspects of the school, including facilities (maintenance, grounds, custodial, and security), financial aid, institutional risk management, and related portions of the school's operating budget. She also assists the Academy's treasurer with maintenance of the school's endowment, including preparation of consolidated quarterly performance reports, monitoring of the endowment spending policy and investment of temporary funds in accordance with school policy and cash flow projections. Pam's responsibilities also extend into human resources and strategic and long-range business planning. Prior to her work in independent schools, Pam served as Credit Analysis Manager/ Cash Management Representative at First National Bank in Albuquerque.

FACILITY RENTAL

To Be, Or Not To Be, A Landlord

Given that most schools have limited facilities available to support various programs and activities, it becomes important to share and manage these facilities in a manner that reinforces and enhances the school's mission. A framework for sharing the school's facilities with the outside community (while minimizing the impact on curricular programming, school employees, and facilities) is essential to the success of this type of endeavor. Establishing and consistently following a structured process for sharing facilities with outside users makes good business sense and can significantly support and enhance the school's mission.

WHY RENT?

Schools allow their facilities to be used by external groups for many reasons. The demands on schools to keep tuition increases as low as possible while increasing faculty salaries, enhancing the physical plant, and offering extensive financial aid have increased significantly as rising costs outpace increases in family income. As a result, quite often a school will attempt to earn additional revenue by renting out facilities when they are not in use for its regular program.

Facility rental may also:

- provide a marketing opportunity to reach out to potential students and their families

- foster reciprocal partnerships with outside entities that may provide benefits to current students

- provide a form of community service in support of groups that advance education or other mission-related interests

It's also important to evaluate the potential negative impact that external facility use may bring. Rentals may bring in revenue, but when examining the full cost of the rental—staff time to clean and maintain the space, insurance, and utilities—the school often just breaks even. Even if a rental program is particularly successful from a monetary standpoint, the strain on physical plant personnel, wear and tear on the facility, and the increase in administrative tasks may impact daily operations and staff morale. There are also potential liability issues in all rental situations, which must be factored into the decision to allow outside use. Finally, it is important to evaluate reputational risk if an outside event is controversial or handled poorly.

Assuming that the school has made the decision to allow outside use of its facilities, the next step is to identify spaces suitable for use by external groups and the times such facilities are available for this purpose. This conversation should involve a number of individuals on campus, including the facilities director, the scheduler of the master calendar, the risk manager, the individual who is responsible for coordinating rentals, and others who may be able to assess the impact of outside use of specific facilities on curricular and extracurricular programming. The key to these discussions is to seek a balance so that campus facilities are used in a manner that does not disrupt student activities, overextend physical plant personnel, cause excessive deterioration of the facility, or increase administrative tasks beyond the available resources. Other factors that should be taken into consideration include the overall impact on the school's master calendar and additional resources that may need to be added to support this endeavor.

POTENTIAL USERS

The next step is to develop criteria for determining who may use the facilities and under what conditions they may use them. For many schools, the largest determinant may lie in the nature of the requesting organization. For example, a school may limit use of its facilities to nonprofits that serve children, organizations that build community, or organizations with close ties to the school. Your school will need to determine whether groups with religious, partisan, political, or sectarian purposes will be allowed to use the facilities, and whether certain groups will be given preference over others. You should also consider whether any particular user groups could trigger Unrelated Business Income Tax (UBIT), or may be expressly prohibited in the school's tax-exempt bond indentures.

As the school contemplates "tenant" criteria, it may be helpful to categorize potential users along a continuum that prioritizes certain organizations over others. For example, a school may choose to rank potential users as follows:

1. nonprofits involving youth, education, or others that contribute to the mission and purposes of the school

2. other nonprofits

3. community groups, e.g., dance or drama groups, choirs, cultural organizations

4. functions sponsored by service clubs

5. industrial or business athletic groups or leagues

6. social functions such as fundraising, wedding receptions, dances, and parties

7. commercial enterprises or activities involving personal or individual use or gain

Once the school has determined who may use its facilities, a decision must be made on how to appropriately charge for use. While there may be some circumstances in which it is appropriate to waive the rental fee, for most users some type of fee is generally in order. You may want to use the potential user criteria enumerated above to develop a similarly scaled pricing structure.

Potential Rental Rates:

1. The user is assessed a fee which covers direct costs, including utilities, personnel services, security, equipment use, etc.

2. The user is assessed a fee which covers direct costs and an indirect cost

charge for processing, administration, etc.

3. The user is assessed a fee which covers direct and indirect costs plus a capital costs charge for normal wear and tear and long-term maintenance of equipment and facilities.

Alternatively, for some schools, it may be appropriate to base rental fees on local commercial rental rates for comparable space.

COMMUNICATION AND THE CAMPUS SPONSOR

Once your school has developed its list of available facilities, determined who will be allowed to use those facilities, and worked out its pricing structure, you'll need to establish a routine contact procedure for potential users. It is often helpful to have potential users complete a facility use request form. In addition to providing the school with the necessary information to make an informed decision, the form can be used to convey the school's philosophy on facilities use and the criteria by which decisions are made.

As part of the rental process, your school may find it beneficial to require outside users to secure a campus sponsor for their event. A sponsor is generally a member of the faculty or staff who has obligated himself or herself to remain present during the event from start to finish. Using a campus sponsor ensures effective communication on important issues like security and maintenance. The sponsor will also have knowledge of and be able to implement the campus emergency plan. In addition, a sponsor will ensure that campus facilities are respected and left clean and that the off-campus group is given access only to those areas described in the use agreement.

SIGNING ON THE DOTTED LINE

Once an outside user has been granted use of a facility, it is imperative that the school enters into a binding agreement with the user. The agreement or contract should identify the specific facility to be used, the date and time of use, and the rental fee. In addition, the agreement should provide a schedule for the payment of fees and deposits. It should also specify a cancellation fee, if appropriate.

Obtain legal advice to craft an agreement that covers all important liability issues. The agreement should contain language specifically stating that the user shall defend, indemnify, and hold harmless the school against all claims involving intentional misconduct, negligence, etc., which might arise out of use of the facilities. The user should also be required to provide a certificate of insurance naming the school as certificate holder or additional insured. In conjunction with its insurance broker, the school should determine acceptable minimum limits for a user's property and casualty coverage and commercial general liability coverage. Such insurance is necessary to protect the school against any financial loss occasioned by property damage or physical injury relating to the user's use of the facilities. The

school should also reserve the right to immediately terminate an agreement in the event that required insurance coverage is not obtained.*

The agreement should also contain:

- acknowledgment that while the school will honor its agreement to keep the space available, should a scheduling conflict occur, school activities take precedence

- language regarding relief from liability for the loss, damage, or destruction of the user's property

- any restrictions on alcohol or smoking

- all building and fire codes

- any restrictions on parking

Often a user will want to employ an outside vendor for its event, such as a caterer or musician. In order to limit liability in this area, your school may wish to establish a list of acceptable vendors who may be employed by outside users for campus events. This way, the school can ensure that all vendors operating on campus have appropriate insurance coverage, including general liability, automobile, workers compensation, and liquor liability (for events where alcohol is served).

Finally, the agreement should contain the stipulation that the user agrees not to allow any other organization to participate in the use of the facility without the written consent of the school and that only the facilities specifically named in the agreement are available to the user.

---

*Editor's Note: NBOA member schools have access to TULIP (Tenant User Liability Insurance Program). This service allows a school to provide prospective tenants with a way to obtain necessary insurance if they do not already have access to it.

The agreement should further specify that the user may not make alterations or improvements to the facility without the school's written consent. It should also state that the school's name may not be used in the solicitation of funds for events not sponsored by the school, and that use of school facilities does not imply the school's endorsement of the event or sponsoring organization.

FOLLOW-UP

Following any outside use of school facilities, it is very helpful to perform a quick review of the event utilizing a basic evaluation form. If the school requires a campus sponsor for outside events, this person is the most logical contact for the follow-up.

A facilities use evaluation form might contain the following questions:

- How was the group to work with while planning the event, during the event, and after the event?

- Did the group leave the facility clean and in good condition?

- Did the group follow the school's policies and procedures?

- Were there any incidents during the event that need to be addressed?

- Overall, how would you rate the group's use of campus resources?

The continued use of school facilities by any group should be made contingent upon the group's taking proper steps to protect your school property and follow the agreement it made with your school. Once you work with a particular user, you will become familiar with that group's willingness and ability to abide by general guidelines.

CONCLUSION

You, as the business officer, will likely be "chief landlord." The more you rent, the more you will learn about which "tenants" work well and which procedures don't, and with time you'll be able to adjust accordingly. With clear communication and strict backup documentation, facility rental can increase revenue at your school and establish valuable partnerships with desired groups in your community.

NB⬤A

Kelly H. Sanderson, CPA

Assistant Vice President for Finance and Administration, Woodward Academy

Prior to her current position at Woodward Academy, Kelly Sanderson served as the Director of Operations and CFO for All Saints' Episcopal School of Fort Worth, Texas. Kelly has 12 years of experience as an administrator in independent schools following 10 years of experience in public accounting. While working In thls industry, she focused on not-for-profit auditing and taxation. Kelly has actively participated in school accreditation visits as part of multiple visiting teams for the Independent Schools Association of the Southwest and the Southwestern Association of Episcopal Schools. She was also a visiting team chairman for the Southern Association of Independent Schools. She has presented training programs for multiple independent school associations, and has actively participated in training activities with Mid-South Independent School Business Officers. One of Kelly's significant responsibilities is the daily management of the Woodward Academy bus company and its nearly 50 employees.

TRANSPORTATION

Taking Charge of the Commute

Atransportation program is a significant commitment for an independent school. This chapter will provide you with guidance to help decide whether or not it's a commitment that's right for *your* school. With advance planning and thorough oversight, a transportation program can greatly enhance the service your school provides to its many constituents: students, parents, faculty, and staff.

A NOTE ON OUTSOURCING

As with other auxiliary programs or specialized services, one critical decision is whether to provide the service through the school or contract with an external company. Using an outside vendor transfers some of the risks and headaches of running a bus service, but also transfers some of the control. The decision should be made in the context of the school's mission, resources, and culture. This chapter focuses on providing transportation services through the school, yet the issues covered here will also arise with an outsourced program.*

COMMUTING

Providing a way for students to commute to and from campus is a common reason for a school to choose to have transportation services. To assess whether or not commuting is right for your school, it helps to ask the following questions:

Is there parent demand?

Parents want transportation, but your school needs to know if parents are willing to pay for it, either by an additional fee or by a tuition increase. In order to determine how much commuting would cost, you and the other senior administrators at your school should complete an analysis of your school's demographics, assessing the residential locations of the student body. Commuting service is a more viable option if a large number of students reside in a concentrated area and becomes less cost-effective if the student body is spread out. Commuting services are also more cost-effective if door-to-door bus stop service is not required. Once you have determined the basic price points, communicate with parents to assess real demand through meetings, surveys, phone calls, etc. Find out whether the demand for service has arisen because both parents work and they struggle to get to your school, or if other factors are at play. Do they want to save time? Convenience? The answers to these questions will help you make a decision that serves your student population, at a cost parents are happy to pay.

Does transportation support your school?

If the purpose of commuter transportation does not support your school's mission and strategic objectives, reevaluate the proposition.

Would your school realize a benefit in enrollment?

If your school struggles with consistent enrollment numbers or seeks to grow in size, commuting services may be a way to address these concerns.

Would your school support bus operations?

Since the employee and financial commitment can be substantial, your school leadership needs to view bus transportation as a key operational component.

Are there other options available?

Can students use public transportation such as trains and buses? Can the school utilize transportation from public schools? In many states, public schools are required to provide bus service to students in the school's town or within a certain radius of the school.

INTERNAL SUPPORT SERVICES

The second (and more typical) reason to provide bus service is to support athletics and extracurricular activities. Having buses available throughout the day to transport teams to and from events can be convenient and reliable. Academic

---

Editor's Note: Should your school outsource this function, it is imperative that the contract with the bus company be reviewed with a critical eye toward risk management. Schools should require the company to name the school as an additional insured on their insurance policies and require evidence that all drivers have received required training and passed thorough background checks.

programs and extracurricular activities can prosper from the flexibility afforded by this in-house mobility.

ESTABLISHING ROUTES AND SCHEDULES

Once a school has decided to further pursue commuting services, it needs to establish routes. Student and family residential data can be imported from admission and business office records software, then organized with a visual mapping software program like Microsoft MapPoint. Administrators can use this information to determine the most concentrated areas of the student body and view areas of potential growth. Parent surveys can also yield information regarding possible bus stop locations. Your school should decide if door-to-door residential commuting service is appropriate or if designated stops (churches, shopping centers, etc.) are the right choice, with the proviso that designated stops should never be on a road with moving traffic. Your school will need to obtain appropriate permission from property owners prior to announcing a designated stop location. Additionally, schools should research local and state legislation for unique and specific guidelines. Regulations regarding interaction with public schools and locations of designated bus stops may exist.

Once routes are established, specific timing details will need to be worked out:

- When must the bus begin the route to arrive at school on time?

- How many stops should be on a single route?

- How much time should be allowed at each stop between arrival and departure?

- Should your school day begin at a later time to allow for commuter bus arrival?

- What time must the bus leave school in the afternoon for the reverse process?

Your school will also need to decide whether it seeks to provide commuting services to students a) only in the mornings, b) immediately upon afternoon dismissal, and/or c) after extracurricular activities. The possibilities can be modified to accommodate the school's needs, and most importantly, support the mission.

Schools must also determine where buses will be parked, and where the student boarding and disembarking processes will occur. Permission may be obtained from local municipalities to temporarily close a street adjacent to your school during specific times of the day to ensure student safety while boarding and disembarking.

WHO WILL DRIVE THE BUS?

Once routes are established and timing is refined, a school should decide upon bus drivers. Some schools use their teachers and coaches as drivers, while other schools prefer to hire specially designated drivers as employees. There are advantages and disadvantages to both. The internal model can be convenient and may offer payroll expense savings, but your school should make sure that training is sufficient (even when a Commercial Drivers License [CDL] is not required), that the employee is an insured driver through your school's insurance carrier, and that the employee's educational duties do not hinder his or her availability to drive. Additionally, labor laws should be reviewed to make sure that the employee is appropriately compensated for all driving time. Conversely, the decision to hire a designated bus driver should include attention and thought to cost, benefits eligibility, supervision, training, and the potential hire's availability to work flexible hours and dates. All drivers must be properly trained and maintain state-required licenses (typically a Class B CDL driver's license with S [school bus] and P [passenger] endorsements to drive any bus larger than a 14-passenger bus). Total hours of work (per day and per week) and daily levels of responsibility should be analyzed to make sure that your driver is safely performing his or her duties. Membership in the Department of Transportation (DOT) is voluntary, inexpensive, and can be extremely beneficial. DOT provides specific guidelines that need to be followed, and is the highest authority governing transportation; it takes priority over state regulations if transportation is across state lines.

BUS PURCHASING

Bus vendors such as Thomas, BlueBird, and Collins provide good products. A vendor's quote for a new school bus does not usually allow for much, if any, price negotiation, nor does it include substantial incentives. The cost of a bus can affect a school's operating budget greatly, so size and price must be carefully considered. A school bus may range in price from about $50,000 for a 14-passenger vehicle to well over $100,000 for larger buses. Schools are encouraged to purchase all available safety options, including higher seatbacks and three-point harnesses or seatbelts. School bus color should be considered as well. Yellow is the most recognizable color for a school bus and is the preferred choice for safety reasons. Having yellow school buses may also be an explicit requirement of state regulations. School logos, radios, and cameras are usually options installed on buses by a separate vendor; these features add to the total cost.

Once a decision is made, the turnaround for delivery of a bus is often several months, so advance planning is necessary. New bus purchases can often be financed over a 7-year term. "Useful life," as defined by years of service, will vary depending upon mileage, but useful life defined by total mileage is generally around 250,000 miles per diesel fuel bus and 100-150,000 miles per nondiesel fuel bus. Typically, the larger-sized buses utilize diesel fuel while the smaller-sized buses can be manufactured for diesel or unleaded gasoline (but not both).

INCORPORATION AND LIABILITY

Your school should evaluate the appropriateness of separately incorporating the bus operations of your school. This decision would likely be made for a school providing commuting transportation services. Legal advice is essential in this area. Risk needs to be assessed, mitigated, and then properly insured.

BUDGETING

Transportation financial records need to be separately maintained, whether or not bus operations are separately incorporated, because the bus operation is a separate legal entity.

Transportation services can be a separate "budget within a budget." The goal is a break-even budget whereby parents pay for all commuting services. The difficulty is that buses are likely to also be used for internal purposes (academics, athletics) when they are not commuting. Thus, the operating budget of your school will incur expenses for bus operations (driver wages, bus maintenance, fuel, loan payments, insurance, etc.), some of which are for commuting services and some of which are for school operations. To determine what share of the expenses are to be recaptured by billing commuting parents for bus fees, detailed records will need to be maintained. A reliable method of allocation can be based upon mileage of all activities. Total expenses would be allocated among commuting activities and internal activities based upon mileage per group, as a percentage of total mileage. The cost for commuting activities would then be billed to parents.

Your school will also need to create a pricing structure. Questions that need to be addressed to do this include:

- Should your school charge the

same price for all parents regardless of distance, or maintain a separate pricing structure based upon distance of each route?

- Will your school charge less for students who ride only one way?

- Should your school provide single bus passes for those who may have only an occasional need to commute?

Budgeting of bus transportation is extremely sensitive to number of riders, in addition to bus maintenance and repair and changing prices in gasoline. Knowing ridership prior to the start of your school year will help to properly plan routes and better enable your school to cover operating expenses.

Based upon availability, sales of single bus passes may be an excellent opportunity to market a school's bus transportation program, and marketing is important. A school bus with prominent logo placement can represent your school throughout a community, city, and state; increase public awareness of your school; and generate interest in enrollment.

PASSENGER REGISTRATION

A school should consider the appropriate timing to extend the invitation to register for services. Each year's pricing will be based upon volatile estimates, so it's important to know which students are eager for the service. Your school will also need to decide whether the contracted service is refundable or nonrefundable. The answer depends upon your school's culture and the pressure that this program places upon the operating budget. Registration before the conclusion of

Year 1 allows for better planning and budgeting for services provided in Year 2. Registration can become the basis for bus rosters, which can then be used daily to maintain student records of participation.

GREEN BUSES

Schools should also consider the viability of utilizing eco-friendly fuels. Biodiesel and compressed natural gas are options available as alternatives to diesel and unleaded gasoline fuel. Most new buses can accommodate the transition, while older buses may not; either may incur conversion costs. In addition to analyzing cost, consideration should be given to the location of providers of alternative fuels as well as their method of transporting fuel, since the product may not be available in desired school bus locations. Additional information is available at *www.biodiesel.org* and *www. eere.energy.gov*.

CUSTOMER SERVICE

Bus transportation generates a new opportunity to provide customer service to students and families. Email can be extremely helpful as a communication tool. A school can use the address bus@ schoolname.org, and set up its email program so that this address automatically forwards to personnel responsible for managing bus issues. Schools should also consider a designated emergency dispatch number, which can be distributed to all parents. The line can be monitored while all buses are operational so that drivers can call for assistance and parents can call with concerns. (However, drivers should

never make or receive phone calls while in transit.) Dual radio and cell phones can be installed on buses that can also include Global Positioning System (GPS). Multiple cameras on buses providing digital information can be used to address disciplinary issues and monitor activities. A transportation link on your school's website with bus schedules and important phone numbers is a helpful tool for the community. Your school could also create a bus reservation system on its internal website (using an open source application) so that school personnel can reserve buses for school activities. Frequent electronic memos to parents can also address issues related to bus activities.

CONCLUSION

As with all issues relating to school administration, there are multiple ways to meet an objective. There is no single method to providing optimum bus transportation, but the goal should always be "safety first!"

NBOA

Chapter Fourteen

ENVIRONMENTAL SUSTAINABILITY

Driving the Green Initiative at Your School

IN THIS CHAPTER:

- How a societal priority became an educational priority

- Starting from scratch with a small budget

- LEED & building green

- Committing your school to carbon neutrality

- Real-life examples

by Wynn Calder

Wynn Calder
Principal, Sustainable Schools, LLC

Wynn Calder directs Sustainable Schools, LLC, working primarily with K–12 independent and private schools to build environmental sustainability into strategic planning, campus operations, curriculum, and community outreach. He directs the Association of University Leaders for a Sustainable Future (ULSF), the secretariat for signatories of the Talloires Declaration. He is also the senior strategist for Green Schools Alliance. In the early 1990s, he worked for six years at Harvard University in the area of academic counseling and admission. From 1984–1986, he taught history and was an Assistant Director of Admissions at Milton Academy. Wynn has been principal consultant on environmental sustainability for the National Association of Independent Schools (NAIS) since 2003, and chairs the NAIS Summer Institute for Leadership in Sustainability. He is also a co-founder of the U.S. Partnership for the United Nations Decade of Education for Sustainable Development (2005–2014). Wynn attended Germantown Friends School in Philadelphia. He received his Bachelor's Degree from Harvard University in 1984 and his Master's from Harvard Divinity School in 1993. Wynn is based in Washington, D.C.

ENVIRONMENTAL SUSTAINABILITY

Driving the Green Initiative at Your School

Kofi Annan, former Secretary-General of the United Nations, puts the concept of "going green" this way: "Our biggest challenge in this new century is to take an idea that seems abstract—sustainable development—and turn it into a daily reality for all the world's people." (2002) Independent schools are especially suited to take leadership in this critical endeavor. They consistently aspire to instill in graduates such qualities as good citizenship, moral integrity, leadership, critical thinking, and indeed, care for the environment. The work of building a sustainable world requires precisely these qualities and more. Choosing to start or expand a "green" initiative at your school can be the ultimate fulfillment of these ideals, and the moment to do so has perhaps never been more urgent.

This chapter makes the argument that as sustainability becomes a societal priority, it must also become an educational priority. There is a growing imperative in the educational community to model environmental, social, and economic responsibility and to prepare students to be leaders in building a more sustainable world. As the business officer, you sit at the nexus of nearly every decision to make your campus more or less sustainable. Your oversight of plant management means you can choose to install energy-efficient lighting. Your role as transportation program manager means you can purchase fuel-efficient vehicles. Your supervision of food services on campus means you get to decide whether or not to order recycled paper products or local produce or fair trade coffee. And, of course, as steward of the school's financial resources, you determine where the line is between saving the planet and keeping the school within a reasonable budget. In increasing numbers, schools are becoming more environmentally sustainable without breaking the bank. And in several areas, such as energy and water conservation and sustainable landscaping, they are saving money.

THE EARTH OUR STUDENTS WILL INHERIT

By almost any measure, humanity is living unsustainably. According to the 2005 United Nations Millennium Ecosystem Assessment, "there is no longer any doubt that every ecosystem that life depends on is compromised and in danger."[1] By some estimates, half of all plant and animal species could be extinct by the end of the 21st century if our current rate of habitat destruction continues. Our students will be the first in human history to inherit a world where climate stability cannot be counted on.

Our social and economic challenges are equally abundant. Americans comprise about 5% of the world's population, but consume nearly 25% of the world's resources. The extent to which we collect and consume "stuff" continues to be the measure of our well-being. Yet ironically, more than 36 million Americans today live in poverty.[2]

If we are to learn to live sustainably over the course of this century, we will need, to a significant extent, to transition from:

- "Take, make, waste" to cyclical production

- Individual-centered mindsets to community-centered mindsets

- Ignoring our impact on the environment & other species to managing our impact on the environment & other species

- "Traditional" energy to renewable energy, e.g., fossil power to solar power

The skills needed to make these transitions are skills that you, as the business officer, already possess. You conserve resources and manage risk on a daily basis. The information needed to make these transitions is also information you (sometimes alone) possess: you know

1 See www.millenniumassessment.org/en/synthesis.aspx. 2 See www.census.gov/Press-Release/www/releases/archives/income_ wealth/007419.html.

how much electricity your school uses, how old the buildings are, how much money you have to work with—in short, you know exactly what factors to consider when rethinking your school's impact on the planet.

DEFINING SUSTAINABILITY

The concept of sustainable development emerged in the 1970s in response to a growing awareness of the need to link economic and social progress with environmental responsibility. The most common definition of sustainable development—the so-called Brundtland definition from the 1987 report of the World Commission on Environment and Development—is development that "meets the needs of the present without compromising the ability of future generations to meet their own needs." Unlike traditional development policy and practice, this definition sought to strike a balance between environmental protection and economic growth in the context of long-term intergenerational responsibility. Applying the principle of sustainable development to your school bears some resemblance to preserving intergenerational equity in endowment management—only with different types of resources.

In the 1990s the concept of sustainability became synonymous with the "triple bottom line," which emphasizes the interrelatedness of the environment, the economy, and society, and the need to ensure the health of all three, both now and into the future. "Sustainability

is an ideal end-state," writes Alan AtKisson. "Like democracy, it is a lofty goal whose perfect realization eludes us."[3] Fundamentally, sustainability is a definition of progress. It implies a dynamic condition that balances ecological health with human well-being and economic viability. Solutions to our societal problems need to make economic sense, take care of people and communities, and protect the environment. If we don't address all three at the same time, then we'll continue to give with one hand while taking with the other.

Most independent schools have promoted social justice, fairness, and equity for decades among their staff, faculty, and students. But they have not typically committed to environmental sustainability or to thinking about the economy, society, and environment in an integrated way. The business officer, however, almost always has to balance a variety of "dueling" bottom lines—managing the reputation of the school while respecting its unique culture, acquiring new technology while honoring old ways of doing things, and funding new programs while knowing where to cut or reduce. For most schools, the sustainability conversation begins with environmental concerns and expands out from there. Business officers are well positioned to facilitate and help manage these new opportunities.

WHERE TO BEGIN

A good place to start is to engage your board of trustees in helping you create a

3 *"The Compass of Sustainability," 1998.*

strategic sustainability plan. From there, or in tandem, you can create a sustainability task force that includes faculty, administration, staff, and students. This is a critical step in moving the campus from curiosity or interest to action. Initially, it is recommended that you conduct a sustainability assessment of the school with both qualitative (student and staff behaviors, knowledge and attitudes) and quantitative (energy and water audits) elements. A campus assessment enables you to understand where you are, to establish a baseline, and to form a realistic plan going forward.[4]

Going green can seem daunting, especially for schools that are just starting to think about this issue. But read on: no matter what your budget, no matter what your resources, there is a sustainability initiative that suits your school and might even save you money. Once you've figured out what it is, you can help drive it.

STARTING FROM SCRATCH WITH A SMALL BUDGET

Numerous small steps can be taken on campus to build a culture of sustainability and positively affect the bottom line. Capturing peoples' passion and imagination, and engaging them in efforts to improve the planet, can bring powerful results at little or no cost.

Recycle:
Start or improve your recycling program (important because this engages the whole school community in a visible way):

introduce more signage, more education (perhaps have a student-led assembly), and better placement of containers. In addition to paper, plastic, and aluminum, start collecting rechargeable batteries, cell phones, toner cartridges, old computers, and find how and where they can be recycled (see ***www.greenschoolproject. com***). Some of these items can be sold to recyclers.

Reduce Paper & Disposables:
In addition to recycling, launch a "reduce, reuse" campaign in all offices and classrooms. This includes printing less and requiring double-sided copying. Consider instituting "waste-free lunches," which encourage students and parents to think about packaging and how much they throw away.

Use Energy-Efficient Lightbulbs:
Switch to compact fluorescent bulbs (CFLs) throughout the school. Although they might cost more upfront, CFLs can last up to thirteen times longer than incandescents, use 70% less energy, and save hundreds of pounds of CO_2.[5]

Instill a Culture of Conservation:
While you're waiting for your shipment of CFLs, begin to encourage habits of conservation within the school community. These include turning out lights, turning computers, TVs, and other appliances off at night, keeping windows closed at appropriate times, disallowing space heaters, turning thermostats down one degree in winter and up two degrees in summer, etc. Over time, these small actions can save the school significant energy and utility expense.

Install Power Meters:

Install power meters in each building to determine how much power you are using and wasting. Meters can be installed with a display screen in a common area to show daily power consumption to the entire campus, inspiring more conservative use of resources.

Install "Watchdog" Gadgets:

There are several inexpensive devices on the market that can make your school more energy-efficient and save you money on utility bills, such as motion sensors for lighting and programmable thermostats.

Buy Green:

Negotiate with your vendors to ensure that you get the most socially and environmentally responsible products available—from recycled paper and non-toxic cleaning products to VOC-free paint and carpeting. Consider joining an independent school green purchasing consortium, or launch one in your region.

Plant a Garden:

Start a small garden (butterfly, herb, native, or vegetable). This can be used for class instruction or a "hands-to-work" program, and can be expanded to grow produce to feed the school community.

Conserve Water:

Consider banning bottled water from school. Promote the healthy consumption of filtered municipal water and encourage students and staff to carry reusable water bottles (preferably steel) for use during the school day. Consider installing waterless urinals, low-flush toilets, sink aerators, and "low-flow" shower heads in your locker rooms. Minimize watering on campus grounds and use drought-resistant plants where possible.

BIG BUDGET ITEMS

Building Green

It has been repeatedly shown that schools can increase their fundraising dollars when building green. As the cost gap between traditional and sustainable design narrows, going green is becoming practice rather than trend.

Think Before You Build

Assess and repurpose existing building space where possible to avoid new construction. Consider making green renovations on your existing buildings your first priority since new buildings—whether energy-efficient or not—use additional resources and energy.

Become LEED-Certified

When people talk about green building, the term "LEED rating" usually comes up. "LEED" stands for Leadership in Energy and Environmental Design, and the rating system is the brainchild of the U.S. Green Building Council. The ratings help focus the design efforts of aspiring green builders and provide public validation and benchmarking for green projects. A recent development in favor of the educational community is a new rating system designed specifically for school buildings. Inaugurated in April of 2007, "LEED for Schools" pays particular attention to issues unique to educational institutions, such as classroom acoustics, master planning, mold prevention, and environmental site assessment. You can seek LEED certification for either new construction or renovations.[6]

6 For more information, visit **www.usgbc.org**.

Hire Green Planners & Architects

Hire building consultants with special expertise in green building or with LEED accreditation. These consultants are familiar with LEED standards and can help you design the process and set the objectives you would use to recruit architects, engineers, and others.

OTHER MAJOR GREEN INITIATIVES

Conduct a Formal Energy Audit & Invest in Upgrades

This audit will enable you to identify major areas of inefficiency in your buildings and invest in technology upgrades and infrastructure changes that will save significant money over time.[7] Consider working with an energy consulting firm or contract with an energy services company (ESCO) to optimize your campus energy use. Generally speaking, working with an energy consultant will be cheaper than contracting with an ESCO. The consultant will require more investment of staff time but the results may better reflect your specific needs. The primary value of an ESCO contract is that you receive integrated design and implementation services with guaranteed operational and financial outcomes.[8]

Shrink Your Carbon Footprint

Commit your school to carbon neutrality by 2020. This is an ambitious goal to set for a school, and is a powerful commitment to the well-being of future generations. In order to accomplish this, consider joining a community of like-minded schools and sign on to the Green Schools Alliance (GSA) Climate Commitment as a "Champion," which commits the school to a 30% reduction in carbon emissions within five years and to carbon neutrality by 2020.[9]

Eat Green

Start a sustainable food initiative with the full engagement of your director of food services. Promote local, organic, and fair-trade food options where possible.[10]

Travel Green

Invest in fuel-efficient and/or electric school vehicles as existing vehicles become obsolete. Create a student and staff-run biodiesel program using campus and local vegetable oil. This can provide real fuel for converted campus vehicles and enhance teaching and research in science courses.

Landscape Green

Launch a green landscaping initiative that includes minimal use of pesticides (including use of environmentally safe turf and pest control products on your athletic fields). Reduce the amount of managed turf grass on campus and increase native plantings. Use drought-resistant plants where possible and if watering is necessary, use drip irrigation.

Teach Green

Work with your sustainability task force to provide opportunities for faculty

7 For more information on energy auditing, consult EPA's Guidelines for Energy Management at **www.energystar.gov**. 8 For a detailed discussion of these choices, consult NAIS's guide on "How to Assess Environmental Sustainability at Your School" at **www.nais.org**. 9 For more information, visit **www.greenschoolsalliance.org**. For information on performing an emissions inventory, see Clean Air Cool Planet's Campus Carbon Calculator at **www.cleanair-coolplanet.org**. 10 For more information, see NAIS's guide, "How to Build and Run a Sustainable Dining Program," at **www.nais.org**.

members to incorporate environmental and sustainability topics in existing courses—and perhaps offer a course on sustainable development. Encourage the school community, through assemblies and speaker series, to explore and discuss the "quality of life" issues that underlie many of our efforts to make our schools more sustainable. (To what extent are our own lifestyles more or less sustainable? Do we consume too much? How much is enough? Is sustainability a cornerstone of our mission? To what extent does our school promote values that are in line with an environmentally sustainable and equitable future? How are we or are we not, as individual teachers, administrators, staff, and students, practicing what we preach?)[11]

REAL-LIFE EXAMPLES

The following brief examples from independent schools illustrate a variety of existing approaches to sustainability.

Energy

Northfield-Mount Hermon School (Northfield, MA) is a co-founder of the Green Cup Challenge, an interscholastic energy conservation competition involving a reduction in average campus electricity use over the course of one month. Through primarily lighting retrofits and campus behavioral changes motivated by the competition, the school saved 45,960 kwh (10.73%) in 2006, equivalent to $5,643.89/ month, and $51,972.71/ year.

Food

The Unquowa School (Fairfield, CT) launched a sustainable dining program in 2006 with the goals of improving nutrition, reducing waste, and supporting the local economy. Working with an outside consultant, school staff met with local farmers and vendors, developed a mission statement, and introduced the initiative with a sustainable meal for faculty at the beginning of the 2006-07 academic year. To date, Unquowa's dining program achievements include reduction in waste, creation of a kitchen garden, a composting program, better food quality and freshness (with organic milk and local cage-free eggs), and incorporation of food awareness and hands-on work into the curriculum. Costs overall have not increased due to creative strategies such offering fewer food choices of higher quality and serving organic milk from gallon containers rather than regular milk from individual-sized containers.

Curriculum

Branksome Hall (Toronto, ON) launched a curriculum initiative as part of its Environmental Sustainability Action Plan in 2007. The school started with a survey of sustainability in all grades. All faculty were asked to research and develop an enhanced focus on sustainability in their courses with an expectation that by 2009, 60% of faculty will implement at least one curricular component—a lesson, unit, resource—that builds student awareness of environmental sustainability and provides skills and habits of mind for meaningful action. This will increase to

---

11 Some of these recommendations are taken from Calder's guide, "100 Ways to a Greener and More Sustainable Campus," written for the Philadelphia Area Independent School Business Officers Association (PAISBOA). See **www.paisboa.org**.

100% by 2010.

Rainbarrels

As water conservation becomes a growing necessity, The Miquon School (Conshohocken, PA) installed rainbarrels in critical locations around campus in spring 2008. Given their location on 10 acres of steeply sloped wooded valley, where they contend with severe stormwater runoff, these barrels are helping mitigate the problem and have become part of their ongoing environmental education program.

Green Roof

Fairville Friends School (Fairville, PA) installed a green roof on a new building in 2008. With this roof they hope to reduce energy consumption from both heating and cooling, sequester carbon dioxide, neutralize acid rain, and extend the roof life.

CONCLUSION

Schools can no longer avoid the reality of their impact on the planet—their use of pesticides, paper, and energy, and their role in instructing the next generation. By being more environmentally sustainable, schools model appropriate behavior, protect the environment, educate future leaders, and save money if they do these well. Nearly every sustainability initiative at an independent school will need to be planned, organized, and managed through the business office in some manner. Understanding the opportunities and challenges you face in this area is the first step toward green-lighting your green initiative. Powerful evidence is increasingly abundant of true change and genuine all-school mobilization in this arena. Once school leaders start paying attention to their institutions' impact on the planet, they almost always get excited about—and enjoy—making their school more sustainable. I encourage you to get hooked on going green, and to do your part to make sustainability a reality.

NBOA